The Politics of Disgust

The Politics
of Disgust

*The Public Identity of the
Welfare Queen*

Ange-Marie Hancock

NEW YORK UNIVERSITY PRESS
New York and London

NEW YORK UNIVERSITY PRESS
New York and London
www.nyupress.org

Library of Congress Cataloging-in-Publication Data
Hancock, Ange-Marie.
The politics of disgust: the public identity of the welfare queen /
Ange-Marie Hancock
p. cm.
Includes bibliographical references and index.
ISBN 0-8147-3658-0 (cloth : alk. paper)
ISBN 0-8147-3670-X (pbk.   )
1. Welfare recipients—United States. 2. Public welfare—
Government policy—United States.   I. Title.
HV95.H256   2004
362.5'82'0973—dc22   2004011429

Manufactured in the United States of America

c 10 9 8 7 6 5 4 3 2 1
p 10 9 8 7 6 5 4 3 2 1

For Kyle Gerard Meriwether
(1950–1991)

Contents

List of Tables   *ix*
Acknowledgments   *xi*
List of Abbreviations   *xiii*

1   Introduction: The Face of Welfare Reform   1

2   Political Culture and the Public Identity of the
     "Welfare Queen"   23

3   The News Media: Constructing the Politics of Disgust?   65

4   Public Discourse in Congress: Haunted by Ghosts of
     "Welfare Queens" Past   88

5   Contending with the Politics of Disgust: Public
     Identity through Welfare Recipients' Eyes   117

6   The Dual Threat: The Impact of Public Identity and
     the Politics of Disgust on Democratic Deliberation   138

7   Epilogue: Public Identity and the Politics of Disgust
     in the New Millennium   152

     Appendix A: Citations for News Media Data Set
        Analyzed in Chapter 3   *158*
     Appendix B: Congressional Record Documents
        Analyzed in Chapter 4   *166*
     Appendix C: Data Analysis Procedures   *168*
     Notes   *185*
     Bibliography   *191*
     Index   *203*
     About the Author   *210*

Tables

3.1. Key Variables in News Media Articles, Frequency   69

3.2. Text Code Overlap: Dimensions of Public Identity   70

3.3. Text Code Overlap: Public Identity and Policy Options   74

3.4. Text Code Overlap: Public Identity and State Program Policy Options   77

3.5. Text Code Overlap: Public Identity and Political Values   80

3.6. Text Code Overlap: Political Values and Policy Options   82

3.7. Text Code Overlap: Public Identity and Consensus for Welfare Reform   85

3.8. Text Code Overlap: Consensus for Welfare Reform and Policy Options   86

4.1. Key Variables in *Congressional Record,* Frequency   93

4.2. Text Code Overlap: Dimensions of Public Identity   96

4.3. Text Code Overlap: Public Identity and Policy Options   98

4.4. Text Code Overlap: Public Identity and Political Values   100

4.5. Text Code Overlap: Political Values and Policy Options   102

4.6. Text Code Overlap: Public Identity and Consensus for Welfare Reform   105

4.7. Text Code Overlap: Consensus for Welfare Reform and Policy Options   106

5.1. Cross-Racial Consensus Regarding Welfare System Problems   134

5.2. Consensus Regarding Community Service Work Requirements, Selected Populations   135

C.1. Dimensions of Public Identity Variable   180

C.2. Dimensions of Policy Options Variable   180

C.3. Dimensions of Political Values Variable   181

C.4. Key Buzz Words and Dimensions   181

C.5. Frequency Table for Data Set of News Media Articles   182

C.6. Frequencies among Media Articles, Political Elites   182

C.7. Frequencies among *Congressional Record* Documents   183

Acknowledgments

I recognize that I am at this point by grace. Far too many begin the journey of writing a book only to have it remain unfinished for far too long. I am truly grateful to family, friends, and colleagues who have provided unflagging spiritual, emotional, editorial, and even financial support. Mentors near and far have shaped my work and commitment to an intellectual life with practical political applications.

My thanks go first to Robin D. G. Kelley and Gerald Horne, intellectual activists of the first order. If ever you have spoken to me, you have heard the honored names "Robin" and "Dr. Horne," emblems of their truly divergent personalities and the shared worship I reserve for them. Jobs, conversations, books, articles and emotional support are just a few of the ways these wonderful Black men were supportive of my career. I can only aspire to be part of the same kind of support system for others as I continue my academic career.

Further, without the work and timely encouragement of Cathy Cohen, Paula Giddings, Craig Calhoun, and Lisa Disch I may have quit long ago. I also thank my earlier academic advisers: Pamela Johnston Conover, Susan Bickford, Norman Hurley, Stephanie Rowley, and Isaac Unah. In many cases I started out as their student and am fortunate to have their intellectual contributions be part of my ongoing work.

This project was supported by the James Irvine Foundation Minority Dissertation Scholar Fellowship and the Faculty Development Fund of the University of San Francisco. Colleague and mentor Pamela Balls-Organista provided much-appreciated ethnic psychology discussion, empathy, and lots of great wine in the final years of writing this book. My politics department colleagues Robert Elias and Roberta Johnson both offered extensive advice on the book proposal that ultimately turned into the pages at hand. In thinking about the politics of disgust from a theoretical perspective, I benefited greatly from conversations with David Kim and Lisa Wagner, who shared their thoughts in preparation for presentations at the Passions of the Color Line: Emotions and Race Conference at the University of San Francisco.

During my brief stint at Pennsylvania State University I worked with some outstanding women scholars who offered feedback on chapters as we shared coffee or wine twice a month. The "Tenure-Track Divas"—Holloway Sparks, Marnina Gonick, and Lisa Miller—all gave incisive feedback on various chapter drafts that improved the book immensely. As we all get our books out in the next few years, we will hopefully all become the "Tenured Divas!"

My sisters-by-choice from around the country cheered me on up close or at a distance depending on my domicile of the moment—New York, Chapel Hill, San Francisco, State College, and now New Haven. Debbie Atwater, Cynthia Boaz, Trevaughn Brown, Ariane Coleman, Robyn Spencer, Tracey Ungar, Teri Washington, and Nicole Webster would listen, cajole, empathize, lecture or simply spirit me away from it all for five days or five minutes. Todd Ellinwood, Anthony Graham, James Taylor, Josh Tower, Greg Weeks, and Steve Wuhs are also friends who remained open to talking about anything but the book!

Last, but certainly not least, I could not have finished this project without the help of some very committed and spirited assistance. Research assistants Kristen Bonatz, Danice Cook, Dana Evans, Patricia Hageny, Heather Ondecin, Elisa Bramble, and Bryant Hall were valuable "foot soldiers" in this enterprise, as were University of North Carolina library staff Marlin Murrell and Glenn Brooks. Former University of San Francisco librarian Kathy Brazee provided speedy service with a smile when my project made an unexpected turn in a different direction, and Patricia Heinecke offered her valuable editing expertise to earlier incarnations.

I thank the first Dr. Hancock—my father Charles—my mother, Theresa, and my sisters, Nicole B. Hancock and Janine H. Jones, for their love and commitment to my vision. I also thank the most recent additions to our family—my brother-in-law, Christopher Jones, and my niece, Taylor Renee Jones—for reminding me that the life of the mind is nothing without the love of family. To recognize the contributions of others in no way suggests they are responsible for whatever failings remain. Without their presence, however, whatever successes are present would not exist.

Abbreviations

ADC   Aid to Dependent Children
AFDC   Aid to Families with Dependent Children
CBC   Congressional Black Caucus
FAP   Family Assistance Plan
HR   House Resolution
NAACP   National Association for the Advancement of Colored People
NWRO   National Welfare Rights Organization
PRWA   Personal Responsibility and Work Opportunity Act (1996)
S   Senate Resolution
SCLC   Southern Christian Leadership Conference
TANF   Temporary Assistance to Needy Families

1

Introduction
The Face of Welfare Reform

Imagine the following scenario. While watching C-SPAN in July of 1996, you observe a member of the House of Representatives reading the following statement:

> Bertha Bridges is still waiting for the end of welfare as she knows it. She and her three children have been on and off welfare since the early 1980s, and she has been unable to hold a job in recent years because school administrators often call several times a week to ask her to pick up her disruptive, severely depressed 13 year-old son for fighting and disobeying teachers. (Appendix B, Document 75A)

If you close your eyes and picture Bertha Bridges, you envision a person "with issues." Despite no overt reference to her economic class or race, "coded" categories abound, including welfare, a disruptive male child, unemployment, and nearly fifteen years of sporadic welfare dependency. We may blame the member of Congress for creating such an image, but the next statement reveals a more complex picture:

> Seventeen months after U.S. News first interviewed her for a cover story on welfare reform, matters have only worsened for the Detroit resident. Several weeks ago her son let three strangers into her house, and they promptly stole Bridges' money, jewelry, clothing, dishes and videocassette recorder. Her son is now back in a psychiatric hospital, his younger sister is starting to imitate him by refusing to complete school assignments and Bridges doesn't know where to turn for help. "I'm living a nightmare," she says. (Ibid.)

1

Here Bridges herself contributes to your mental picture. Her life, most charitably, could be characterized as spinning out of control. A harsher view would see her as an incompetent mother nurturing the next generation of pathology. Importantly, the role of the media in the process of public debate is also made clear: a magazine is given as a source of information reliable enough to be included in the public record. This is the face of welfare included in the *Congressional Record* for the floor debate regarding HR 3734, now the Personal Responsibility and Work Opportunities Act (PRWA) of 1996.

When citizens like Bertha Bridges are thrust into the public sphere for political purposes, the potential for "reasonable" democratic consideration of policy options is bleak. Reading the first excerpt from the *Congressional Record* triggers a comparison of Bridges to stereotypes about welfare recipients. This act of cognition occurs so quickly that before we read her own words (as quoted by a journalist), we have given her an identity that acts from that point forward as an interpretive filter. Whether her words reinforce or contest the identity assigned by the reader, any political claim she may make later in the article is still considered in the context of that identity. After those two paragraphs and the rest of the article, the debate of HR 3734 continues, with the identity lingering in our minds. What are the political implications of this image for our democracy? This book explores one compelling answer to this question.

Bertha Bridges's story triggers a specific identity in many American minds. The identity, although shaped by political elites, academicians, and the media, draws on citizens' preexisting beliefs about women who exist at the intersection of marginalized race, class, and gender identities. The harsh light under which Bridges found herself in July of 1996 is emblematic of the political context in which HR 3734 was developed and ultimately signed into law.

Political context,[1] a key product of political culture, is commonly thought of as a primary influence on policy decisions. In this vein, historical and contextual changes in political culture and public discourse receive a share of the responsibility for the preservation of democracy (Almond and Verba 1963, 5; Merelman 1984; Barber 1998; M. Williams 1998), not the destruction of it. However, political culture encompasses more than the shared beliefs, values, and norms that coalesce to form a political context at a particular political moment. It also includes identities learned by means of experiences and relationships in institutions like families, schools, the media, and voluntary associations (Conover et al. 2002, 5).

Certain identities, such as race and gender, are salient in American political culture due to long-standing beliefs of politically important differences between people of different races and different genders. Often at the insistence of members of marginalized races and genders, such differences have historically received attention in the public sphere to promote shared values such as equality and freedom (M. Williams 1998). We might call this demand for attention a demand for democratic attention.

Many theorists agree that in democratic politics a specific form of attention is required, one that requires thinking collectively with others while "judging for one's self" (Bickford 1996, 139). Democratic attention is a necessary component of democratic deliberation because we deliberate about uncertain things that are within our collective power to do (27). In other words, as we collectively figure out what to do, the democratic process requires us to consider the multifarious opinions of other citizens in rendering our personal judgment.

The use of democratic attention in the political sphere is intended by democratic theorists to "create a sense of genuine public interest" in solving particular social problems (Barber 1984, 13). In the area of welfare politics, however, Congressman Scott McInnis (R-CO) perverts democratic attention into an ideological justification for a specific policy that restricts the rights of welfare recipients. The critical feature of this attention, its intent to separate welfare recipients from worthy American citizens, has serious implications for the potential of participatory forms of democracy in the United States. Such perversions of democratic attention are part of what I define as a "politics of disgust."

A developed democracy usually turns its attention to issues about which there is a genuine debate, but the underlying assumptions—the unquestioned consensus about certain topics—influence democratic deliberation before, during, and after a specific policy or issue debate. By defining *deliberation* as an activity conducted in common by citizens (Barber 1998, 25), the democratic process retains republican aspirations of citizen development and enhancement of individuals' capacities (see Young 1990; Barber 1984). For the process to function, however, some preexisting consensus must exist: "Still, not everything can be up for deliberation at the same time. Aristotle [in *Nicomachean Ethics*] notes that there must be some agreed-upon or assumed factual background for deliberating" (Bickford 1996, 28). Yet as many political theorists now agree, political facts are largely shaped by norms conditioned by history and experience. The question remains: Whose history and which experiences shape this assumed factual background?

Public identities of marginal citizens represent one critical part of this assumed background. In developing public identity as a specific construct suitable for political psychology, I do not intend to discredit other more theoretical connotations of the term. My project, in fact, is to link political theory with empirical political science to develop a bridge term that explains the representations that stories like Bertha Bridges's create in the audience's mind.

Previously, theorists such as John Rawls and Susan Bickford have characterized public identity as a public presentation of the self, based upon what we as citizens are able to agree upon (Rawls 1985 quoted in Bickford 1996, 5). To further her point, Bickford argues, "We may bolster our courage by reminding ourselves that criticisms are not of our most intimate selves, but of how we have performed, how we are acting in public" (150). I argue that the public presentation of the self is not the sole component of public identities in contexts of inequality. Taking issue with theorists who overstate the role of agency in the political sphere, I demonstrate that public identities endure over generations and impoverish the potential for empowered participation by citizens saddled with such identities in processes of democratic deliberation. The ability to adopt an identity at will has been proven time and again to remain a pipe dream for citizens consigned to the margins of the public sphere. As Bickford herself acknowledges, the actor, in the language of Hannah Arendt, cannot also assume the role of interpreter for the spectator (162; see also Arendt 1958, 1982).

My logic here does not intend to argue that agency is impossible. What I want to argue is that one's public identity is conditioned not simply by one's own speech and action but also by others' perception, interpretation, *and* manipulation—particularly for those citizens who lack political equality. In this sense, I extend Arendt and Bickford's work into a realm of emotionally charged political context—the politics of disgust. A politics of disgust is first marked by traditional signposts of inequality; for example, members of marginal groups, even when granted the power of speech, find their voices devalued or disrespected, increasing their isolation and alienation from the public sphere (Young 1997, 64; Taylor 1994,

70). Democratic deliberation then devolves into conversations "routinely marked by vast differences in status, power and privilege" (Kinder and Sanders 1996, 285). The persistent influence of public identities contributes to the breakdown of deliberation, largely because of the more unique characteristics of the politics of disgust I discuss in the next section.

The politics of disgust occurs despite the relatively "open and permeable body of people in active roles that influence public opinion and shape public affairs" (McCloskey and Zaller 1984, 3), or the opportunity to cause a little "gender trouble" in micropublics, as Judith Butler (1990) and Nancy Fraser (1992) might have us do. Because political culture under conditions of consensus tends to be successfully transmitted by elites to the general public (McCloskey and Zaller 1984, 234; Zaller 1991, 1216; Zaller 1992, 1996), the unacknowledged consensual absence or misrepresentation of a marginalized group can predictably stunt the dissemination of accurate information and thus the development of accurate attitudes about them (Taylor 1994, 25).

Moreover, such social constructions of groups are continually reinforced by existing government policy (Schneider and Ingram 1995, 443). Socially constructed target populations are "the cultural characterizations or popular images of the persons or groups whose behavior and well-being are affected by public policy" (Schneider and Ingram 1993). Such social constructions, Schneider and Ingram argue, are based upon stereotypes about particular groups of people from politics, culture, the media, and history, among other influences. Yet both theoretical and empirical critiques of their theory center upon the lack of conceptual clarity of key constructs such as "social construction of target populations" (Lieberman 1995; Schroedel and Jordan 1998). In this book I offer a concept that builds upon their notion of social construction while incorporating several innovations that improve empirical utility, using the insights of political psychologists studying social identity. Several recent scholars have emphasized the social construction power of extant public policy (Schram 1995; Campbell 2000); I want to focus upon other equally important contributors to what I define as the public identity of a target population. I argue that elite manipulations and cues of public identities provide a feedback arrow to the start of the policy-making process, shaping government policy by means of public identity's role in democratic deliberation.

The Politics of Disgust

> It seems that more than ever the compulsion today is to identify, to re-
> duce someone to what is on the label. To identify is to control, to limit.
> (Madeleine L'Engle 1995)

Identities and emotions are two aspects of our common humanity. Each
of us has one or more identities that we accept; we each have one or more
identities ascribed to us by others regardless of whether we accept them.
Much attention has been given to the possibility of overlaps and discon-
nects between these identities of differing origins in both political theory
and political psychology. Similarly, emotions in politics have long been an
issue of discussion among political theorists; feminist theorists have made
the strongest case for the appropriateness of emotions in politics (see,
e.g., Collins 2000; Bickford 1996; Young 1990). I am extremely sympathetic to this ontological position, yet the susceptibility of citizens to an
emotionally charged political context can pose serious problems for
democracy.

   I argue that the public identity of welfare recipients—created from the
misperception that they are all or mostly single mothers who are poor and
African American[2]—interacts with a context I term the politics of disgust
to produce legislative outcomes that are undemocratic both procedurally
and substantively. The remainder of the book analyzes the national welfare reform discourse in 1996 from historical, empirical, and theoretical
angles to make this case.

   But first it is essential to define what is unique about a politics of disgust, as distinct from other more popular terms like contempt or demonization. The politics of disgust is characterized by four features in our
representative democracy. As I alluded to above, the politics of disgust involves a perversion of democratic attention. In this political context the
process of deliberation lacks the type of attention (to *all* citizens' claims)
that democratic theorists deem necessary for a democracy. I initially document the perversion of democratic attention from a historical perspective in chapter 2 when I discuss the roots of the public identity of the
"welfare queen," which is grounded in two discursive themes about Black
women traceable to slavery: their laziness and their fecundity. I return to
it throughout the case study.

   Second, the political context within which so-called democratic deliberation occurs is conditioned by monologic, rather than intersubjective,

communications among citizens. As the character Sheldon Runyon (played by Gary Oldman) in *The Contender* so aptly puts it: "People will believe me because I'll have a very large microphone in front of me." It is this particular aspect of the politics of disgust that renders public identities like that of the "welfare queen" so resistant to change following contestation. Chapter 3 discusses the results of a study[3] of national print media coverage of welfare reform in the months leading up to the passage of the Personal Responsibility and Work Opportunities Act in 1996.

Third, the politics of disgust can exist beneath the radar screens of many citizens because even "well-intentioned" citizens in the public sphere succumb to a pitfall of what Hannah Arendt calls "representative thinking." This pitfall, when studied by political psychologists, is usually called correspondence bias. In addition to these mistakes in political thinking, the politics of disgust is marked by a fourth and final feature: a distinct lack of political solidarity between citizens who are and citizens who are not part of the target population of the legislation at issue. Chapter 4 demonstrates the failures of representative thinking and mistaken solidarity among African American and female members of Congress evident in the 1996 *Congressional Record*. I turn first to the common cultural context of emotions like disgust.

Emotion scholars in psychology have determined that humans are programmed (that is, hardwired) for at least six core affects: anger, fear, disgust, happiness, sadness, and surprise (White 1994, 222). Although emotions are "prototypically social and moral" (221) and carry moral weight, emotional responses to stimuli are couched within cultural frames, or interpretive grids of tacit social understandings, social representations, and practices that reflect and enact these understandings in daily life (Kitayama and Markus 1994, 95; see also Keltner and Haidt 1999). Thus emotions, while seeming to be "gut" reactions over which we have no control, are in reality learned within what Charles Taylor calls "a common space" in which my and others' experiences are shared and interpreted (1994, 35).

Politically speaking, emotions serve to regulate power relationships (Frijda and Mesquita 1994, 77) and instigate politically relevant behaviors such as sharing, bonding, and correction. Associations with emotional components, moreover, are learned faster and rendered salient to an individual when expressed by another individual. This finding has distinct ramifications for the durability of public identities such as that of the "welfare queen" and, more generally, for the difficulty even well-intentioned, politically "progressive" citizens have unlearning racism or sexism.

Culturally focal events, those that are important subjects of daily discourse, have clear norms that dictate how to interpret such topics and how to respond to them (Frijda and Mesquita 1994, 68). Thus the universe of possible welfare reform policy options is circumscribed by norms regarding how we interpret the process of welfare reform and those assumed to benefit from it. Not only do the norms themselves exist but cultures possess explicit verbal categories to identify events with particular associated meanings and affective evaluations. In chapters 3 and 4, I find buzz terms like "culture of poverty" and "welfare as a way of life" to be part of a semantic network surrounding welfare reform in 1996. The semantic network permeating the discourse regarding a certain topic contains the coding to be used by individuals regarding a particular event. In one sense, this is good news because it supports the assertion that emotions, although hardwired into all of us, are expressed and learned in culturally specific ways, implying that they can be unlearned.

Yet while social constructions may in fact change over time (Schneider and Ingram 1993; Lieberman 1995), one building block of social constructions, stereotypes, often does not change. Racial stereotypes in particular tend to be closely held and immune to contradictory information (Link and Oldendick 1996). The resilience such lessons demonstrate in the face of change, even among those of us who recognize the peril at the bottom of such a slippery slope, leads us only to guarded optimism about the potential for agency among marginalized citizens in democratic contexts with significant socioeconomic stratification.

In fact, one of the above functions served by emotions, that of bonding, may in its political form strengthen the role of core cultural frames in perpetuating the emotional responses we have to racialized stimuli. As Kitayama and Markus note, "societal integration may well require that the foundations of cultural models or schemas be largely taken for granted, and that their propositions be transparent or 'go without saying'" (1994, 344). This idea of preexisting, uncontested consensus that precedes democratic deliberation again points out how the cultural frames through which we learn our quasi-instinctive emotional reactions are protected from being successfully challenged by the actual political purpose they serve.

Further, democratic theory notes that each instance of democratic deliberation must necessarily proceed from some shared background of information. Although the background information itself can be debated, it occurs under a process separate from the question "What is to be done next?" This separate process of debating the background information in welfare policy has been consistently thwarted by the politics of disgust. I point out the role of the politics of disgust in maintaining the hegemony of the "welfare queen" public identity in each chapter.

The politics of disgust is an emotion-laden response to long-standing beliefs about single, poor African American mothers that has spread, epidemiologically, to all recipients of Aid to Families with Dependent Children/Temporary Assistance to Needy Families (AFDC/TANF) and to recipients of other welfare programs, including Social Security Income (SSI) and related programs for what citizens previously considered "the deserving poor." Disgust, as defined by the *Oxford English Dictionary*, has a two-pronged definition that speaks to the political context in which Bertha Bridges and her sister welfare mothers found themselves in 1996. Both prongs speak to the role of psychology more generally and emotions specifically in social constructions like the public identity of welfare recipients. In particular, this definition of disgust helps to explain the inner workings of the perversion of democratic attention, one significant part of the politics of disgust.

The first relevant *Oxford* definition, that of a "strong repugnance, aversion, or repulsion excited by that which is loathsome or offensive," lists a "disagreeable person or action" as a cause for "profound instinctive dislike or dissatisfaction." Within the sphere of democratic deliberation, the public presentation of one's emotion affects not only the subject of that emotion but has an interactional effect that turns our attention, even as democratic spectators, toward the subject in a search for evidence to justify such a reaction. Democratic theorists assert we reveal our public identity—who we are—as we speak our opinion; emotion scholars note that we can also reveal (intentionally or not) perceived aspects of the identity of the subject or person about whom we are speaking. When talking about someone else, or his or her political needs, as in the case of what to do about welfare policy, the goal of politics is to influence others' opinions toward your own, as Aristotle's definition of political rhetoric implies. Importantly, speakers persuade by causing listeners to feel in particular ways; though manipulation is not the goal, neither is it absent from the discourse (Bickford 1996, 42). Psychologists Frijda and Mesquita explain it more succinctly: "My disgust defines an object as potentially disgusting . . . [and] may instigate in others a search for disgusting attributes [within the stimulus]" (1994, 74). Thus the public presentation of Bertha Bridges, or of a set of folks eating crab legs outside the Capitol who "looked like they were on welfare," in the words of one senator, in a context of the speaker's personal disgust provokes a search in those of us exposed to the reaction for evidence to justify or contradict our own reaction of disgust. In this sense, the terms of the discussion have already been set; any openness to Bertha's words are already circumscribed by the cued emotion of disgust.

The second relevant point raised in this definition is the knee-jerk reaction disgust represents: a "profound, *instinctive* dislike or dissatisfaction." This suggests that the reaction is somehow out of the hands of the perceiver, that he or she cannot control the reaction. This is often the construction commonly put upon emotions, that they are indeed "gut" reactions that cannot be changed and, what is more important, should not be. This primordial reaction, which maintains our link to the animal world (see Haidt et al. 1993), is then extrapolated to other emotions brought into the political world, a site where one's intellective actions represent a very basic expression of one's humanity (Arendt 1958, 22).

Such actions as the public presentation of the self are subject to interpretation by others; it is out of the hands of the actor him- or herself. Yet some contemporary theorists hold fast to the possibility that perceivers can control their interpretations (see ibid.). Bickford suggests that representative thinking has democratic potential, though with limits: "My concern is not so much with what others actually feel, but with how my own self would feel [in their position]: 'I still speak with my own voice'" (Bickford 1996, 85).

While Bickford acknowledges this can be tricky (86), Gwendolyn Mink gives a powerful example of representative thinking gone horribly wrong. During the deliberations concerning the 1996 PRWA, several women legislators confided that in the past they had witnessed personal acquaintances suffering from lack of paternal child support within their middle-class environs. Putting on their representative thinking caps, they pushed ardently and succeeded in making paternal identification and pursuit of child support conditions of welfare benefits receipt.

On the surface, this seems an example of why we need more women representing women. However, as Mink notes, a significant percentage of women on welfare who are single mothers are also survivors of domestic violence. Requiring paternal identification or salary garnishment served either to alert abusive former partners to the location of the survivors or to exacerbate the already traumatic process of leaving a violent relationship by antagonizing the abuser (Mink 1998; see also Polakow 1997; GROWL 2002). In either case, it was the women on welfare who bore the brunt of these effects. Several states have since scrambled to enact policies for exemption from the paternal identification requirement in cases of domestic violence. Notably, the federal government does not require them to do so; hence women on welfare are subject to the whims of state legislators. Chapter 5 provides evidence of the specific problems associated with the policy of paternal identification.

Political psychologists would term this error of representative thinking a case of correspondence bias. We as individuals use ourselves and our social environment as anchors, as reference points from which to begin the political judgment process. The use of ourselves as an anchor is not inherently problematic. It is problematic, though, when we fail to correct for situational constraints in our thinking such that bias occurs, with results like those described above. That women legislators used their personal experiences, therefore, was not inherently troubling. That they failed to acknowledge the economic-class-based differences in access to services and protection for survivors of domestic violence, however, is partly an effect of the politics of disgust.

This third piece of the politics of disgust—the failure of representative thinking and the influence of correspondence bias—also emanates from a colloquial use of the term *disgust*. In many African American communities, to be "disgusted with someone" means to be fed up with the person's excuses or shenanigans and to be ready to run roughshod over his or her express wishes or desires. As a child, I knew that I was reaching the limits of my loving but strict parents' patience when my actions were termed "damned disgusting." It's critical to note in this example, though, that while my parents categorized my actions as disgusting, they always loved me and never put me as a person in the same category as my actions, a key condition for a citizen's potential for democratic redemption. In chapter 5, I discuss the lack of potential for democratic redemption attributed to welfare recipients that emerges from the words of welfare mothers themselves.

Social psychologists have found that in processes of social judgment—processes in which judgments are made in common among individuals—the explanation of a particular outcome, the "why it happened," in other words—plays a significant role in the evaluation process and the kind of judgment that emerges. For example, attributions of negligence ("she should have known better"), responsibility ("she was coerced by power-ful forces"), and blame ("the consequences were intentional and thus there is no excuse") are each determined by the explanation provided by the subject and its common interpretation by those who are judging (see Shaver et al. 1999).

Over the history of welfare politics in the United States, publicly ac-cepted explanations of women's poverty have changed as the perceived race of the prototypical recipient has changed. The politics of paternalism for White Protestant widows and southern European immigrant mothers was prevalent during the nineteenth and twentieth centuries prior to the New Deal. The "maternalist" arguments presented by women activists often included the attribution of negligence as a partial justification for behavioral components of the policy. "Mothers of the race" needed to comport themselves appropriately to raise proper nineteenth-century male Americans. A vote for "widows' pensions" became a vote for the "American way" (McClintock 1993; see also Sapiro 1990 and Skocpol 1995).

As greater numbers of women of color obtained benefits between the 1940s and the 1970s,[4] a politics of contempt emerged as a by-product of the more general compassion fatigue following the turbulent 1960s and recession-dominated 1970s. The persistent misdiagnosis of pov-erty causes in the past has produced new buzzterms, such as "cross-generation dependency" and "welfare as a way of life," to again explain poverty from an individualist perspective. The manipulation of this com-passion fatigue involved a cueing of racial hostility by linking race, poverty, and crime to White working-class citizens' uncertainty about the national economy in the 1970s and 1980s (Edsall and Edsall 1991). The emphasis upon individual blame later produced the exact term "welfare queen."[5]

The attribution of individual blame conflates a person's public action —receiving government benefits—with his or her private identity. The intransigence of the politics of disgust is tightly linked to the collective moral judgments that accompany the emotional reactions of disgust. The PRWA of 1996 trampled on welfare recipients' constitutional rights (Mink 1998), reflecting the loss of patience with and a perceived lack of redemptive potential among welfare recipients in their current situation. Reforms included in the PRWA focused on the private lives of welfare recipients in more restrictive ways by requiring paternal identification, receptivity to the prospect of heterosexual marriage, and reproductive restrictions as conditions for receipt of benefits. Indeed, the push for marriage as a solution to poverty has increased in the years since 1996; it was a major plank of President George W. Bush's proposed renewal of the PRWA in 2002.

The PRWA passed with bipartisan consensus; both Democrats and Republicans supported the move to "end welfare as we know it," as President Bill Clinton had promised (Mink 1999, 174; Mink 1998). Bipartisan consensus on the bill was eclipsed, however, by consensus as to who welfare recipients really were. Even those who usually demonstrate solidarity with welfare recipients were hard pressed to argue against the bill in a way that suggested any allegiance to welfare beneficiaries. Acting in solidarity "requires regarding others as capable of taking an interest in the world and speaking for themselves, capable of political action and therefore meant to be listened to . . ." (Bickford 1996, 77). The politics of disgust lacks this notion of solidarity, an absence that was reflected in the 1996 welfare reform debate.

In an analysis of the floor debates of the bill in the House and Senate, those who voted against it justified their vote as a vote in favor of needy children. Few, if any, stood in solidarity with welfare recipients during that election year. Chapter 4 presents the evidence that their legislative votes ignored welfare parents and supposedly went directly to the children.

The focus on children by both supporters and opponents of the 1996 PRWA legislation is especially salient because 1996 was a presidential election year, with its attendant media circus. In fact, the bill was passed and signed into law just prior to the Democratic and Republican National Conventions, where claiming credit for "ending welfare as we know it" abounded. The heightened media attention surrounding elected officials during an election year highlights the final part of the politics of disgust: a communicative context marked by gross inequality.

The PRWA did not proceed through the legislative process without challenge or contestation. Welfare recipients and their activist allies contacted their representatives and senators, and, when denied a seat at the table, disrupted congressional subcommittee hearings on the bill to present themselves and their opinions publicly. The protests turned out to be a mere blip on the radar screen; they were covered by one national newspaper (*Washington Post*) in a brief paragraph in *one* article out of a representative sample of 149 articles in five national newspapers during the period HR 3734/S 1751 was deliberated. The challenge was insurmountable and forces us to acknowledge the limits of agency to present oneself in a context in which others can portray you with the aid of a "very large microphone."

Despite all of our American commitment to viewing empirical and theoretical politics from the individualist perspective, the sociopsychological processes I am describing here—linguistic conventions, socialization practices, scripts for daily behavior—are also simultaneously social facts—external realities that can exist relatively independently of the wishes, desires, hopes, or plans of any particular participating individual (Kitayama and Markus 1994, 341). Their susceptibility to manipulation and distortion, as evidenced in this politics of disgust, reflects the asymmetrical availability of power to various members of the population seeking to shape such core cultural ideas.

The politics of disgust creates a context that is difficult to contest successfully, thus leading to its perpetuation. The four features I have described above can be and have been challenged separately, but viewing them as a coherent entity helps to explain why we have not made the progress we desire toward a fuller democracy. A politics of disgust has further implications for members of oppressed groups because it reinforces silence and invisibility among those brought into the public sphere as part of another citizen's ideological arguments, e.g., those of Congressman McInnis (see above). This outcome leads specifically to the question of public identity as a contributor to the political context.

A Conceptual Definition of Public Identity

Identity is not socially constructed solely by the winds of political context; this would deny humans any agency. But certain manifestations of one's identity, such as modes of expression, are learned through interactions with others (Taylor 1994, 32). The misrecognition that occurs among many citizens includes the "unconscious assumptions, reflexive reactions of well-meaning people in ordinary interpersonal interactions, media and cultural stereotypes" (Young 1990, 41; M. Williams 1998). Public identity as a political psychological construct reflects the influence of political culture upon the dialogical interaction between actor and spectator. In this sense, it represents a fundamental step in bridging the gap between political theory and political psychology.

Public identities underlie competing issue frames, reinforcing the structures of suggested relationships among citizens, government, political practices, and political values. Public identity represents a bridge concept first and foremost because it attends to the dynamic relationship between actor and spectator. Charles Taylor (1994) emphasizes the way in which one's identity is developed dialogically—in relation to others. His analysis focuses on the repercussions for interpersonal interactions when citizens misrecognize one another and act according to norms corresponding to an inaccurately attributed identity.

An example of this phenomenon would be the behavior demonstrated by a southern White woman in accordance with her belief that the only young African American woman in a luxury box for a football game is more likely one of the food-service workers than Reyna Walters, the 1998–99 student body president of the University of North Carolina at Chapel Hill. The roots of this behavior may be correctly traced to prior experiences with young African American women and/or a public discourse that includes cultural images of student body presidents as primarily male and always White. But beyond this indirect influence upon interpersonal experiences, public identities provide a common foundation for democratic deliberation among citizens even when the subjects of such identities do not themselves participate in the process.

Public identities are constituted of stereotypes and moral judgments of multiple group identities (e.g., race, class, gender) ascribed to groups that are the subject of legislative policy. Importantly, they are generally based upon the perceptions of non-group members specifically for the advancement of facially race- or gender-neutral public policy goals. Public identities are socially constructed and include stereotypes but differ from stereotypes for several reasons. Earlier research has demonstrated that the social construction of target populations is more complex than simple stereotypes, due in part to the way stereotypes function and are susceptible to change: "Stereotypes tend to be loosely held images highly susceptible to change given new information about the target of the stereotype" (Link and Oldendick 1996, 152). Yet despite Lieberman's (1995) and Schneider and Ingram's (1995) argument that social constructions change over time, certain social constructions such as attitudes about race tend to be held firmly and are only reinforced, not transformed, over time, despite ongoing contestation (Link and Oldendick 1996, 152).

The cueing of public identity by political elites or the news media involves two distinct cognitive behaviors: the assignment of specific traits and behaviors to an individual (stereotyping), and moral judgments based on the explanations for said traits or behaviors. Thus, public identities also differ from traditional stereotypes because of the number of cognitive processes involved. Last, public identities function more dynamically in the goal-oriented context of politics. Although stereotypes are learned more passively, through exposure and observation, public identities are developed and shaped for political goals, as ideological justifications for public policy with little attention to their dissemination as such.[6]

The role of moral judgment is likewise a critical component of public identity as an empirical measure of the social construction of target populations. Lieberman (1995) argues that the social construction of a group can remain the same in content (e.g., African Americans) and change in valence. While this may in fact be possible, what occurred in welfare policy discourse was an actual change in who was perceived to benefit from the policy. As the public identity of welfare beneficiaries shifted, so did citizens' positive feelings toward "who benefits" and, most importantly, the legislative policy options considered appropriate. I link the misperceptions embodied in the public identity of the "welfare queen" directly to policy options considered legitimate solutions in chapters 3 and 4.

Chapters 3 and 4 also highlight the importance of an analysis that is attentive to the intersections of race, class, and gender. Both chapters reveal that something beyond race drives the public identity of the "welfare queen" by demonstrating the role of the "welfare queen" in the Black women's club movement, civil rights movement, and Million Man March (chapter 2), as well as among Black members of Congress (chapter 4). If race is truly the decisive factor, we have no explanation for findings of antiwelfare sentiment among Blacks (Kinder and Sanders 1996; Cose 1999). Similarly, something beyond gender drives the public identity of the "welfare queen" as demonstrated in chapter 4's content analysis of feminist lawmakers such as Senator Barbara Mikulski (D-MD). It is important to note that the identity cued remains stable regardless of which side of the aisle or political issue one stands on.

Earlier work has focused exclusively on race (Gilens 1995, 1996; Gilliam 1999) or gender (Mink 1998), with nodding acknowledgment of the other. Research on welfare politics is often classified as "race in welfare politics" (e.g., Quadagno 1994) or "gender in welfare politics" (e.g.,

Abramovitz 1996). This book seeks to bridge that gap by design and explicitly introduce the role of class. Significantly, this approach begins to account for the durability of the public identity of the "welfare queen" over nearly seventy years of national welfare discourse despite overwhelming evidence debunking its legitimacy. If, as Schneider and Ingram argue (1995), social constructions of target populations change over time, why does the "welfare queen" linger in our collective memory?

The concept of public identity and its potential for weighting unfairly the public judgment process presents a serious obstacle in terms of democratic public policy debate and implementation. The individual who is tied to a particular public identity is often challenged to change herself or risk further isolation and suppression in a context where the opportunity for change is limited by structural considerations. Neither alternative fully satisfies the goals of democracy: empowered participation in the political process, freedom, or justice. The political context in which such deliberations occur interacts critically with public identities. When triggered in the public sphere, public identities again exert influence, this time more indirectly, in the public judgment process. First, as discussed above, exposure to public identity within a particular political context leads some citizens to devalue other citizens' claims to resources prior to vetting the claims themselves.

Second, lawmakers' status as citizens leads them to similar exposure to the political context and public identities, shaping the public policy options considered in the legislative process. In both instances, the public sphere represents the political context where acts of public judgment occur. How does this condition the judgment process? The prevailing political context in the public sphere will influence the capacity of individuals to express their experience, a key dimension of participation.

Citizens cast as the subjects of public identities that marginalize them, based on multiple aspects of their identities, are potentially further alienated from political participation than traditional resource-based models of voting behavior may suggest. Directly influenced by the products of political culture, individuals' public identities can negate formal assurances of equal participation in the public sphere in two ways. First, a prevailing political context that is continually filled with negative stereotypes, moral judgments, and frames concerning a particular group of individuals lumped together based on shared characteristics ascribed to them by others lessens the motivation to express one's lived experiences in the public sphere (Soss 1999; M. Williams 1998). Second, a group's fellow citizens are similarly constrained in their abilities to accurately interpret and attend to the communicated experiences of marginalized individuals (Young 1990, 1997; Taylor 1994) despite any of their best intentions. Both outcomes allude to the power of public identity and the politics of disgust. Welfare recipients' confrontation with the public identity of the "welfare queen" and the politics of disgust is discussed in chapter 5.

Critical Theory and Social Justice

Theories of minority politics have long drawn on multiple academic disciplines to adequately explain phenomena that have more than theoretical relevance. Many scholars who pursue this type of interdisciplinary work face the challenge of producing research that is empirically rigorous *and* contributes to the transformation of society. Yet the task is never more relevant than it is in the twenty-first century, when globalization and the increasing diversity of American society demands new structures, new paradigms, and new ways of being "at home in this world" (Arendt, 1973).

The challenge to political scientists, recently made in the *New Republic,* is similarly instructive. Jonathan Cohn suggests that political scientists have an obligation to do work that is "not merely interesting as an intellectual enterprise, but also helps us govern ourselves" (1999, 25; see also Schram 1995). The call for work that is relevant to the practice of American politics today is clear.

This project has benefited from earlier attempts to remedy the vestiges of racism and sexism that linger despite earlier efforts at eradication. The chapters in this project progress from a critical perspective in the sense that they recognize the power of ideologies and discourses in shaping relations of power and the material conditions of American citizens' lives. My general argument stems from this fundamental assertion.

The political outcomes of 1996 regarding welfare reform are part of an ongoing process of historical and social constructions of single Black mothers that culminates (for the purposes of this study) in the passage of the Personal Responsibility and Work Opportunities Act of 1996. The evidence of public identities presented to Americans as fact rather than manipulation validates Fraser and Gordon's (1997) philosophical argument about the encoding of facts with values in the arena of welfare politics.

Cognitive dependence on frames—suggested shortcuts in political think-ing—in place of critical thinking about the facts within them also impov-erishes the policy-making process.

The evidence presented also supports theoretical assertions by Mar-cuse (1965) and Habermas (1984), as well as social psychological re-search in social judgment (Eiser 1990). All three authors argue for the im-portance of language as a constructor of subjectivity prior to political participation by marginalized citizens (Marcuse and Habermas) and the role of linguistic cues in evaluating claims and claimants (Eiser 1990). Chapters 3, 4, and 5 in particular build on these points through content analysis of welfare reform discourse in 1996.

Content Analysis: Words That Matter

Language plays an essential part in constructing inequality in American political culture. Document analysis is a specialized type of content analy-sis that consists of a systematic examination of forms of communication to reveal patterns objectively (Marshall and Rossman 1995, 85; Hodson 1999) that is an increasingly widespread method in political science. The greatest strengths of this approach are its unobtrusive and nonreactive features. Data are collected in a natural setting and can provide a com-prehensive account of major events, crises, or social conflicts (Marshall and Rossman 1995, 100–101). The two data types used here, newspapers and the *Congressional Record,* are uniquely suited to this purpose. More-over, the easily quantifiable qualities of document analysis make it amenable to statistical analyses, facilitating analysis, validity checks, and triangulation, ultimately combining the strengths of quantitative and qualitative analyses (Marshall and Rossman, 1995, 100; Hodson 1999, 65). The document analyses I discuss in chapters 3 and 4 are intended to supplement, rather than supplant, the sociohistorical analysis presented in chapter 2. Further, the validity of results is enhanced when the same method and coding protocol are applied to separate data sets, as I do in this project.

Any commitment to social justice and democratic deliberation does not obviate the need for rigorous empirical investigation. Grounded the-ory and document analysis methods complement the goal of unveiling inequality with a more positivist emphasis on confirmation, reliability, and validity. This project is a blend of both approaches, for it is both a *"welfare queen" = intersectional identity*

theoretical and empirical enterprise. To enhance the accessibility and readability of the book for a wide audience, I provide technical details of the empirical analysis in Appendix C for interested readers.

Empirically Investigating Intersectional Identity

The intersections of Bertha Bridges's race, gender, and class described earlier indicate that it is fruitless to extract the influence of one characteristic to the exclusion of others. For Bridges and others like her, it is not *intersectionality* solely because they are single, or poor, or Black that they remain marginalized. It is because they are single, poor, Black mothers simultaneously, each day of their lives, that they are marginalized. In developing a political psychological operationalization of public identity, I seek to move us forward in our evaluations of democracy and equality. Throughout the book, I am attentive to the ways in which racism, sexism, and classism interact to compound marginalization. An intersectional approach is critical to this pursuit.

The notion of intersectionality has yet to gain a firm foothold in the domain of political science; within the past decade national empirical studies such as the Civic Voluntarism Study (Verba et al. 1995) compartmentalized citizens according to a singular "politically relevant characteristic," leading only to an additive rather than multiplicative approach. In evaluating the potential for empowered political participation, also known as agency, among marginalized citizens additive models risk underestimating the severity of their isolation within the political system.

To illustrate its role as a "bridge" concept between theoretical and empirical political science, public identity in this book embraces intersectionality by operationalizing more theoretical treatments of one particular intersectional identity (Collins, 1990; Crenshaw 1991, 1995; Lubiano 1992), the "welfare queen." The concept of public identity contributes to an area of identity research that continues to struggle with a unitary framework at both the theoretical and empirical levels. Earlier empirical work has documented racial and gender consciousness among African American women, making a strong argument for an intersectional explanation of their politicization (Wilcox 1997, 89). Yet some of these findings are dependent also upon respondents' level of education, implying some potential conflation with economic class. Class potentially contributes to the division between politically active African American women and those who are inactive. Earlier work did not have the concept of public identity, a specifically intersectional construct, to use in its research. Public identity provides an exciting opportunity for more penetrating analysis.

The concept of public identity continues the evolution of the definition of citizenship—the gateway to empowered political participation—beyond its earlier boundaries. The entry of race and gender identities into notions of citizenship has exploded the Framers' construction of "we the people" to produce public policy that ushered wider participation into the democratic process. Public identity, as an intersectional construct, further demystifies the ideal of a static, monolithic American citizen. The shift to a term that embraces intersectionality potentially moves the discussion beyond the notion of additive oppressions to a more sophisticated, emancipatory construction (McClure 1992, 112).

Evidence justifying such a shift is compelling. The resistance of public identities to contestation centers on the competing axes of inequality or power that mutually construct public identities. Part of the intransigence of public identity in the political sphere also emanates from its location between the macro- and microlevels of political analysis. Although residing in the discourse (macrolevel), public identities cue microlevel political thinking because they draw upon long-standing beliefs citizens obtain via socialization. For example, long-standing beliefs regarding Black mothers' hyperfertility and laziness, two primary content dimensions of the "welfare queen" public identity, have roots in slavery. The two dimensions act as organizing themes for more recent stereotypes and moral judgments contained in contemporary portrayals of the "welfare queen." Intersectional analysis brings new attention to the threads forming the fabric of one's life.

Outline of the Book

This book investigates the role of the "welfare queen" and the politics of disgust in discourse about welfare politics. Previous empirical research has confirmed that the politically potent construction of a welfare recipient has a specific gender (West 1981; Mink 1998, 1999; Abramovitz 1996) and race (Gilens 1995, 1996; Gilliam 1999) among U.S. citizens, joining more theoretical allegations (Collins 1990; Lubiano 1992; Mink 1998) of the same point. Thus, my focus in this project is on more macrolevel evidence of public identity in the discourse as a supplement for evidence provided elsewhere concerning the presence of public identity in citizens' minds (Feldman and Zaller 1992; Gilens 1995, 1996; Kinder and Sanders 1996; Cose et al. 1999; Gilliam 1999). In the ensuing chapters, I establish the concept of public identity by tracing the evolution of a specific identity, the "welfare queen," in two areas of the public sphere: media discourse and political discourse.

First, I detail the evolution of the public identity of the "welfare queen," tracing its roots to the first Black women in America (chapter 2). I then conduct content analyses of two distinct discourses, the news media and politics, for evidence of the "welfare queen" in the 1996 welfare reform debate (chapters 3 and 4). Having documented evidence of the politics of disgust, I then explore its impact on welfare recipients' lives (chapter 5). This portion of the study represents the empirical investigation of public identity.

Next, I discuss the implications of public identity and the politics of disgust for participatory forms of democratic theory (chapter 6), which seeks to bring us closer to the goal of equality and justice for all. I return to the noble goals of our American democracy and discuss the implications of public identity's impact on democratic deliberation and political outcomes. In the epilogue, I review the most recent plan to renew the PRWA put forth by the Bush administration and passed to date by the House of Representatives. I conclude by briefly discussing the potential for fighting a battle against the politics of disgust on all four fronts. Can the Berthas of the world gain enough of the power of self-definition to eventually eradicate the public identity of the "welfare queen"?

2

Political Culture and the Public
Identity of the "Welfare Queen"

It is the social responsibility of Black women writers to address the
hard questions, even those that Blacks don't want to talk about.
Just as the discourse of criminal violence pathologizes Black men's
lives, welfare discourse pathologizes the lives of Black women.
(Evelyn C. White, *Yari Yari* Conference, New York University,
October 1997)

Evelyn White's words reveal the widespread impact of the
public identity of the "welfare queen," beyond the lives of welfare recipients themselves. The consensus apparent among elites and dominant
groups about welfare recipients is further echoed among American citizens (Gilens 2001; Cose 1999; Kinder and Sanders 1996). Yet the reality
of who welfare recipients are is continually ignored in favor of long-
standing stereotypes and moral judgments about the prototypical beneficiary. In other words, the public identity of welfare recipients masks the
true demographics and needs of welfare recipients.

In *Why Americans Hate Welfare* (2001), Martin Gilens provides
ample evidence of gross error among White American citizens about the
race, residence, and behavioral traits of people who receive benefits from
programs commonly termed "welfare." Much of the explanation, according to Gilens, lies in the erroneous belief that Blacks lack a commitment to the work ethic (76). Though Gilens does not interrogate the falsity of this claim, Kinder and Sanders (1996) provide compelling evidence
that African Americans and Whites share a commitment to principles of
economic individualism such as industry, as well as similar levels of antiwelfare attitudes (see also Cose 1999; Joint Center for Political and Economic Studies 1997; Dawson 1994). Conflation of all welfare recipients

with single, poor Black mothers largely reflects the supercession of inegalitarian traditions of race, gender, and class over the facts concerning the demographic characteristics of welfare recipients.

Gilens asserts that this attribution error originates in a "centuries-old stereotype" (2001, 78) that is replicated and perpetuated by both the print and electronic media. He finds a pattern of association between negative coverage of poverty and the use of pictures of African Americans that is both widespread and consistent over time (118). What Gilens glosses over in his analysis of antiwelfare attitudes are other powerful contributors to the public identity of the "welfare queen." These factors emerge from the fact that the portrayals were not simply Black faces; they were Black *female* faces (see, e.g., 125). Gilens's analyses of race or class and nodding acknowledgment of gender obscures additional aspects of the public identity of the "welfare queen" produced by an intersectional analysis that can examine race and class and gender simultaneously.

Without concepts like public identity, rigorous empirical analysis from an intersectional paradigm is difficult. While the media play a critical role in reinforcing this identity, social scientists lacking intersectional analyses risk complicity (whether intended or not) in reinforcing the public identity of welfare recipients as single, poor Black mothers because their research is subsumed into the national discourse (see Collins 1998a). Such discourses delegitimize the political claims of marginal groups (Young 1997; Collins 1998a). In this chapter and the two that follow, I examine from an intersectional perspective the permeation of the "welfare queen" public identity within American political culture.

Although finding one's voice has long been an objective for Black women (Collins 1990, 94), the challenge for the twenty-first century has become whether anyone is listening (Collins 1998a) and whether the filter of public identity prevents effective democratic listening (see Bickford 1996). Because this analysis focuses on the conflation of public identities of welfare recipients and single, poor African American mothers, it explicitly centers the project in the everyday lives of single, poor Black mothers. In so doing, it validates experiential knowledge (Collins 1990, 209) and "makes sense of people where they are rather than where we would like them to be" (Kelley 1996, 13). The extensive quotation of single, poor Black mothers' words in this chapter (and in chapter 5) is designed to challenge traditional academic treatments of this group, which contribute to a public sphere that devalues and marginalizes them.[1]

Chronicling the political situation of single, poor African American mothers illustrates the challenges posed by public identities to welfare recipients' empowered participation in the national debates surrounding welfare reform and, ultimately, public policy that addresses their needs as articulated by the mothers themselves, not other citizens. In this sense, chapter 2 explains via sociohistorical analysis an assertion made in chapter 1 regarding the impact of a politics of disgust. Ample evidence is provided to show Black women's efforts to exercise political agency and counteract different aspects of the politics of disgust. Conflation of all welfare recipients with single, poor Black mothers largely represents the conflation of racism, sexism, and classism with the facts concerning the identities and behaviors of welfare recipients. The consensus apparent among elites and dominant groups reveals their power to disseminate their opinions, to persuade the American public of such opinions' validity, and to marginalize alternative opinions in the national discourse (see VanDijk 1993, 45). Yet without a comprehensive, integrated attack, the "welfare queen" identity lives on, as we will see in the empirical content analysis of welfare discourse in 1996.

This chapter, which loosely spans three historical stages of welfare politics, provides a sociohistorical profile of the evolution and construction of a "welfare queen" public identity that continues to be a product of elite and dominant group consensus, despite ongoing contestation from above and below. The development of the "welfare queen" public identity has been shaped by inegalitarian traditions of racism, sexism, and classism from the dark side of an American political culture of freedom and rugged individualism. The "welfare queen" public identity, a contemporary moniker applied to welfare recipients, has two organizing dimensions: hyperfertility and laziness. This chapter reveals the origins of these content areas; chapters 3 and 4 test their relationship to policy outcomes in 1996.

Further, the more general emphasis in American political culture upon individual-level explanations for sociopolitical problems rather than systemic explanations (Merelman 1984, 1; see also Mullings 1997) is exacerbated in a political context of disgust. In particular, judgments of compliance with the American political value of individualism have even greater political impact when the public identity of welfare recipients is cued. Among White Americans, Gilens found support for cutting welfare jumped from 63 percent to 71 percent when the question asked about cutting spending for "people on welfare" as opposed to "cutting spending on welfare" (2001, 64). Why are "people on welfare" considered (to borrow a phrase from chapter 1) so "damned disgusting"?

It is again important to note that privileged African Americans have joined their European-American counterparts to embrace many aspects of the public identity of the "welfare queen." As I detail the context of welfare politics in the United States, I pay special attention to long-standing beliefs about single, poor Black mothers by elites and dominant groups across race and gender and class boundaries. The pathologizing discourse focused on the poor mothering skills of Black women. These inegalitarian stereotypes and moral judgments legitimated discriminatory treatment of Black women by civic groups, legislators, and government bureaucrats. When welfare recipients stood up and said, "Enough," the continuing consensus among elites, the media, and academics led to cultural cooptation and ultimately backlash.

Bad Black Mamas

The stereotype of Black women as bad mothers dates to slavery, when the terms "Jezebel" and "Mammy" represented oversexed and asexual women respectively (White 1985) who shared in common neglect of their own children, in favor of having sex (the "Jezebel") or tending the master's children (the "Mammy"). Single, poor Black women now have more nuanced "controlling images" (Collins 1990, 76) that have a material impact on their lives, including that of the "welfare queen." The idea of "controlling images" of women standing at the intersections of race, class, and gender has been examined most thoroughly from a theoretical perspective (see, e.g., Collins 2000, Lubiano 1992, Crenshaw 1995). This chapter proceeds from a more historiographical perspective to foreground the two components of an empirical "controlling image," the stereotypes and moral judgments that constitute the public identity of the "welfare queen."

"Welfare," a program originating in the late nineteenth century for the "worthy white widow" was quickly characterized as one dominated by the "immoral Black 'welfare queen'" (Roberts 1997), as Black women, limited by institutional and implementational constraints, pursued the equal access constitutionally guaranteed to them. The portrayal of bad mothers emanating from slavery became a part of the assumptions undergirding the implementation of New Deal programs, as the state sought to regulate maternal behavior.

During the first wave of welfare politics prior to and during the New Deal, the construction and implementation of facially neutral public assistance policies were influenced by long-standing beliefs of race, gender, and class domination held by those advocating for (not merely against) poor relief. In the absence of a larger social movement, single, poor African American mothers fought their battles individually to ensure their families' survival. With the advent of the National Welfare Rights Organization (NWRO) in the 1960s, however, single, poor African American mothers recognized that political institutions were responsible for their discriminatory experiences with the welfare bureaucracy. Instead of choosing to psychologically withdraw from the political process, the NWRO was the product of support-seeking activities which ultimately fueled collective action (West 1981). Their work was reinforced by a 1960s political culture containing collective action frameworks (see W. Gamson 1992) that encouraged resistance. As those frameworks disappeared, issue frames within political culture drew on the same long-standing beliefs of race (Gilens 1995), gender (Mink 1998), and class domination, as well as newer images of single, poor African American mothers as political activists to again silence their voices in the welfare discourse. During this third period of welfare politics, the underlying assumptions of all dominant welfare issue frames coalesced into a single controlling image, the "welfare queen."

The public identity of the "welfare queen," a product of the political culture, effectively stymied single, poor Black mothers' empowered participation in the public sphere, and limited the success of various policy prescriptions to end poverty. To comprehend the roots of this occurrence, we must look first at early government involvement. From its very start, "woman-centered" social welfare policy has meant "mother-centered" social welfare policy, introducing the state as an agent regulating maternal behavior.

Enforcing Victorian Womanhood

Long before there were "welfare queens," pink Cadillacs, or public housing projects, American citizens sought to capitalize on the American value of charity toward the less fortunate by pursuing state funding for poor, single-female-headed families. The expression of this political value of charity involved rhetorical and legal arguments from reformers and women's groups that can be interpreted as a brand of cultural feminism often described as maternalism. Yet, although the activism may have challenged gender norms, the construction of motherhood and the policies women's groups pursued in welfare politics are better described as paternalistic maternalism. Early social policies championed by elite and middle-class women involved judgments by these women of "what was best for" the poor mothers considered the real target populations of the proposed policies (Skocpol 1995, 72).

The paternalistic maternalism reflected in the rhetoric of women's groups like the National Women's Congress exemplified the correspondence bias aspect of the politics of disgust, complete with concomitant unintended political consequences. For example, White women's groups argued in the courts for the "protection of the 'mothers of the race' from overwork," persuading judges of the need for legalized gender discrimination such as maximum-hour laws and minimum-wage-law invalidations (Skocpol 1995, 25, 99). The need for a social welfare program like Aid to Dependent Children (ADC) was in part created by the lack of access to economic independence reinforced by women's groups' brand of paternalistic maternalism.

Although Skocpol correctly notes that American upper- and middle-class women were able to make greater gains in maternalist social policy than their sisters abroad (1995, 27), as with Gilens, her work in American political development treats gender and race (as well as gender and class) as mutually distinct categories rather than interrelated (see, e.g., 114–115, 122–123, 126, 221). The maximum-hour laws and minimum-wage laws were designed (and enforced) for a target population that did not include African American women. The political culture underlying support for widows' pensions as states approved such programs prior to the New Deal featured notions of racial, class, and gender hierarchy, often woven into a call for nationalism.

In addition to the appeal to American nationalism, women's activism on behalf of poor-relief programs became a part of a generalized effort to maintain race, ethnicity, and gender hierarchy through the regulation of sexuality and fertility of women (Collins 1998b, 77; see also Skocpol 1995, 25; McClintock 1993).[2] Single, poor Black mothers were urged by elites of both races to look toward Victorian ideals of motherhood as the solution to their problems. However, the structure of political and economic institutions prevented such aspirations from coming to fruition, given a U.S. political economy dependent on Black women's inexpensive labor as domestic servants and agricultural workers. When the fantasy failed to translate into reality, emphasis focused mostly on individual-level, behavioral explanations, leaving single, poor Black mothers in the same political and economic position.

Mothers of the Nation

Exhorting American nationalism, advocates for widows' pensions presented poor-relief programs as a way of assuaging concerns about the purity and perpetuity of American democracy in an era of racial strife and influxes of immigrants. Many women's arguments for public poverty-alleviation programs were tied to nationalist ideology, which is itself predicated upon a specific theory of gender difference (see Collins 1998b; McClintock 1993; Landes 2001). Nationalism requires a specific construction of women as mothers to justify many of its political prescriptions. Although considered the part of the nation who transmitted and produced the national culture, women, as biological reproducers of the nation, also represented the boundaries to be preserved by means of restrictions on sexual and marital relations (McClintock 1993, 62). Having been brought into the nation symbolically through their husbands (McClintock 1993; W. Williams 1991), widows' pensions were thought to extend beyond the deaths of their husbands the privilege afforded to married White women. Their positions would be preserved by public assistance after their husbands' deaths.

The rhetoric of maternalist social policy came in paternalistic wrapping. Victorian notions of motherhood overlapped with nationalist portrayals of mothers' primary roles as the caretakers of future American citizens in the discourse surrounding widows' pensions. Advocates for widows' pensions argued that the only way for these mothers to produce worthy citizens was through reform and renewal of maternal practice (Mink 1999, 93). In others words, to be a "good mother," one had to embrace Victorian notions of motherhood (Collins 1990, 78; 1998b; McClintock 1993). Remaining within this circumscribed ideological position of women's inclusion without a direct demand for women's political agency enabled poor-relief programs to pass through state legislatures well before women's suffrage.

White American women's arguments for widows' pensions followed in the same vein as those for Christian Temperance and women's suffrage: exploiting White American males' fears of the "browning" of the United States by embracing their specified role as "mothers of the race." Members of the Women's Christian Temperance Union, the National Congress of Mothers, and the General Federation of Women's Clubs were "well-placed to press upon legislators and public opinion across the land the "moral values" for new social policies designed to protect women workers and their children (Skocpol 1995, 27). As "culture bearers," they encouraged their female compatriots to transfer the important elements of American citizenship, including industry, economic individualism, Christianity, and the social hierarchy (of race, class, and gender) to their male children in particular. Mothers' responsibilities varied according to racial group, part and parcel of the arguments for regulating sexuality and marriage to maintain racial purity (Collins 1998b, 69).

White southern American women, strong in their beliefs in women's suffrage and Christian Temperance, shaped the racial rhetoric of the proposed widows' pensions. The women's club movement remained overwhelmingly segregated until well into the twentieth century (Giddings 1984). The political legitimacy of women's action in the public sphere to the overwhelming majority of White American women in the club movement was infused with a specific race as well as a specific gender as they continued to benefit from the intersection of racial and economic privilege afforded them in the United States.

An important part of preserving racial and ethnic hierarchy in the United States involved the limited embrace of Eastern and Southern European immigrants. To White American women, the argument for widows' pensions proposed "Americanizing" European immigrants like the Irish and Italians, teaching them the ways of domestic science to prevent the country from being overrun by the unclean elements in society. Playing the race card, as long as it advanced the gender card, received little critical attention at the time.

Saving Our Sisters: The Work of the Black Women's Club Movement

Despite all of the efforts of clubwomen and other well-intentioned middle-class Blacks, the socioeconomic and cultural status of Black women prevented their being presumed virtuous. Stereotypes of Black women as overly fecund and licentious lingered from slavery, when such beliefs had been used to justify White males' sexual abuse of Black women, including rape, forced prostitution, and forced reproduction of the slave population. Black women's bodies had been regulated through laws delineating the status of their children as slaves (regardless of the father's status); through court decisions preventing sexual abuse from falling within the definition of cruel punishment; and through an economic and cultural context that encouraged forced prostitution.[3] Moreover, after the Civil War ended, the Freedmen's Bureaus perpetuated Black women's oppression by shrugging off claims of domestic violence or abandonment by Black men as reason to qualify as a single Black mother for federally guaranteed assistance.[4] These conditions continued well into the twentieth century (Davis 1981).

The activism of the Black women's club movement further brings into focus the dilemma of political resistance within the confines of the American political culture. The clubs' efforts on behalf of racial uplift preached the ideals of Victorian motherhood as an individual-level solution to the problems faced by single, poor Black mothers. Their efforts, much like those of White American women, produced programs (both public and private) that in practice reinforced the idea of women's dependency, despite their rhetorical calls for economic independence. Such charitable and political work also alienated poor Black mothers from the Black middle class (Gaines 1996).

The exclusion of single, poor Black mothers from access to widows' pensions (Amott 1990) increased the focus of an already focused Black middle class. The transformation of Black women from "de mules uh de world" to persons deserving of just treatment and, more practically, of access to government aid and protection became a major project for Black middle-class American women. Like White American women, however, this form of social and political activism traded intersecting hierarchies; in this case, they traded gender and class biases in pursuit of racial transformation. In a political culture of southern apartheid and northern hostility, denied the gender protection guaranteed to White southern women, the Black women's club movement sought to combat the dominant minstrel images of licentious females and male buffoons with an emphasis on patriarchal gender conventions (Gaines 1996, 78). In fact, despite the fact that several leaders in the club movement personally challenged gender conventions by marrying later than typical of the period, most had very traditional views of marriage (Giddings 1984, 95–96). As "culture bearers," they urged their daughters to counteract fears of the predatory behavior of White southern men by living beyond moral reproach and by gaining the protection of a husband.

Similarly, Black clubwomen's emphasis on domestic science represented an attempt to imprint middle-class values on a population lacking middle-class socioeconomic standing for the general cause of racial uplift (Giddings 1984, 97; Gaines 1996). In so doing, they embraced the philosophy of Booker T. Washington (Giddings 1984, 101) in terms of self-transformation, an explicitly individualistic approach (Simpson 1998). Like Washington, Black clubwomen taught the "gospel of the toothbrush," personal and household hygiene, discipline, thrift, piety, and "proper" child-rearing techniques. Yet the relationships between members of Black women's clubs and their less fortunate sisters was not one of equals (Collins 1990, 153; Giddings 1984). Although united in the goal of racial uplift, Black clubwomen lamented out-of-wedlock childbirth as immoral, low-class behavior.

The focus on domestic science shared by Black and White women's clubs had distinct political implications. Their activities and political pressure were primary factors in changing the American political culture to accept government's responsibility to "promote the general welfare" by actively assisting the poor and needy. The political strategies used to obtain state poor-relief programs provided the political socialization that eventually aided White American clubwomen in obtaining the vote, as well as federal social programs. Black clubwomen, through their private programs, helped single, poor African American women in service of their cause, racial uplift, and succeeded finally on the political stage in the struggle for passage of antilynching legislation. Looking at the isolated victories of both races as a whole reveals a larger intervention made within a political culture of government noninterference. Together, these changes laid part of the groundwork for the New Deal.

Their political success, however, was a double-edged sword. The ideological justifications utilized to support these social programs reinscribed hierarchy in three ways. First, they reinforced women's role as traditional mothers, mere conduits in the production of future citizens with no independent identity of their own. This lingering construction of womanhood also reinforced American nationalism, muting the challenge to the structural inequality and American individualism that social programs like widows' pensions could potentially represent. Female autonomy was simply never the intention (Sapiro 1990, 45, 51) because in part, the public identity of "woman" was associated exclusively with the roles of wife and mother. No independent existence was assumed and clubwomen did not attempt to force such consideration.

Tied to a nationalism that enforced racial hierarchy, widows' pensions became one more aspect of U.S. citizenship denied to single poor, African American mothers. Racialized arguments for widows' pensions implied that the target population consisted of White Americans and European immigrants only. White American clubwomen took up the cause for European immigrants, relegating poor Black mothers to the care of an already burdened and marginalized population of Black middle-class women. Yet despite their shared race and gender, single, poor Black mothers' needs (as articulated by the mothers themselves) receded even further from view.

To the degree that they were presented at all, the perceived needs of single, poor Black mothers were articulated in the public sphere by class-privileged Black women. In championing social policies "for the good of less privileged women" (Skocpol 1995, 72), Black clubwomen similarly focused on individual-level proposals for social transformations. Drawing largely on the philosophy of Booker T. Washington, they presumed that urging behavior that was consistent with Victorian and middle-class values would ultimately produce social and economic stability in the lives of single, poor African American mothers and their families. This emphasis on maternal behavior, particularly regarding child rearing and fertility, is usually missed by analyses focusing exclusively on race (e.g., Gilens 2001) but remains a key component in contemporary discussions of the public identity of the "welfare queen."

The rhetorical arguments used to agitate for widows' pensions and other poor-relief programs reveals the degree to which single, poor African American mothers were excluded from participation in their own empowerment. The exclusion proceeded intraracially as well as interracially. The failure of class-privileged women of both races to fully incorporate the articulated (instead of presumed) needs of single, poor Black mothers illustrates the necessity of intersectional analysis across race and class boundaries. The correspondence-bias aspect of the politics of disgust led to emphases on reform of maternal behavior as the catalyst for improving the economic standard of living for single mothers and their children. The political cultural orientation toward individualist remedies for poverty and reform of maternal behavior coalesced with beliefs originating in slavery about poor African American women. These long-standing traditions in American political culture became assumptions undergirding the implementation of federal public assistance programs and are evident during the next two stages of welfare politics.

The New Deal: A Fair Deal for Black Mothers?

The Great Depression acts as a great divider of history for most Americans, but the majority of poor and working-class Black women saw little change between the two eras. Long-standing beliefs of hyperfertility and laziness among single, poor Black mothers remained firmly entrenched before, during, and after the Great Depression. While by 1932 all states had mothers' pension programs, worthy mothers were most often widows (thus the term "widows' pensions"), not single mothers nor deserted or divorced mothers (Abramovitz 1996, 60). Within the framework of patriarchy, the ideological assertion that a woman's proper place was in the home was conditioned by a mother's race and class. As a result, extension of mothers' pension programs to single, poor Black mothers was sporadic (West 1981, 290) and maintained an emphasis on reform of maternal behavior to conform with the Victorian standards previously discussed.

By this time, the beliefs about single, poor Black mothers' hyperfertility and laziness were mapped onto norms of "proper" maternal behavior. Black mothers were judged as failing to conform to these standards. Further, the combination of stereotypes and moral judgments interacted with the historical context of the Great Depression and a fledgling welfare bureaucracy. The interaction of public opinion and context conditioned the implementation of public policy during the wide expansion of the welfare state as part of the New Deal. The experiences of single, poor African American mothers at this time reveals the intersecting roles of race and gender in the implementation of New Deal social welfare policies.

Dependent Children without Dependent Mothers

When Title IV of the Social Security Act created the Aid to Dependent Children (ADC) program in 1935, the federal mandate evened out the financial differences among state programs but not the differences in implementation. Importantly, the Social Security Act also created a Social Security program that was the product of a deal between President Roosevelt and southern Democratic congressmen. In exchange for the latter's support of the legislation, the administration excluded two large employment sectors from consideration for Social Security benefits (both old-age insurance and unemployment benefits): domestic service and agricultural work (Quadagno 1994, 20), the two sectors employing most African Americans, particularly in the South.

ADC began to gain the public perception that it was a program for "undeserving single mothers" (Abramovitz 1996, 64; Quadagno 1994; West 1981) after survivor benefits in Social Security shifted most widows—the mothers considered deserving of help—to Social Security benefits. This turn of events led to the public perception of ADC as a program for both morally corrupt single mothers and African Americans who were ineligible for Social Security. Yet the typical ADC recipient remained "a West Virginia mother whose husband had died in a mine accident. Honest, hard-working, God-fearing, white Protestant folk. Rural" (West 1981, 18). The intertwining perceptions of morally corrupt single mothers and Blacks, though the product of a longer history, became tightly affiliated with public policy at this stage of American political development (Quadagno 1994; Abramovitz 1996; Amott 1990; West 1981). This lingering conflation of race with welfare programs for the undeserving poor continued to have serious political ramifications in the 1990s (Gilens 1995, 1996, 2001).

Although the public believed ADC served unworthy African American mothers, the racial composition of its recipients did not quite match that perception. Prior to World War II, no more than 14 percent of all African American applicants were granted ADC (Abramovitz 1996, 71). The African American community showed a greater openness to sustaining women on their own (Gordon 1990, 35), yet the implementation of federal programs (especially but not only in southern states) routinely featured selective use of loosely defined regulations to deny Black women welfare benefits (Amott 1990, 288; Roberts, 1997; Mink 1998). To obtain ADC benefits, applicants were subject to a "morals" test that was tantamount to providing state oversight of women's sexual and childbearing behavior, in addition to the long-standing regulation of parenting. The relevant clauses were vague and hence ripe for abuse by ADC bureaucrats seeking to maintain the racial and economic status quo. In addition, African American applicants were told they could find a job; that they were capable of work and did not need government assistance. State implementation policies, such as that of Louisiana, deemed some mothers to be "more suitable as workers than as mothers" (Mink 1998, 47).

Pinkie Pilcher of Greenwood, Mississippi, illustrates this point in her letter to then-president Franklin Delano Roosevelt, relating this experience:

> I was in the office a few days ago. A woman was there she had five children and a husband not able to work. They told her to go hunt washings. . . . The white people don't pay anything for their washing. She cant [*sic*] do enough washing to feed her family. (Lerner 1973, 401)

Intimidation designed to preserve the racial and economic status quo were also part of the varied interpretations of ADC rules and policies (Abramovitz 1996; Roberts 1997; Amott 1990; West 1981). In her letter to President Roosevelt, Lutensia Dillard of the Colored Women Democrat Club of Woodland Park Biteley, Michigan, wrote a more direct political appeal:

> We can't get any Welfare help unless we sign our homes over to the welfare. We do not want to be beggers [*sic*] . . . Our club were and are still for you and all of your supporters, one hundred percent. . . . We aren't getting a fair deal. Some of our boys are being drafted for service for our country and here we are in a free land are not aloud [*sic*] to work and make a living for their wives and childrens. (Lerner 1973, 405)

These letters are examples of poor Black women speaking for themselves in 1941 in response to discriminatory local policy implementation. Despite the fact that African American women have worked throughout their history in the United States, they continued to suffer from being stereotyped as lazy, which originated during slavery. Mainstream Americans consistently judged poor Black women as immoral for failing to conform to the American political value of industry, when in fact they were working and/or suffered extreme unchecked employment discrimination. This moral judgment continued to serve as a filter through which many Americans heard the political claims advanced by the movement for welfare rights in the 1960s and 1970s (Edsall and Edsall 1991).

The justification for extraordinarily low numbers of Black women receiving Aid to Dependent Children was reported by a southern local office worker: "The number of Negro cases is few due to the unanimous feeling on the part of the staff that there are more work opportunities for Negro women and [the staff's] intense desire not to interfere with local labor conditions. The attitude that they have always gotten along, and that 'all they do is have more children'" (quoted in Roberts 1997, 206). The work opportunities referred to by this worker were the lowest paid and least economically empowering, because of the re-entrenchment of southern racial apartheid after the turn of the century and following World War I. Black women were employed in the same positions of domestic service and field labor as during slavery, and often received little remuneration. Many White Americans—including some in policy decision-making positions—subscribed to stereotypes and moral judgments of African American women as lazy and ripe for childbearing, but these beliefs are clearly challenged by the words of the above single Black mothers in the 1930s and '40s.

Rosie the Riveter Retains Racial Privilege

The post–World War I years signaled a rise in so-called pink-collar jobs, clerical and low-level administrative positions that were increasingly accessible to women with certain job skills or comparable education. Pink was not the only color associated with these occupations. After World War II, job-training programs funneled single, poor Black mothers into domestic service and other service-related industries. This practice joined with continued discriminatory implementation of the ADC program. In response to the reluctance to hire African American women for jobs paying livable wages, the U.S. Women's Bureau created training programs for service jobs only, despite overwhelming shortages in clerical positions (typists, stenographers) and white-collar positions (nurses, teachers, social workers, medical aides) (Abramovitz 1996, 68). Further, African American women were judged "inherently unfit and uneducable" (Mink 1998, 45).

Southern states committed egregious but not isolated discrimination. During the 1940s and 1950s, southern ADC offices systematically and routinely approved lesser monthly allotments for African American mothers than their White counterparts. Moreover, half of those Black mothers who applied were (illegally) denied benefits outright between 1950 and 1960 (West 1981, 19). Discriminatory ADC implementation remained a fact of life for them until the 1960s. Contrary to the belief in laziness, statistics reveal that in 1961 single Black mothers receiving ADC who were also working outnumbered White single mothers similarly situated by a ratio of two to one in southern states (Abramovitz 1996, 69).

In addition to discriminatory implementation to avoid disturbing "local labor conditions," the anonymous southern ADC worker quoted above also described the interaction between long-standing beliefs and government bureaucracy regarding the reproductive proclivities of single, poor African American mothers. Regulations related to women's marital and childbearing choices focused on ferreting out fraudulent claims by means of "man-in-the-house" rules, forbidding an adult male from living in the home with the mother and her children. Many of the regulations were enforced with midnight raids: social workers literally visited to check for welfare fraud (Abramovitz 1996, 72; Mink 1998, 93; West 1981). Moreover, until 1968, a mother's childbearing behavior could legitimize the denial of benefits altogether; in *King v. Smith* (1968) the Supreme Court overturned Alabama's policy, ruling that states could no longer deny assistance on the basis of a mother's *alleged immorality*. The policy at issue had rendered 16,000 children (90 percent of whom were African American) ineligible for benefits (Mink 1998, 50). Thus, facially neutral policies clearly had a disparate impact on single, poor African American mothers, in part due to entrenched beliefs about their sexual behavior.

Based on the words of single, poor African American mothers and welfare workers themselves, the manifest role of public perceptions of single, poor African American mothers in the administration of ADC is clear. It is especially important to note that these perceptions derived from the mothers' multiple identities. It was not merely because they were single, or African American, or mothers, or poor; it was because they were all of these simultaneously that they were denied assistance, funneled into service-level job training, and subjected to "midnight raids." Notably, the events of these years further hardened hierarchies among women when race- and class-privileged women later became the overwhelming majority of social workers and social welfare bureaucrats (Mink 1998). But the hardening did not solely occur along the solitary plane of race or class. While the experience of racism seems to have taken center stage in this discussion, race alone was not automatically a unifying force in welfare

politics, as the women of the National Welfare Rights Organization dis-
covered in their search for allies among middle-class African American
churches and civil rights organizations.

"Every Woman Is One Man Away from Welfare": Subscribing to a Culture of Resistance

The above statement, coined by Johnnie Tillmon, the first chair of the National Welfare Rights Organization (NWRO), reveals the organization's
impact on political culture. The statement became a mantra for mainstream women's rights organizations as they decried the "feminization of
poverty" during the mid- to late-'70s and early '80s. The construction of
welfare as a feminist issue, however, originated with the NWRO in 1968.

Part of the legacy of African American civil rights activism centers
upon the change it engendered in American political culture. The modern
civil rights movement, which served as an inspiration and laboratory for
numerous social movements, fundamentally altered norms, beliefs, and
practices in a way that enhanced the participatory nature of American
democracy. Similarly, the NWRO also contributed to the mainstream political culture. Its history provides an example of how welfare motherhood served as a site of empowerment during the organization's brief existence, enhancing (albeit temporarily) the cause of participatory democracy. Preexisting political conditions conducive to collective action and
social activism encouraged group consciousness among single, poor
Black mothers through an emphasis on self-definition, self-valuation, self-
reliance, and self-transformation. Their activism, we will see, also falls
within a larger tradition of Black women's activism that focuses simultaneously upon the struggle for group survival and the struggle for institutional transformation (Collins 1990, 141–142). Yet it differed from the
earlier efforts of clubwomen in its willingness to challenge gender, class,
and race norms in the Black community.

The women of the NWRO confronted the falsity of their public identity head on, resulting in new experiences of political participation that
forced limited elite acknowledgment of their intersecting race, gender,
and class identities in the making of public policy. Sparked by a larger
political "culture of resistance," the NWRO, through its conflictual
relationships with larger social movements, ultimately presented an

alternative to existing models of political empowerment through self-definition and self-determination. The durable beliefs of poor Black women's laziness and hyperfertility were finally challenged in the nation's public discourse.

The NWRO served two purposes. Its chapters exemplified microlevel support seeking for individual welfare recipients through its member chapters, and in its entirety it exemplified macrolevel collective action, peopled overwhelmingly by single, poor Black mothers. No other organization influenced public discourse on social welfare policy by strenuous attempts to provide to such mothers self-definition and determination as did the NWRO. Its framework for collective action developed in dialogue with American and African American political cultures. The framework, which includes a common sense of injustice, political agency, and identity (W. Gamson 1992, 7), was shaped at every turn by this dialogic process. The ten-year life span of the NWRO serves as an organizing thread to review single, poor Black mothers' collective feelings of injustice, agency, and identity during this era of welfare politics.

The Struggle for Group Survival: Recognizing Injustice

Founded in 1967 as an umbrella for various local grassroots organizations, the NWRO had two political goals: decent jobs with adequate pay for those who could work and adequate income for those who could not (West 1981, 39; Abramovitz 1996). In pursuit of these goals, the NWRO used micro- and macrolevel strategies: solving individual grievances in attempts to gain access to legally guaranteed assistance and collective agitation, respectively, for change at welfare agencies (Abramovitz 1996, 129; West 1981, 40). Although not originally defined as such, the NWRO became an organization populated by single, poor Black mothers, given the reality of racially discriminatory welfare policy implementation and organizers' mobilization efforts, which occurred primarily in heavily Black urban areas (West 1981, 3).[5]

The NWRO overtly challenged stereotypical beliefs about single, poor Black mothers, as well as the state's tendency to regulate poor Black women's bodies. It addressed common misperceptions about welfare mothers, as this comment from Anne Henderson of Milwaukee, Wisconsin, demonstrates:

If you think that I'm gonna have a baby—and watch that child grow up with no food or clothing; and then watch him go to school where teachers don't teach him anything; and worry that he's gonna become a pimp or start shooting up dope; and finally, when he's raised, see him go into the army and get really shot up in there—if you think I'm gonna go through all that pain and suffering for an extra $50 or $100 or even $500 a month, why you must be crazy. (Milwaukee County Welfare Rights Organization 1972, 82).

This statement explicitly confronts the hyperfertility thesis and challenges the notion that single, poor Black mothers are bad mothers who care more for themselves than their children. Henderson clearly speaks to a mother's love that prefers not to bring children into a world of poverty, inadequate education, crime, and militarism. Single, poor Black mothers were well aware that the public identity of the "welfare queen" existed, and their awareness had an impact on the self-esteem of the mothers themselves.

Johnnie Tillmon concurs in part with Henderson, explaining the link to self-esteem:

The notion that AFDC mothers are immoral is another way of saying that all women are likely to become whores unless they're kept under control by men and marriage. Even many of my own sisters on welfare believe these things about themselves. (Tillmon 1972, 116)

Her incisive confirmation of what social psychologists term stereotype internalization (Crocker et al. 1998) comes from a woman not steeped in the academy but who after nineteen years of agricultural labor, domestic service, and laundry service received $363 monthly to raise three teenagers in 1973 when her health failed (West 1981, 89; Abramovitz 1996).

NWRO members and leaders similarly confronted the long-standing belief of laziness. Statistics from 1972 reveal that only 15.9 percent of the AFDC recipient population was able-bodied (Milwaukee County Welfare Rights Organization 1972, 75) as Congress debated stricter work requirements at the urging of Senator Russell Long (D-LA). Further, the overwhelming majority of that population were already working or in job training. Single, poor Black mothers vehemently disputed their unwillingness to work, as evidenced by the words of Marie Bracey, from Wetumpka, Alabama:

> We want jobs. We need jobs. And we poor people want to work. But we do not want to give up our rights, our dignity, and life, and then go and get the lowest wages for the job which will not adequately take care of, or benefit in the way of helping, our children. (Milwaukee County Welfare Rights Organization 1972, 112)

Acting in a similar vein, Johnnie Tillmon took a survey of 600 residents of her housing project in Watts, California, and presented the government with her results. Of those surveyed, 599 wanted jobs and training. So Tillmon and ADC Mothers Anonymous set up a job-training program, but their request for government funding was rejected (West 1981, 92; Nadasen 2002). As is evident from the above words and actions, the NWRO and its members clearly sought to change persisting misperceptions of single, poor Black mothers.

The history of the NWRO indicates that the organization began as a number of local grassroots organizations of women seeking help with their welfare agency encounters and social support. These support-seeking responses to negative experiences, which are common in the face of discrimination, furnish the foundation for the sense of injustice[6] communicated by the above personal statements. Through the experiences of social support and problem solving, women involved in local groups were able to reinterpret their experiences by recognizing that their experiences were not completely of their own making. Such an understanding restored some of their self-esteem and encouraged collective action for structural change while providing access to information and resources so they could ameliorate their individual situations.

Developing "Mother Power": Emerging Senses of Agency

The experiences provided by involvement in the NWRO combined with the political culture to support the second component of building a psychological framework for collective action: a sense of agency. Although the African American political culture, particularly the civil rights movement, represented a challenge to the American political culture, its impact was constrained by what Joshua Gamson (1996) and Cathy Cohen

(1996, 1999) define as "boundary drawing." Single, poor Black mothers received two conflicting messages from the civil rights movement: the power of numbers as a moral force for change, and the force of boundaries drawn to exclude them from the benefits of such changes. The presumed logic of shared race or gender identity producing a predisposition to political solidarity did not hold for members of the NWRO seeking solidarity with African American churches or national feminist organizations. In this sense, the NWRO came face-to-face with one aspect of the politics of disgust: the lack of solidarity with similarly (but not identically) situated potential allies. Fortunately, members' experiences with the NWRO helped to negate the debilitating force of boundary drawing, but the boundaries limited the possible degree of systematic transformation.

Many policy proposals presented to the country by the civil rights movement materially benefited the portion of the African American population who could take advantage of antidiscrimination policies related to buying homes, attending college, blue- and white-collar employment, and so on. The overwhelming majority of women and children who constituted the backbone of the civil rights movement possessed the basic resources commonly considered necessary for political participation, including some secondary education, employment, and family economic support. Similarly, the strategies employed by the movement, assimilationist in nature, attempted to counteract enduring beliefs that Blacks lacked the cherished American political values held by middle-class Whites. As a direct strategy countering the psychological development of prejudice among Whites, it was in some ways successful. But the strategy also drew a boundary, consciously and unconsciously, between deserving Blacks who were quintessentially American in morals and values despite their race, and undeserving Blacks, whose "lower class behavior" (to use the language of the Black women's club movement) left them outside what Cathy Cohen (1999) terms "the boundary of Blackness."

The degree of political isolation and the refusal of others to stand in solidarity were quickly revealed when the NWRO sought political and financial allies. Despite a base constituency of single, poor Black mothers, few race-, gender- or class-based organizations responded to its appeals (West 1981, 15; see also Abramovitz 1996). Importantly, organizations focused along singular axes of oppression shunned members of the NWRO based on multiple aspects of their identities. For example, the NWRO received no support from the largest independent institution in the African American community, the Black church. Even though NWRO Executive Director George Wiley acknowledged the antiwelfare sentiment among the Black middle-class church population (West 1981, 31), the alienation of the NWRO by Black ministers was attributed simultaneously to the Black church's typical prejudice against single mothers because of its focus on men as heads of families and the growing push at the time to restore the Black family (ibid., 229). Thus the lack of support can be described accurately only with an approach that acknowledges the intersections of race, gender, and class. As a result of such boundaries within African American political culture, the highest levels of support for the NWRO were received, ironically, from White Protestant groups.

The financial contributions of White Protestants dwindled, however, as they noticed and reported upon the lack of support from Black churches, a point not lost on the NWRO either. The NWRO's experience with the Poor People's Campaign in 1968 and the words of NWRO members themselves reveal the organization's frustrating attempts to find major African American and feminist organizations willing to stand in solidarity with them.

The NWRO began as an organization seeking to build a "poor people's movement." Its idea for a poor people's march on Washington developed well before the efforts of Martin Luther King Jr. and the Southern Christian Leadership Conference (SCLC) (West 1981, 215; Giddings 1984, 312–313). Until the proposed 1968 march, SCLC and King largely ignored the NWRO, despite its ten thousand members. It took a heated meeting between leaders of both organizations[7] before SCLC publicly acknowledged the contributions of the NWRO and went on record in support of welfare rights and organizing. King's ignorance of welfare rights issues was striking (Giddings 1984, 313), and the NWRO insisted on improved working relations before pledging its support for the SCLC's Poor People's Campaign (West 1981, 215).

Leaders and members of the NWRO clearly understood that other civil rights organizations presented obstacles just as daunting as those of the welfare bureaucracy. Garnette Reddic of Milwaukee, Wisconsin, condemned the neglect of government and political organizations:

> You can bet we see ourselves as some kind of political football, and we're tired of all the "sportsmen" kicking us around. (Milwaukee County Welfare Rights Organization 1972, 76)

Along these same lines an unnamed Black female NWRO leader in 1970 took Black leaders to task at the NWRO national conference for not acknowledging that welfare was a relevant issue:

> The power structure knows we're fighting. . . . They [our opponents] come in all colors. Some of us say the power structure is all white. It's a lie. It's not all white. There's the black power structure which looks down on us worse than the white power structure. . . . We say the white man is splitting us up. Wrong! We're splitting up ourselves. The white man doesn't separate us. We separate ourselves. (West 1981, 230)

Both of the above examples highlight the necessity of the NWRO's being a vehicle of political participation by and for single, poor African American mothers. By observing the successes of the civil rights movement and participating in their own work to provide support to members and welfare justice for the nation, the members of the organizations that constituted the NWRO gained the consciousness that collective action can alter material conditions. The messages gleaned from the American and African American political cultures, though, told them that anything they sought would be achieved alone, not in solidarity with leading organizations.

Agency, as the second component of a collective action framework, was critical in moving masses of single, poor African American mothers to act publicly. The socialization effects of such political action were noted by several members, including Johnnie Tillmon:

> You have to learn to fight, to be aggressive, or you just don't make it. If you can survive being on welfare, you can survive anything. It gives you a kind of freedom, a sense of your own power and togetherness with other women. (Tillmon 1972, 116)

The socialization provided by political action reinforced the sense of agency, and also began to change the self-defeating identity possessed by many single, poor Black mothers involved in the NWRO.

"I Am Somebody": From Identity to Consciousness

Tillmon's coactivists also found that the NWRO and its chapters fostered a rising group consciousness and anger that politicized women and added their voices to discussions of welfare reform (West 1981, 6). Mildred Calvert of Milwaukee, Wisconsin, echoes Tillmon's conclusions:

> After I joined the organization, they took me and helped me settle the problem. . . . Then I started getting interested in the meetings and listened to what these people were saying and I realized that these people *were* doing something about a situation that has existed all these years but nobody before had ever thought enough of it to do anything about it. . . . That's when I learned of the welfare laws and the Supreme Court decisions . . . and I started wanting to learn more. (Milwaukee County Welfare Rights Organization 1972, 27; emphasis in original)

Later in the narrative, Calvert ceases talking about "these people" and shifts to the pronoun "we":

> I started learning about the Wisconsin welfare cuts coming . . . so we went to . . . Madison to protest the cuts. That when I really started learning . . . how bad the system is, how we are really hated and how people could make you feel degraded and how humiliating it really is to be a welfare recipient to a person who just really doesn't understand . . . all of a sudden, I realized what we were up against, and then I was determined to fight. I was determined. (Milwaukee County Welfare Rights Organization 1972, 29)

Calvert's words describe experiences of political socialization that encouraged not only agency as part of collective action but also confrontation with the public identity of welfare recipients and the politics of disgust. Her words speak clearly about this confrontation. While the self-categorization process had been peppered with experiences with government that produced disempowerment in the past (see, e.g., Milwaukee County Welfare Rights Organization 1972, 27–28), the NWRO fostered an identity of citizenship and political participation among its members, lessening the sense of stigmatization, alienation, and powerlessness (West 1981, 119; Tillmon 1972; Milwaukee County Welfare Rights Organization, 1972). The identification process was the product not solely of political socialization but also of the organizational structure, which nominally and later tacitly encouraged indigenous leadership (West 1981, 22). With three elected chairs and an executive committee from the rank and file throughout its life span, the NWRO clearly urged members to become leaders as they developed their talents.

The earlier comment of the unnamed NWRO organizer regarding opponents of all demographic types applies to this feature of the NWRO as well. The NWRO faced struggles externally and internally because of the "devalued identity" of poor Black women (ibid., 4). Indigenous leaders, as they increased their political experience and strengthened their positions, accused staffers and organizers (who were overwhelmingly White, middle class, and male) of taking unauthorized power (ibid., 58). The collective memory developed through acting and working together for change soon took precedence over the "professional recommendations" of the staff. Consequently, as the organization became of, by, and for single, poor Black mothers, the NWRO lost economic and political support *within* as well as outside the organization (ibid. 77).[8]

While the interlocking nature of race, class, and gender identities as multiple jeopardies left poor Black women with the lowest chance for appearance and effective action in the political sphere, this predisposition did not prevent poor Black mothers from achieving some success due to the efforts of the NWRO. Facing bankruptcy, a more conservative political climate, and diminished support (financial and political), the NWRO closed its national offices in 1975. Many supporters dropped out as the reward structure within American political culture shifted away from direct action and political protest (West 1981, 8, 77). Moreover, many members ultimately found the risks of aggressive political protest and leadership too high over the long term (ibid., 79).

Yet the NWRO's work on behalf of single, poor African American mothers is an example of Black women's community work writ large. The organization fought for group survival and succeeded collectively by means of their "militant" responses to welfare cuts in seven states: California, Massachusetts, Minnesota, Nevada, New Jersey, New York, and Wisconsin. It also lobbied successfully against "suitable home" and "man-in-the-house" policies that violated the mothers' constitutional rights (Abramovitz 1996, 129; Mink 1998; West 1981).[9] Its microlevel strategies of helping the mothers gain access to benefits legally due to them resulted in millions of dollars in increased benefits paid directly to welfare mothers regardless of race (West 1981, 295; Funicello 1993). These aspects of the struggle for group survival, however, represent only half of the NWRO's contribution to Black women's activist tradition.

The Pursuit of Institutional Transformation

The NWRO simultaneously pursued institutional transformation explicitly through its legislative lobbying against President Nixon's Family Assistance Plan and its use in the courts of the sequential test case strategy previously employed brilliantly by the NAACP to fight racial segregation. Single, poor Black mothers active in the NWRO also sought to transform their public identity by demonstrating their similar political values (e.g., their willingness to work) and pushing for reform of the welfare system to foster economic independence. The words of NWRO members and leaders quoted in this section clearly reflect a subconscious effort to challenge the generally held beliefs of hyperfertility and laziness. The pursuit of the two related goals—decent jobs at decent wages and a guaranteed income for those who could not work—reflect their long range goal of transforming the welfare system.

To the NWRO members themselves, their experiences demonstrated the impact of their public identity, devalued in a public sphere that lacked their voices. The welfare rights movement signified more broadly the recognition by single, poor Black mothers that participation was not going to occur at the invitation of political elites, dominant groups or institutions, or even those who claimed to represent them (e.g., the civil rights movement). The most ironic counterclaim to the "dependency" encoded in the public identity of these women was the "mother power" of the NWRO members doing things for themselves.

The NWRO's impact was not limited to the thousands who participated in the welfare rights movement. As mentioned at the beginning of this section, the vision of welfare as a women's issue, embraced by mainstream feminists during the 1970s and 1980s, was originally articulated by Johnnie Tillmon. Thus it was the NWRO that contributed a previously absent analysis to the political culture. The contribution, part of the empowering process of breaking silence, cemented the critical importance of participation in the public discussion of welfare politics.

The NWRO's intervention in the public discourse also included several other actions related to participatory democracy. It forced political leaders on various occasions to reopen the debate and reconsider the policy articulations of principles like the right to work or the right to welfare for the poor. Also, it reinforced the right of poor people to participate in policy discussions that affect their lives (West 1981, 384), a critical component of a more participatory democratic framework in American politics.

Hence, the NWRO was an important influence upon American political culture.

Yet the consensus emerging among dominant groups and political elites cannot go unnoticed. As the organization became increasingly of, by, and for single, poor Black mothers in practice, the NWRO was left without resources, favorable public support, and a voice in the public sphere. The public beliefs in Black women's hyperfertility and laziness exhibited an amazing resiliency, which can be interpreted as part of the ongoing politics of disgust. The NWRO's breaking of the silence, although empowering to its members, had two unanticipated consequences. First, the NWRO found few who were willing to stand in solidarity with its struggle for welfare rights as part and parcel of both the civil rights and women's movements. Second, the transformation of public and private leadership from middle-class Whites to welfare recipients themselves rendered the NWRO's public interventions vulnerable to appropriation for other ends (see Collins 1998a, 56; L. Williams 1995) in a communicative context marked by gross inequality. The vulnerability was due to not only the public identity of welfare recipients but also elites' validation of certain interpretations and models used in public and academic discourse (Collins 1990, 228), which ushered in the stage of cultural cooptation.

Cultural Cooptation

The breaking of silence about oppression does not occur in a vacuum. An intervention into the public discourse generates both rhetorical and policy-related retaliation (see Collins 1998a, 50, 190). The political activism of the NWRO incurred increased counterattacks during its last five years (West 1981)—rhetoric and public policy that strengthened the links in the public sphere between single, poor Black mothers and moral judgments of their failure to conform to American political values. These links continued to be grounded in the long-lived beliefs about poor Black women's laziness and hyperfertility. Single, poor African American mothers had previously been deemed "inept or reckless producers in need of moral supervision" (Roberts 1997, 18). After the heyday of the NWRO, their political activism and limited success led to more hostile characterizations: politically savvy rational actors, "calculating parasites deserving of harsh discipline" (ibid.).

The politics of disgust played on, including the perversion of democratic attention and a communicative context marked by gross inequality. For example, Senator Russell Long (D-LA) specifically characterized Black women as "brood mares" during Senate hearings in the early 1970s (West 1981). These inhuman images of parasites and horses loomed large against the backdrop of welfare reform during the 1990s. I return to this example in chapter 5.

The demise of the NWRO in 1975[10] protected such counterattacks from systematic, widespread challenges. The new conservative politics, working through sophisticated strategies of control to draw boundaries among American citizens, also drew lines excluding welfare recipients based on citizens' perceptions that they were overwhelmingly poor African American women (Collins 1998a, 32; see also Edsall and Edsall 1991). As in earlier sections, I begin with the rhetoric of dominant groups and elites, demonstrating the interactions between the beliefs in single, poor African American mothers' hyperfertility and laziness, and a welfare reform–minded national government.

(Re-)Sowing the Seeds of the Politics of Disgust

The arena of welfare politics lost its hard-won characteristics of contestation following the demise of the NWRO; a conservative, value-based consensus had developed among political elites. During the recession-plagued 1970s, elite and dominant-group frames of the welfare reform issue associated single, poor African American mothers with the decline of the American way, especially with regard to the political value of economic individualism: charting one's own path without the help of government. The focus on a combination of new and old ways that poor, single Black mothers supposedly had failed to conform to political values of industry, individualism, and heterosexual marriage served to negate many of the strides made by the women of the NWRO.

Following their active participation in public policy debates during the early 1970s, AFDC recipients were described as having become fat, lazy, and exploitative. Increased public attention to a heavily Black underclass during a period of a skyrocketing crime rate in Black communities produced a backlash among working-class ethnic White voters in the North and lower-income White populists in the South (Edsall and Edsall 1991, 28). Using the twin traditions of racism and classism, conservative political elites persisted in framing the issue of welfare "dependency" as one of Black women's individual social behavior—especially after the implementation of numerous civil rights laws at the national level. By attacking the problem as a crisis in values, such conservative political elites were able to silence liberal challenges from elites who feared charges of racism by those who considered value-based arguments to be inherently prejudiced (Moynihan 1996, 58). Framing the issue in terms of individual behavior simultaneously justified moderate White working-class Democrats' emotional reactions of anger and resentment toward government demands that they finance (through taxes) the redistribution of resources to Blacks and minorities whom those Democrats deemed "undeserving." In other words, the "crisis-in-values" elites had the larger, more effective microphone.

As the economy took a downward turn into recession, distress grew among formerly loyal Democratic voters who perceived their jobs, homes, and children to be at risk. The White working-class/middle-class male was seen as in need of protection from big government, which required more revenues to cover welfare payments and its payroll and at the same time imposed racial preferences (Edsall and Edsall 1991, 9, 12). The Republican Party's ability to articulate and capitalize on increased feelings of resentment and contempt led to the legions of "Reagan Democrats" in 1980 and 1984.

As the economy began to recover, the debate about welfare reform continued. By triggering citizens' predisposed moral judgments of single, poor Black mothers, Republican efforts at welfare reform remained a dialogue about values (Moynihan 1996, 229) and individual behavior. Following the lead of his predecessor, Ronald Reagan, who coined the term "welfare queen" in a speech, President George H. W. Bush introduced the dilemma of cross-generational dependency into the political lexicon. The rumblings of bipartisan consensus also began to be heard at this time as the otherwise liberal Senator Daniel Patrick Moynihan (D-NY) returned to his thirty-year-old argument: the disintegration of families would emerge from the "individual and group behavior in the inner city . . ." (ibid., 178).

The 1990s featured a Democratic president who gained electoral advantage with a promise to "end welfare as we know it." Yet little changed regarding approaches to reform; the options focused on work and childbearing. President Bill Clinton's "New Democrat" contribution advocated implementation of time limits to prevent prolonged welfare dependency (ibid., 184). Yet the value-based attacks continued, growing in vehemence. In response to the perpetually popular opinion of Black women's overactive childbearing behavior, one popular North Carolina bumper sticker distributed in 1998 at the State House in Raleigh read "Can't Feed 'Em, Don't Breed 'Em." These characterizations were protested by precious few members of the country's political elites.

Similarly, mass public opinion followed the hostility of political elites and dominant groups. The NWRO lost most of its political allies and financial supporters (both organizations and individuals) as it became politically unfeasible to continue such partnerships. Despite the embrace of welfare as a women's issue in the late '70s and early '80s, the trend was not toward a revitalization of a movement of single, poor African American mothers but toward a common concern for women as mothers of children (West 1981, 374), continuing a long tradition of the focus on women as childbearers to the exclusion of women's economic independence.

Importantly, the inner-city riots in the late 1960s and the political agitation by single, poor Black mothers for welfare rights served as further grounds for White Americans to look upon antipoverty programs as African American programs (Quadagno 1994). This trend continued into the 1990s; welfare policy attitudes are strongly influenced by racial attitudes (Gilens 1996, 593; 1995; 2001). The images of NWRO members protesting contributed to the existing association of welfare with African American mothers, encouraging the ongoing conflation of race and poverty among the news media (Associated Press 1997, A2; Gilens 1996, 2001)[11] and rendering the public identity of welfare recipients susceptible to manipulation by elites in an unequal communicative context.

The link between the activism of the NWRO and welfare attitudes is further buttressed by the finding that the influence of beliefs about Black welfare mothers on welfare issues is more politically potent—about twice as strong—as the influence of beliefs about White welfare mothers (Gilens 1996, 599; 2001). In fact, negative beliefs about Black mothers receiving public assistance are about 2.5 times more likely to be associated with negative attitudes about welfare mothers than negative beliefs about similarly situated White mothers (Gilens 1995, 600). This perception is attributed to the exaggerated salience for White Americans of Black overrepresentation among the poor due to the political culture (Gilens 1996, 602). The historical argument of racialization of welfare programs among White citizens (Quadagno 1994) has been buttressed by empirical evidence (Gilens 1995, 1996, 2001).

But is race the sole dominant factor among Americans' hostility to welfare? If this were the case, then we could expect strong support for welfare programs among African Americans, who logically should bear no racial hostility toward their fellow African Americans receiving public assistance. Yet, as I have suggested more generally, the politics of disgust is not limited to the "rich White male establishment." The public identity of the "welfare queen" highlights individual behavior as the primary cause of poverty, drawing particularly on the political values of economic individualism and sexual morality. The findings described below indicate that the politics of disgust occurs within the African American community as well. Moreover, they underscore the need for additional studies using an intersectional approach to identity in the discipline in order to ascertain intraracial effects.

First, economic individualism is a political value framed by Blacks and Whites in very similar ways. Contrary to the beliefs of an admittedly declining number of their White counterparts, African Americans actually conform to many conceptions of political values as elucidated within the larger political culture. Their conformity to economic individualism mirrors that of Whites despite an overwhelming percentage of Black families in poverty (Kinder and Sanders 1996; Dawson 1994). Indeed, the 1992 National Election Survey (NES) reports a solid majority of African Americans share the mainstream view of individualism: 62.5 percent. This finding challenges the dominant belief among White American respondents that most African Americans subscribe to a "culture of dependency" that seeks something for nothing (Kinder and Sanders 1996, 139). Similarly, both African Americans and White Americans articulate the strongest commitment to the American political value of equality (ibid., 152). Even though key differences persist between African Americans and White Americans on public policy issues (Sniderman et al. 1991), their shared political values counter persistent inegalitarian issue frames positing African Americans as fundamentally different from mainstream Whites.[12] This consensus serves as a double-edged sword, however, with regard to welfare reform as I next relate.

One other specific example stands out. A huge political rally, later characterized as antiwelfare, occurred October 16, 1995, in Washington, D.C., at the behest of the top Black male leaders in America with the support of millions of African Americans, the Million Man March. In particular, the Million Man March united African American men of all ages in a "Day of Atonement" designed to begin the process of restoring Black men to their "rightful" place as head of the Black family. The language used at the rally emphasized the values of economic individualism and sexual morality, castigating welfare mothers for their dependency on the federal government rather than on African American men.

The Million Man March, as a showcase for Black nationalism, reflected several of the same problematic constructions of motherhood reflected in appeals to Victorian notions of motherhood during the nineteenth-century rise of American nationalism. These constructions included a focus on Black mothers as culture bearers (see Collins 1998b, 171) within a two-parent patriarchal heterosexual family and censure of those women who fail to fulfill such functions (ibid., 172). The boundary drawing present at the Million Man March included a line of demarcation between women deemed worthy of patriarchal protection through their compliance to the above family model (either in word or deed) and those deemed unworthy through their turn to the government or themselves for economic independence.

The Million Man March is a contemporary example of the approach to racial uplift utilized by privileged African American males in the civil rights movement and in Black religious organizations[13]—the empowerment of Black males through the celebration and pursuit of "intact" heterosexual families with a male head of household. Twenty-nine percent of march participants surveyed stated that the primary reason for their attendance was to show support for Black families; 25 percent came to show support for Black men taking more responsibility for their families (Taylor and Lincoln 1998, 63). This explanation suggests not merely a gender divide but a class divide as well when compared to a more recent poll of African Americans of both genders. In a sad twist, the Million Man March coincided with the debate of the first welfare reform bill during the 104th Congress, HR 4, which passed overwhelmingly and was then vetoed by President Clinton. The irony of a march designed to uplift the Black family when many poor and Black families' sustenance was on the line a few blocks away was lamented by an African American man, one of the few alternate constructions of the Million Man March by African American men (Appendix A, 5).

Little has changed in Black public opinion since the 1992 NES or the Million Man March. The misperceptions of welfare recipients shared by Whites and Blacks persist. A 1999 poll demonstrated the latter's embrace of both economic individualism and patriarchal/heterosexist standards of sexuality: 63 percent believed "people depending on welfare" was a "big problem" for Black families, compared to 53 percent of Whites, and 51 percent perceived "too many parents never getting married" as a serious problem for African Americans, as compared to 49 percent of White respondents (Cose 1999, 35; see also Simpson 1998). It is clear that the African American political culture continues to draw an increasingly hostile boundary between deserving African Americans and welfare recipients presumed to be single, poor African American mothers. The inherent logic of the results of this study again focus on individual-level, rather than structural, explanations and solutions.

The focus on individual-level behavior modification was perpetuated by the architect of the New Jersey welfare provision denying additional benefits for mothers bearing children while on welfare, also an African American male. Succumbing to the belief in Black women's hyperfertility, he made national headlines for proposing a policy to control the practice of women on welfare having more children for extra welfare money. This "family cap," a proposed solution to the "exploding" welfare population, was intended to coerce women into "proper" sexual behavior, and implied that women who have additional children while receiving public assistance do so for the money provided by the state. Theirs was a rational, individual-level act of self-interest that had been refuted in the early 1970s by Anne Henderson's words (see "The Struggle for Survival" section). Again, to the degree that women receiving benefits do have increased birth rates, structural explanations such as the lack of access to affordable birth control and abortion services (the latter due to the Hyde Amendment) were ignored in the justification for the family cap policy (Roberts 1997; see also Davis 1981). More recent studies, noted in chapter 5, reveal *no* association between birthrates and welfare receipt (see also Schram 1995, xxvii). Indeed, the long-standing beliefs, now coupled with a predilection for individual-level solutions, conditioned a public identity of single, poor African American mothers that included yet another moral judgment: welfare mothers did not deserve government assistance, largely because they were responsible for their own poverty. Again, the interventions proposed by African American elites are not always substantively different from those of White American elites. The lack of solidarity among logical allies again reveals evidence of the politics of disgust. Further, something beyond race plays a role in shaping the public identity of welfare recipients.

Neither intervention—the Million Man March nor the New Jersey "family cap"—has alleviated single, poor African American women's poverty. Now deemed the face of welfare cheats, they did not join the 1996 political debate surrounding contemporary welfare reform on their own terms; they were marginalized by political elites of all races and ideologies. Their marginalization within the public sphere created conditions conducive to manipulations of social welfare policy with few or no political repercussions for elected officials.

The mix of successes and failures of the NWRO and its ultimate demise present dramatic proof of the limits of coming to voice without simultaneously coming to power (see Collins 1998a, 76). The emancipatory intervention of the NWRO as a group of and for the rights of single, poor African American mothers has been reinscribed to reinforce the assumptions that underlie the issue frames of contemporary welfare reform. A general shift away from governmental activism culminated in the 1990s with public officials' castigation of "welfare queens." The public identity of the "welfare queen" presents the most critical proof of the consensus among dominant groups, political elites, and the mass public regarding single, poor African American mothers.

A Contradiction of Terms

The public identity of the "welfare queen" is the indigent version of the Black matriarch controlling image (Collins 1990, 74): a dominant mother responsible for the moral degeneracy of the United States (C. Murray 1986; Mink 1998; Lubiano 1992; Collins 1990; Amott 1990). Wahneema Lubiano, a former welfare recipient who is now a professor of English and African American Studies at Duke University, gives the following contemporary definition:

> Within the terms specifically of, or influenced by, the Moynihan Report and generally of the discourse on the "culture of poverty," "welfare queen" is a phrase that describes economic dependency—the lack of a job and/or income (which equals degeneracy in the United States); the presence of a child or children with no father and/or husband (moral deviance); and finally, a charge on the collective U.S. Treasury—a human debt. (Lubiano 1992, 337–338)

The public identity of the "welfare queen," as enumerated above, crystallized into a political symbol during the Reagan administration, when the president, taking up the cause once championed by Senator Russell Long, lambasted "welfare queens" in speeches for living off the hardworking American taxpayers. However, as earlier sections of this chapter demonstrate, the term *welfare queen* simply gives a name to long-standing beliefs regarding single, poor African American mothers. Specific currents within the political culture created the designation to serve as the public identity of welfare recipients in the United States with bipartisan roots.

The public identity of the "welfare queen" is a construct designed to justify ideologically specific forms of public policy. As we have seen in this chapter, the influence of public identity, while subject to challenge and intervention, is also subject to the politics of disgust, leaving it largely out of the hands of those who are characterized by it.[14] The introduction of the term into the American lexicon is akin to the term "inner city" in that it is a code word; it denotes a certain "type" of individual with certain "pathological" behaviors that prevent her from sharing in the American dream. The public identity described here, then, is a product of stereotypes and moral judgments about individuals presumed to share a specific intersection of race, class, and gender identities, and of the tendency toward individual-level explanations found more broadly in American political culture. That the "welfare queen" is of a specific race has been demonstrated in earlier research (Gilens 1995, 1996, 2001; Gilliam 1999). The case study begun with this chapter provides a more comprehensive analysis that also accounts for class, gender, and political values such as individualism.

The Civil Rights Roots of the "Welfare Queen"

Although the term *welfare queen* is an explicitly political creation, the cognitive structure it is intended to trigger stems from a larger academic discourse dating to the work of African American scholars E. Franklin Frazier and Kenneth Clark as well as of sociologist Oscar Lewis, the coiner of a related term, *culture of poverty*. The transition from academic discourse to political discourse occurred through the now-well-known efforts of the late Senator Daniel Patrick Moynihan (D-NY), author of *The*

Negro Family: The Case for National Action (1965), more commonly known as the Moynihan Report.[15]

In searching for an explanation of the enduring poverty among African Americans, Moynihan, then a member of the Johnson administration, cited the work of Frazier and others attributing poverty to the pathological structure of the Black family. The single-female-headed households in the Black communities Moynihan studied did not match the American norm of a two-parent heterosexual household. Considered sensitive to the influences of racism for African American communities, Moynihan stressed the Black family structure as one that included mothers who were "too strong," who prevented Black fathers from assuming their rightful position as head of the household (P. Murray 1995).

Moynihan's work, although perhaps well-intentioned,[16] exacerbated the impact of individual-level behavioral approaches, sparking a wide body of research and policy analysis in this vein. Similarly, long-standing beliefs about single, poor Black women, including lower morals and hyperfertility became guiding assumptions underlying subsequent social science research (Collins 1998a, 101). In another curious mix of race, class, and gender politics, the Moynihan Report received the approval of civil rights leaders, including Martin Luther King Jr. (SCLC), Roy Wilkins (NAACP), and Whitney Young (Urban League).

Perhaps because of this approval, the Moynihan Report also helped shape Black attitudes toward single, poor African American mothers, encouraging Black male chauvinism (Giddings 1984, 329) and hardening the lines of demarcation between the poorest African Americans and their more affluent counterparts. Several prominent scholars (Robert Staples, Joyce Ladner, and Andrew Billingsley, in particular) presented voluminous research to refute the Moynihan findings, but the emphasis on individual-level solutions remained strong in the American and African American political cultures.

Moynihan later oversaw the proposed Family Assistance Plan (FAP) of the Nixon administration, which was vehemently opposed by the NWRO and some of its allies. Although FAP subscribed nominally to the notion of a guaranteed income, the levels proposed would cut family benefits to less than half of what most welfare rights advocates believed would enable a family to survive. The eventual defeat of FAP was the highlight of the waning years of the NWRO. Again, however, a closer look at race, gender, and class politics reveals evidence of single, poor African American mothers' political marginalization. A most glaring example was the lack of support from the newly created Congressional Black Caucus, which did not publicly reject the FAP and join the NWRO in fighting it until the conference committee met to iron out differences in Titles IV and V of the enabling legislation (West 1981, 318). Members of the Congressional Black Caucus had a similarly complicated relationship with welfare recipients in 1996 (see chapter 4).

The Long Shadow of Daniel Patrick Moynihan

Thanks to Moynihan's role in the political sphere, his sociological interpretation of the Black poverty problem remains hegemonic.[17] Moynihan, considered a liberal Democrat, contributed to the bipartisan consensus surrounding the public identity of the "welfare queen" during his tenure in the Nixon administration (West 1981). More recently, he further fanned the politics of disgust with his statement that welfare recipients "were essentially failed persons" (Moynihan 1996, 58). Charles Murray (1986) and Lawrence Mead (1986) both owe a debt to Moynihan's original report and his subsequent work in Congress in formulating their politically conservative arguments for welfare reform. All three men predicate their research findings and policy prescriptions on the public identity of the "welfare queen." This bipartisan, cross-ideological consensus about the terms of the debate mirrors the cross-racial consensus I described above.

The historical foundation presented here portends yet more convincing evidence of consensus among elites and dominant groups in upcoming chapters. As the public identity of the "welfare queen" went largely unchallenged, policy options remained focused along the road begun by the women's club movement: individual behavior modification. Allegations of rampant fraud and abuse "uncovered" by a fourth estate focused on investigative journalism following Vietnam and the Watergate scandal contributed to the changing public perceptions of the welfare rights movement. Although some members of the media earnestly sought answers to the age-old question of Black poverty, they, like Moynihan, reinforced the public identity of the "welfare queen."[18]

What is the legacy of such investigative attempts? Print media reports use African Americans 65 percent of the time as the face of poverty; electronic media at an even higher rate, to the point where each is used as a proxy for the other in coverage on an alarmingly frequent basis (Associated Press 1997, A2; Gilens 1996; see also Soss 1999).

The tone of calls for behavior-modification policies shifted from a desire to paternalistically socialize welfare mothers to questions of deserving benefits. Requests for benefits or changes in policies signified in citizens' minds that recipients were asking for more than they deserved. *Dandridge v. Williams* (1970) gave judicial force to public opinion that public assistance is a privilege, not a right. I investigate the influence of public identity upon congressional policy deliberation in chapter 4.

In academic discourse, the views that influence policy makers remain hegemonic—those of Moynihan, Murray, and Mead. Further, the "symbolic racism" thesis asserts that because overt racism is less acceptable in public, issues coded by race serve as a method for Americans to express racially conservative views (Mendelberg 2001; Simpson 1998). This phenomenon has been found to impact welfare politics (Feldman and Zaller 1992; Gilens 1995, 1996, 2001). Single, poor Black mothers, as the centerpieces of such discourse, are cast at best as incompetent mothers struggling to survive in a bewildering world. At worst, they are presumed to be lazy, baby-making system abusers in violation of the country's most cherished political values. In the contemporary era of welfare politics, no NWRO stands ready to seriously challenge public identity in the national discourse.[19] I investigate the prevalence of public identity in the news media in chapter 3.

The impact of the "welfare queen" public identity on the political culture is undeniable. What theorists call a narrative or controlling image of the "welfare queen" has distinct political and policy ramifications. She is judged at all levels to be shirking her duty to carry her part of the load as a citizen. She usurps the taxpayers' money, produces children who will do the same, and emasculates the titular head of her household, the Black male. In the language of the national family, she avoids contributing her fair share to the national well-being, either as a "bearer of American values" or as a contributor to the U.S. political economy.[20] Particularly with regard to a language of family that implies rights, obligations, and rules (Collins 1998b, 71), those who are presumed to be avoiding their contributions are prevented from sharing in the complete spoils of citizenship granted them by way of their location in the political system.

The boundary drawing among Americans in general and among African Americans in particular reveals that political hierarchy locations are maintained through a complex system of sticks and carrots within political culture, disguising the force with which such norms are enforced.

Those to whom the public identity of the "welfare queen" is attributed most frequently find themselves at the bottom.

The transition from the activism of the NWRO to the construction of the public identity of the "welfare queen" exhibited several examples of boundary drawing evident within American and African American political cultures. The contemporary political context also demonstrates the ongoing marginalization of single, poor Black mothers. What may have been previously considered a politics of neglect or contempt is now firmly entrenched in a politics of disgust. So far, evidence of correspondence bias/representative thinking, a communicative context marked by gross inequality and the lack of willingness among traditional allies to stand in solidarity have at varying points been part of single, poor African American mothers' experiences with welfare (or prewelfare politics). The next two chapters investigate the political context in the final era of welfare politics at issue in this book: the discourse surrounding the PRWA of 1996.

The Persistent Conflation of Public Identity and Welfare Policy

We have seen that enduring beliefs about the reproductive tendencies of poor African American women and their (mis)perceived failure to comply with the virtues of industry and individualism interacted with the formation and implementation of welfare policy at the federal level, based on the social construction of the perceived target population. As the perceived target population changed in race, class, and marital status, so too did the policy options discussed.

As the single, poor African American mother became the public face of welfare, long-standing beliefs about her fused with the identity of a prototypical welfare recipient. Both nature and nurture arguments supported beliefs about fecundity and lack of a work ethic. Although the attempts of clubwomen implied "good motherhood" could be learned, the same stereotypes and moral judgments were deemed genetic traits by scientific racists (Hoberman 1997; see also Collins 1998a). More importantly, no matter the origin, both inegalitarian beliefs tend to be accepted as fact across races and between genders. These "facts," although patently untrue, combine with a political cultural orientation toward individualism to produce policy proposals that encourage behavior modification of individual mothers rather than systemic change (Funicello 1993; Roberts 1997).

The individualist orientation dates to the earliest notions of poor-relief programs (when White women were the target population), but it persisted with increased vehemence following the activism of the NWRO, in part because NWRO members developed methods of collective action that were successful in achieving many of its objectives for welfare recipients regardless of race or gender. Following that activism, welfare recipients' claims have been persistently ignored or excluded unless they fit the desired elite political script (see Sparks 2003).

The widescale denigration of certain citizens' political claims is at the center of what I term the politics of disgust. All four aspects of the politics of disgust emerge from this brief sociohistorical analysis. Early actions of the White and Black women's club movements revealed examples of representative thinking gone wrong. An exclusive focus on individual transformation did not lift welfare recipients, particularly the percentage who were Black, out of poverty. Structural considerations like the exclusion of certain labor categories from Social Security or the discriminatory implementation by welfare bureaus were not accounted for when antipoverty policies failed to serve their purpose.

When single, poor African American mothers attempted to explain the reasons for policy failure and articulate their own needs, the public identity of welfare recipients helped prevent their political claims from being classified as legitimate—effectively preventing their empowered participation in the public discourse. This widescale assault upon certain citizens' political claims is another critical implication of what I've defined as the politics of disgust.

In public discourse about welfare policy, policy options are discussed across political parties, races, and genders without recognition of the role of public identity. The "welfare queen" public identity serves as a filter through which related policy options are discussed, selected, and implemented with little or no effective contributions from those affected most. Because the communicative context is marked by gross inequality, public identities such as that of the "welfare queen" perpetuate the exclusion of marginalized citizens, even in the face of contradictory facts regarding welfare recipients.

What remains troubling for American democracy are the roles a politics of disgust and the "welfare queen" public identity have played in perpetuating this stratified communicative context. Indeed, the NWRO's activism has been subsumed into a cultural argument that systematically distorts the voices of single, poor African American mothers, leading to a political context for welfare reform that continues the trend of reinforcing dependency rather than encouraging economic empowerment.

The words of New Deal welfare applicants and NWRO activists illuminate evidence of a fourth component of the politics of disgust: political isolation. The refusal of major civil rights and feminist organizations to adopt the expressed agenda of the NWRO as their own despite the clear, overt overlaps among their respective constituencies again prevents long-term systemic transformation that would empower welfare recipients. West (1981) notes possible competition for funding between the NWRO and other organizations as a cause of the lack of political solidarity. A more charitable explanation may focus on the inability of more affluent citizens to identify with the NWRO membership. Quite simply, most Americans of any demographic group do not come into periodic contact with single, poor African American mothers. Thus, contravening information that could challenge the public identity of the "welfare queen" (in a manner similar to contact theories of racial integration in schools) is largely unavailable to them.

The argument for an intersectional approach to identity is significantly strengthened by the history presented above concerning the enduring marginalization faced by single, poor African American mothers within their racial group and their gender group. That Black women and men are willing to believe many aspects of the public identity of the "welfare queen" reveals a class-based axis of oppression suffered in addition to the race and gender axes noted by Evelyn C. White in this chapter's epigraph.

Incredibly, although welfare discourse does pathologize Black women's lives, the public identity of the "welfare queen" now appears in the pathological portraits of crime among Black men. This extension of the "bad mother" image, one that dates to slavery, demonstrates a public identity's power to cross policy arenas. The argument that many of these "sons" are being raised "without fathers" and "mothers can't teach them how to stay out of trouble" is increasingly linked to the same types of dimensions that characterize the "welfare queen" public identity: the mothers are producing another generation of citizens who will drain the resources of the nation if not through welfare dependency for daughters then through the prison-industrial complex for sons. We saw this identity cued by the excerpt from the *Congressional Record* included in chapter

1: Bertha Bridges raising a disruptive male child, with no visible adult male figure. The public identity of the "welfare queen," then, is characterized by dimensions corresponding to laziness (drains national resources, doesn't work, crime, system abuse) and hyperfertility (overly fertile, teen mothers, cross-generation dependency, single-parent family).

The resonance between the political and popular cultures is striking. The number of National Basketball Association (NBA) and National Football League (NFL) athletes who, as they celebrate winning the championship, wave "Hi Mom" instead of "Hi Mom and Dad" or "Hi Dad" is crossing increasingly with a picture of such athletes convicted of drug or gun possession, rape, or even murder. Recent movies about the same professional sports reveal similar images. Bertha Bridges (see chapter 1) is just one small part of Evelyn White's commentary on pathologizing welfare discourse. The public identity of single, poor African American mothers, as portrayed in the media and Congress, is becoming the icon (or controlling image) for Black women as a collectivity.[21] Evidence of this controlling image in the national news media is covered in the next chapter.

3

The News Media
Constructing the Politics of Disgust?

Most Americans say they feel disgusted by the current welfare system—not because of its wastefulness, but because it undercuts the ethical cornerstone of an honest day's work, according to a nationwide survey released April 24. (Appendix A, 31; emphasis in original)

The above epigraph, from one newspaper article in a survey sample of 149 such articles published in 1995–1996, puts the emotion of disgust at the forefront of the welfare reform debate. Although the 431-word article concerns the welfare system's responsibility, it links the emotion of disgust and its purported origin in a failure of welfare recipients to conform with the American political value of hard work to a series of policies having to do with the behavior of welfare mothers. Consider another finding of the survey by Public Agenda: "The public feels strongly that mothers on welfare should also be *required* to work, with 76 percent of respondents saying it is *unfair* to *allow* them to stay at home with their children when mothers who work cannot afford that luxury" (Appendix A, 31; emphasis mine).

The refusal to recognize that raising children is work persists in the United States across various economic strata, and not merely with regard to welfare recipients. But the intersection of this gender bias with poverty emboldens many of the one thousand Americans surveyed to enact the politics of disgust to run roughshod over the desires of some welfare recipients to raise their children full-time. Of course, the majority of welfare recipients for a variety of reasons already work or participate in some sort of program designed to produce employment—be it job training or the pursuit of secondary or higher education (Polakow 1994, 11;

Appendix A, 122). But the perception that they are not doing something valuable in exchange for their benefits illustrates the long path journeyed from widows' pensions and Aid to Dependent Children in the early twentieth century to the public identity of the "welfare queen" in 1996.

In chapter 2, I present a public identity of the "welfare queen" that has emerged over the past century of U.S. welfare politics as the perception of the race, class, and marital status of the welfare target population has changed. In this chapter, I empirically test data to determine the level of visibility of the "welfare queen" public identity. Poring over news coverage of welfare reform in 1995–1996, I ask, does the print media fan the politics of disgust?

I have alluded to three interlocking channels through which the public identity of the "welfare queen" is disseminated and perpetuated: political discourse, academic discourse, and media discourse. The foundation for this first of two content analyses is a 149-article data set derived from five newspapers printed and distributed nationally: the *Christian Science Monitor*, the *Los Angeles Times*, the *New York Times*, the *Wall Street Journal*, and the *Washington Post*.[1] The newspapers were selected for their size (number of pages), circulation (number of readers and frequency of issues), perceived editorial ideology, and geographic diversity.[2] I examined the data to determine whether the news media is indeed a dissemination channel for the public identity of the "welfare queen,"[3] and to what degree this identity is associated with policy options regarding welfare reform in 1996.

An analysis of the race-, class-, and gender-coded discussion lurking within the political culture also produced new findings challenging earlier research focusing solely on the influence of race in welfare politics. In the interest of brevity, I provide one or two representative excerpts to answer each question, as well as descriptive statistics from the quantitative portion of the content analysis.[4]

Chapters 3 and 4 provide the results of empirical tests of the argument initiated in chapter 2, that the public identity of the "welfare queen" is a coherent construct of the perceived target population of AFDC, a combination of stereotypes and moral judgments organized into two conceptually distinct content areas: hyperfertility and laziness. To determine whether the "welfare queen" public identity plays a role in public discourse, I analyzed the news media data set in search of answers to four questions:

1. Is the public identity of the "welfare queen" a coherent construct of stereotypes and moral judgments? In other words, is it more than just a stereotype?

Once I examined whether public identity is in fact a coherent construct, I turned to the argument I presented in chapter 2, that public identity did condition the policy options considered and thus the political outcome of the 1996 PRWA. In this sense, I also sought to address the criticisms of the Schneider and Ingram (1993) typology of socially constructed target populations, noted in chapter 1, by using public identity as an empirical proxy in the policy analysis. My test of the public identity construct centered on this question:

2. Does the public identity of the "welfare queen" get directly associated with specific policy options considered viable in the 1996 welfare reform discourse?

Scholars who attempt to develop new concepts or new uses for traditional concepts often encounter questions about whether the concepts are in fact capturing some preexisting variable or concept. To isolate the role of the "welfare queen" in the 1996 welfare reform debate, in the third section of the chapter I briefly consider my analyses of two additional explanations for the content of the welfare reform policy options. I first focus on a political-values explanation, much like that articulated in the epigraph of this chapter. Welfare reform arguments could be couched instead in frames of traditional political values such as industriousness, economic individualism, or self-sufficiency, or the Republican Contract with America's emphasis on shrinking the size of the federal government. Thus my next question considered the influence of political values:

3. Is the public identity of the "welfare queen" merely capturing the role of political values, an oft-cited influence upon policy options and therefore political outcomes?

In that same *Christian Science Monitor* article, the words "most Americans" or "the public" were used interchangeably in reference to a single survey of one thousand Americans who agree by large margins about the appropriate policy solutions to the welfare "problem." Perhaps widespread public support for welfare reform led to the policy options ultimately included in the PRWA—an example of democracy in action. Instead of depending upon the public identity of the "welfare queen," perhaps this consensus for reform determined in some way the policy options discussed. Thus, the last question I investigated asked:

4. Does the public identity of the "welfare queen" merely reflect Americans' consensus favoring welfare reform regarding policy options discussed?

Several themes stemming from the qualitative content analysis emerged to support chapter 2's argument. This analysis proceeded to explore the race-, gender-, and class-coded media discourse to expand upon previous research that emphasized race only (e.g., Gilens 1995, 1996, 2001); gender only (Mink 1998, 1999), and class only (Piven and Cloward 1977). My findings reinforce the urgent need for intersectional analysis and the impact of the politics of disgust by analyzing the discursive context in which the 1996 welfare reform debate occurred. I conclude the chapter by noting the relationship between the results of this empirical analysis and the second aspect of the politics of disgust: a communicative context of gross inequality.

The Public Identity of the "Welfare Queen"

In the sample, I find significant support for the presence of both stereotypes and moral judgments cued simultaneously by the public identity of the "welfare queen." Table 3.1 displays the dimensions of the "welfare queen" public identity, listing their frequencies in the national media data set.

The most prevalent dimensions of the "welfare queen" *Public Identity* are *Don't Work* (159 text units), *Teen Mothers* (111), and *Drug Users* (88). One artifact of these results, though, is the influence of one long article (74 text units) coded at *Drug Users*: a profile of one welfare mother in the Sunday magazine section of the *Los Angeles Times*. I exclude that article as an outlier for most of this chapter's analysis. Following that exclusion, the most frequently coded aspects of the "welfare queen" *Public Identity* are *Don't Work* (159), *Teen Mothers* (111), *Overly Fertile* (76),

TABLE 3.1
Key Variables in News Media Articles, Frequency

Variable/Dimension	Sample Frequency (Text Units)
Public Identity of "Welfare Queen"	621
Don't Work	159
Lazy	32
Teen Mothers	111
Overly Fertile	76
Illegitimacy	75
Drug Users	88
Crime	38
Inner-City Resident	14
Single-Parent Family	52
Culture of Poverty	47
System Abusers	46
Duration of Welfare	40
Cross-Generation Dependency	14
Drain of National Resources	1
Good Mothers	1
Policy Options	1,280
Workfare	183
Teen Mother Policies	49
Family Caps	56
Paternal Solutions	47
Block Grants	142
Time Limits	80
Immigrant Benefits	150
Medicaid Denial	79
State Programs	713
Food Stamp Reform	55
Political Values	173
Care for Children	81
Welfare System Accountability	50
Industry	12
Economic Individualism	6
Heterosexual Marriage	0
Christianity	7
Parental Responsibility	8
Small Government	3
Consensus for Welfare Reform	48
Among American Public	19
Among Taxpayers	0
Bipartisan Support	33
Among Branches of Government	12

TABLE 3.2
Text Code Overlap: Dimensions of *Public Identity*

	Overly Fertile	Don't Work	Lazy	Cross-Generation Dependency	Single-Parent Family	Drug Users	Crime	Teen Mothers	Duration on Welfare	Culture of Poverty	Illegitimacy	System Abusers	Inner-City Resident
Overly Fertile	—												
Don't Work	3	—											
Lazy	2	17	—										
Cross-Generation Dependency	2	0	1	—									
Single-Parent Family	5	8	1	0	—								
Drug Users	0	4	1	1	3	—							
Crime	2	2	1	3	2	21	—						
Teen Mothers	42	7	0	3	10	1	1	—					
Duration on Welfare	4	8	3	1	2	2	1	7	—				
Culture of Poverty	4	7	3	1	2	2	4	4	4	—			
Illegitimacy	15	3	0	5	2	6	3	37	5	8	—		
System Abusers	2	10	6	1	1	1	1	1	1	3	1	—	
Inner-City Resident	1	2	3	0	1	1	3	1	0	1	3	1	—

and *Illegitimacy* (75). This analysis of the data more correctly portrays the characteristics of the entire article sample.

In addition to the largely negative stereotypes and moral judgments about welfare recipients that were gleaned from the literature, the idea that welfare mothers qualify as *"Good Mothers"* to their children was considered an important possibility to document, if present in the data. This dimension and another, the charge that welfare recipients *Drain National Resources* were each found in only one text unit of a single document, respectively. The remaining discussion thus discounts the role of either dimension as part of the coherent construct of the "welfare queen."[5] No articles were discarded from the sample based on this finding.

Of the 149 media articles, 109 (73%) had some or all of their text units coded with dimensions of the public identity variable. No text units are coded on all fourteen dimensions of **Public Identity**; this is unremarkable because the dimensional coding collects around several stereotypes and moral judgments that are in two conceptually distinct domains.

A more interesting question is whether codes of several dimensions significantly overlap with others of the same content domains. As I argue in chapter 2 from a historical perspective, the two primary long-standing beliefs about single, poor African American mothers are their lack of work ethic and their hyperfertility. Following an extensive review of the literature from multiple ideological perspectives, including the culture of poverty, rational choice, and self-efficacy models (see Steele and Sherman 1999, 399), data similarly congealed around these two categories. An index search analysis produced a matrix of overlapping codes that indicate two content dimensions, each with an attribution of a specific behavior/characteristic and one or more moral judgments about said behavior or characteristic. Table 3.2 presents evidence of the multiple overlapping codes.

The content area previously described as lack of work ethic included the specific stereotypical behavior *Don't Work* with the moral judgment of *Lazy*. Using these two dimensions, we see that the stereotyped behavior and the moral judgment occur together in 17 of 32 (53%) of the text units coded *Lazy*. An example of this overlap is provided below from the *Washington Post*:

> Lawrence E. Townsend, Jr., director of the Department of Public Social Services in Riverside County, Calif., which is conducting a large-scale experiment in putting welfare recipients to work, said the key elements

to success in putting clients to work are requiring the participation of all able adults so that recipients know they cannot escape the requirements, and focusing on getting a job—any job—as quickly as possible. (Appendix A, 146)

The above selection contains both components of the content area, plus a third, *System Abusers*. First, Riverside County's "experiment in putting welfare recipients to work" presumes that welfare recipients are not already working or are not newly unemployed; if this were the case, they would then be put "back to work." This places the text unit at the code of *Don't Work*. Without the presumption, there is no need for the experiment. The next section of the sentence involves two moral judgments: "requiring the participation of all able adults so that recipients know they cannot escape the requirements. . . ." The statement again presumes that they do not want to work, involving a judgment that they are *Lazy*. Moreover, the words "so that recipients know they cannot escape the requirements" implies that recipients would rather get something for nothing, a clear abuse of the system of public assistance. Accordingly, the entire text unit is coded for all three dimensions of public identity. However, when the intersection of the three overlapping codes was tested using the entire data set, it produced only three documents and three text units with simultaneous codes. Thus, a more parsimonious inclusion of *Don't Work* and *Lazy* as the primary work-ethic content dimensions seems to prevail. This combination occurred in 13 of 62 (21%) of the possible documents coded at *Don't Work* and in 13 of 24 (54%) of the possible documents coded at *Lazy*.

The second content area, concerning single, poor African American mothers' fertility, was explored as well. It is the content area left unacknowledged by an exclusive focus on the racial stereotyping of welfare recipients. Dimensions coded included the stereotype that most welfare mothers are *Teen Mothers* (111 units in 33 documents) and head a *Single-Parent Family* (52 units in 32 documents), as well as moral judgments that welfare mothers are *Overly Fertile* (76 units in 37 documents) and that their children bear the mark of *Illegitimacy* (75 units in 40 documents). Here the overlap is much more striking, convincing me that the public identity that is cued in welfare discourse is not merely one of Blacks, as Gilens or Quadagno might suggest, but that it is one of Black *women* as especially devalued *mothers*.

The stereotype that many or most welfare mothers are *Teen Mothers* and the moral judgment that they are *Overly Fertile* overlap in a whopping 22 of 33 documents (67%) discussing teenage mothers and 22 of 37 documents citing hyperfertility (59%). Table 3.2 also lists these results. The degree of overlap between *Teen Mothers* and *Illegitimacy* is even more striking: 26 of 33 *Teen Mother* documents (79%) and 40 *Illegitimacy* documents (65%). The data appear to reveal another conceptually specific content area within the public identity of the "welfare queen." A selection from the *New York Times* illustrates the overlap:

> The bill to be considered by the House would bar the use of Federal money to provide cash welfare benefits for a child born to a woman already receiving public assistance. Most states now provide extra money to indigent families for each additional child, and some Republicans say that encourages women to have more babies—a contention disputed by the Children's Defense Fund and by some economists. The House bill would also deny cash assistance to children born out of wedlock to women younger than 18, and to the women as well. (Appendix A, 60)

Here, the discussion focuses on the reproductive practices of women on welfare. The text first discusses treatment of women having additional children while receiving public assistance. In this unit, the judgment that women are having too many babies because of a check is introduced—a reference to the *Overly Fertile* welfare mother, though the contention is challenged by the Children's Defense Fund and some economists. The next sentence then focuses on the issue of *Teen Mothers* with a mention of the proposal to "deny cash assistance to children born out of wedlock to women younger than 18. . . ." The association between public assistance and teen mothers is thereby introduced. The term "out of wedlock" is only marginally less pejorative than "illegitimate." Thus the second judgment, marking single mothers as mothers of "out of wedlock" children is present as well, indicating an image of welfare mothers that corresponds to the second content area of the "welfare queen."

Again, the coding of this text unit on all three dimensions—*Teen Mothers, Overly Fertile,* and *Illegitimacy*—led me to test whether the content area should include all three categories. A larger association of eight documents and nine text units indicates a possible association, but one to be tested with additional data.

The frequency with which many dimensions of the "welfare queen" public identity appeared in the data set—109 of 149 randomly selected

TABLE 3.3
Text Code Overlap: *Public Identity and Policy Options*

Public Identity	Policy Option									
	Block Grants	Time Limits	Workfare	Teen Mother Policies	Family Caps	Paternal Solutions	Immigrant Benefits	Medicaid Denial	State Programs	Food Stamp Reform
Drain on National Resources	0	0	0	0	0	0	0	0	0	0
Overly Fertile	3	5	4	16	38	4	7	2	10	2
Don't Work	4	7	57	1	2	3	2	2	77	3
Lazy	0	6	17	0	0	1	0	0	10	0
Cross-Generation Dependency	0	0	1	0	1	0	0	0	1	0
Single-Parent Family	3	1	3	2	4	14	2	0	13	0
Drug Users	0	0	26	0	0	0	0	0	5	0
Crime	0	0	6	0	0	1	1	0	5	0
Teen Mothers	9	9	6	48	27	3	16	1	12	2
Duration on Welfare	2	14	9	4	6	0	5	0	19	0
Culture of Poverty	2	2	8	3	1	2	0	0	11	0
Illegitimacy	10	4	6	22	23	0	7	1	8	0
System Abuses	2	1	6	1	0	2	1	0	12	0
Inner-City Resident	0	3	6	0	1	2	0	0	4	0

articles—and their overlap in multiple text units provide evidence to support chapter 2's argument. The public identity of the "welfare queen" disseminated by the news media includes both stereotypes and moral judgments in a coherent construct with two content domains—lack of industry and hyperfertility. Both domains occur repeatedly throughout the sample, demonstrating both the pervasive quality of this public identity and its roots in stereotypes and moral judgments not simply of Blacks but of Black women in particular. Only an analysis attending to race and gender *simultaneously* produces this comprehensive result.

The Relationship between *Public Identity and Policy Options*

Next, let's turn to the influence of the public identity of the "welfare queen" I assert in chapter 2. If *Public Identities,* as an empirical operationalization of socially constructed target populations, underlie *Policy Options,* then ostensibly evidence of this association would appear in the national media data set.

I have demonstrated so far that there are two substantive content areas that constitute the public identity of the "welfare queen." Historically, evaluations of welfare recipients' lack of work ethic and hyperfertility became serious catalysts for policy options as the social construction of welfare recipients shifted from White to Black and from widow to never-married single mother. These evaluations, I argue, prompted specific individual-behavior-based policy prescriptions in the area of welfare politics. I test this assertion here with the 1995–1996 media data set.

Table 3.3 gets right to the heart of the matter. As noted earlier, because of the substantive content-based difference among the dimensions of both variables, no text units are expected to overlap on all fourteen dimensions of *Public Identity* and all ten dimensions of *Policy Options.*[6] Still, the level of overlapping coding among the dimensions of *Public Identity* and the dimensions of *Policy Options* are starkly different from those of either competing explanation: *Political Values* or *Consensus for Welfare Reform.*

Looking at the work-related dimensions of *Public Identity, Don't Work,* and *Lazy* noted above, we see significant overlap with the options of *Workfare* and *State Programs. Workfare* and the *Public Identity* dimension *Don't Work* have 57 text units of common coding, and *Lazy* (17 text units) has fewer instances of overlap, partly because of its lesser frequency in the entire dataset. Fifty-seven text units of overlap represents 36% of the *Don't Work* coding, and 17 text units represents 53% of the total coding for *Lazy*.

On the other hand, *System Abuse* and *Workfare* appear to be weakly correlated. The 6 units of overlap represent only 13% of the text units from that node. Yet clearly, in many text units, the idea that welfare recipients are getting something for nothing is clear. Congresswoman Lynn Woolsey (D-CA) provides an example of the overlap of all three dimensions with the policy option of *Workfare* in her comments to the *Washington Post*:

> "When some people sit at home getting a check while other people have to work two or three jobs to make ends meet, of course working people are furious," she says. "But I have faith in the American public that they will invest in welfare if it puts people back to work."
>
> As, once upon a time, it did for her. (Appendix A, 151)

Clearly, the judgment that welfare recipients are lazy and abusing the system is communicated in the first statement of Congresswoman Woolsey's quotation, when she makes a clear distinction between welfare recipients and working people, as if the two groups were mutually exclusive. The judgment is linked to policy considerations when she said, "[T]hey will invest in welfare if it puts people back to work." The qualitative analysis encourages us to look more closely at what the quantitative analysis perhaps overlooks.

The work-related content area of the "welfare queen" public identity is also correlated highly with the *State Programs* dimension of *Policy Options*. This association is partly explained by the fact that the overwhelming majority of state-initiated welfare reform programs prior to 1996 were some version of *Workfare*. Breaking *State Programs* into four nominal categories—recognition of existing *Successful Programs,* the possible *Impact of the Reform* on the states, state applications for *Federal Waivers,* and state *Contingency Plans* depending on the passage of federal legislation—gives us a more detailed view of the association between **Public Identity** and this dimension of **Policy Options**. Table 3.4 reveals, as does Table 3.3, that *Don't Work* has the strongest association, but to ongoing state programs deemed successful by their advocates, and the application for permission to design programs (17 of the 26 text units associated with *Don't Work*).

The News Media | 77

TABLE 3.4
Text Code Overlap: **Public Identity** *and State Program* **Policy Options**

	State Program *Policy Options*			
Public Identity	Successful State Programs	Impact of National Reform on States	State Applications for Federal Waivers	State Contingency Plans
Drain on National Resources	0	0	0	0
Overly Fertile	1	2	2	0
Don't Work	12	7	5	0
Lazy	3	1	1	0
Cross-Generation Dependency	0	0	0	0
Single-Parent Family	0	1	3	0
Drug Users	21	0	0	0
Crime	4	0	0	0
Teen Mothers	2	5	1	0
Duration on Welfare	1	3	1	0
Culture of Poverty	2	2	0	0
Illegitimacy	1	1	1	0
System Abusers	1	2	1	0
Inner-City Resident	0	0	0	0

State Programs are also correlated with *Lazy* (10 units) and *System Abusers* (12 units), and *Duration on Welfare* (19 units). One example of the correspondence among the work-related dimensions of public identity comes from a welfare worker discussing the state of Oregon's welfare-to-work program with a *Los Angeles Times* writer:

> [Susan] Warner, a newcomer to the welfare bureaucracy, has been startled, she says, by the "helplessness" of some of her clients. Some seem afraid to work. Others are eager, but inarticulate. To the handful that refuse, Warner says firmly that they can "participate in the opportunity that we give them, or they can choose to do it their own way, without public assistance." (Appendix A, 88)

Warner specifically described the clients she works with, and to some degree they seem to represent on the surface confirmation of the "welfare queen" public identity in their work habits. The last sentence of the text unit clearly ties together the new policy of working for welfare to the implication of "tough love": "To the handful that refuse, Warner says firmly that they can 'participate in the opportunity that we give them, or they can choose to do it their own way, without public assistance.'" Clearly, the idea of recipients who don't work is tied to the idea of those who refuse to work—the difference between *Don't Work* and *Lazy,* cueing a cognitive link between the stereotyped behavior and the moral judgment. This text unit presents evidence of underlying attributions of traits and moral judgments that constitute public identity, then links them to policy options such as state welfare-to-work programs.

The other content area, hyperfertility, also presents strong numbers of overlapping codes. Welfare recipients are socially constructed as *Teen Mothers* and *Overly Fertile,* and **Policy Options** such as *Teen Mother Policies* and *Family Caps* are then discussed in the same thought. The social construction of the *Overly Fertile* welfare recipient occurs in 41% of the text units discussing *Teen Mother Policies* and in 67% of the text units mentioning *Family Caps* as a policy option. The dimension of *Teen Mothers* follows suit, with a predictable increase in overlap with *Teen Mother Policies*—97% (48 of 49 text units coded at *Teen Mother Policies*) in addition to strong overlap with *Family Caps*—48% (27 of 56 text units coded at *Family Caps*).

An example of a text unit with coding on all four dimensions comes from the *Los Angeles Times*:

> Many Republicans in the House and some in the Senate believe that cutting teenagers out of the program and capping family benefits are essential to reversing the high rate of out-of-wedlock births, which they regard as a cause of many of society's social ills. (Appendix A, 102)

In this text unit, both *Teen Mothers* and *Overly Fertile* welfare recipients are seen as responsible for the "high rate of out-of-wedlock births." The text unit is also coded at a third dimension of **Public Identity**: *Illegitimacy.* This second moral judgment associated with the reproductive content area of the "welfare queen" public identity also maps onto the **Policy Options** of *Teen Mother Policies* and *Family Caps.* Of the units coded for *Teen Mother Policies,* 22 units (45%) also allude to *Illegitimacy.* Further, 23 of 56 (41%) of text units coded for the **Policy Options** of *Family Caps* allude to *Illegitimacy.* The overlap between **Public Identity** with regard to the content area of reproduction is thus undeniable.

An additional point worthy of mention emerges from the last few words of the text unit. Unlike dimensions of **Political Values** such as *Care for Children,* "high rates of out-of-wedlock births" are explicitly posited as a "cause of many of society's ills" and therefore legitimate grounds for policy making. This example thus not only elucidates the logical link drawn between reproduction-related dimensions of the public identity of the "welfare queen" and the substantive policy options discussed but also distinguishes between the use of social constructions and the most frequently expressed *Political Value, Care for Children,* in welfare politics discourse.

Considering Competing Explanations

As I mentioned earlier, previous policy research has emphasized the roles of political values and majority public opinion as key contributors to how issues are framed in media coverage of political elite discourse. In this section, I test these two explanations to determine whether either *Political Values* or *Consensus for Welfare Reform* was more closely aligned with welfare reform policy options in 1996. I consider both as particularly plausible, given the context in which the PRWA became law: a presidential election year.

Political values are often mentioned as an influence upon policy options that are considered and then ultimately passed by legislators. The political values I included in the analyses are again the result of an extensive literature review of various ideological arguments concerning welfare reform. Many of the values are recognizable from both sides of the congressional aisle as "American": *Industry* (working hard), *Economic Individualism, Care for Children,* and *Welfare System Accountability.* Also included in my analysis are values talked about specifically in conjunction with the "Republican Revolution" of the party's 1994 Contract with America: *Heterosexual Marriage, Parental Responsibility,* and *Small Government.* The frequencies for each of these dimensions of *Political Values* are listed in Table 3.1.

To consider whether *Public Identity* is simply capturing the influence of *Political Values,* I conducted another index search. If, in fact, my concept of public identity is merely a proxy for value-driven discussions of welfare reform, then we can expect to find a tremendous amount of overlap in coding of text units at *Public Identity* and *Political Values.* Table 3.5 presents the quantitative matrix documenting overlapping qualitative codes between dimensions of *Public Identity* and *Political*

TABLE 3.5
*Text Code Overlap: **Public Identity and Political Values***

Public Identity	Political Values							
	Industry	Economic Individualism	Heterosexual Marriage	Christianity	Parental Responsibility	Small Government	Care for Children	Welfare System Accountability
Drain on National Resources	0	0	0	0	0	0	0	0
Overly Fertile	2	1	0	1	0	0	4	0
Don't Work	0	0	0	0	0	0	3	0
Lazy	0	1	0	0	1	0	1	3
Cross-Generation Dependency	0	1	0	0	0	0	1	1
Single-Parent Family	0	0	0	0	2	0	3	1
Drug Users	0	0	0	0	0	0	2	0
Crime	1	1	0	0	2	0	1	0
Teen Mothers	0	1	0	1	0	0	5	0
Duration on Welfare	0	4	0	0	1	0	0	0
Culture of Poverty	2	0	0	0	1	0	3	1
Illegitimacy	0	2	0	2	0	0	4	0
System Abusers	0	0	0	0	0	0	1	1
Inner-City Resident	0	0	0	0	1	0	1	1

Values. Even after accounting for the smaller overall evidence of text units coded at *Political Values,* the number of text units that overlap on various dimensions is small; the table is riddled with zeroes, ones, and twos for the most part.

The most frequent instances of overlap occurred with the *Political Values* dimension that articulates *Care for Children* and the *Public Identity* dimension of *Teen Mothers.* It is important to note the distinction here: *Care for Children* is cued as care for the offspring of *Teen Mothers, not* care for *Teen Mothers* as children themselves. An excerpt from the *Washington Post*'s Robert Kuttner illustrates the point:

> To the right, the goal is not punishing children, it is deterring teenagers from having children. Ending the welfare mess may require more poverty for a generation or two, but that is the price [of] inducing responsible behavior and middle class values. (Appendix A, 106)

This text unit refutes the idea that welfare reform is going to "punish children," in direct response to allegations repeatedly made elsewhere by the Urban Institute and Children's Defense Fund. The first sentence clearly separates the teenagers supposedly having children on welfare from the alleged victims, children, and argues, in fact, that strict treatment of teenage moms on welfare and an increase in child poverty may be a price worth paying "to end the welfare mess." For these reasons, the unit is coded as a part of the *Care for Children* dimension of *Political Values* as well as the *Teen Mothers* dimension of *Public Identity.*

But perhaps *Public Identity* is not a proxy for *Political Values;* instead, *Political Values* might be associated directly with *Policy Options.* This possibility would seriously wound my argument about the role of *Public Identity* in policy discourse. Table 3.6 presents the results of my exploration of this alternative. Again, we see a table full of zeros, with the exception of the *Care for Children* dimension, which features 34 text units that share coding with *State Programs.* Despite the fact that this represents less than 5% of the 713 units coded at *State Programs,* it is important to note that it represents 42% of the 81 total text units coded at *Care for Children.* A further analysis seems warranted.

A closer look further supports the result of the first analysis. The majority of text units (26) sharing *State Programs* and *Care for Children* coding focus on the impact of the proposed reform rather than using *Care for Children* as a driving force that should somehow influence

TABLE 3.6
Text Code Overlap: Political Values and Policy Options

Policy Options	Industry	Economic Individualism	Heterosexual Marriage	Christianity	Parental Responsibility	Small Government	Care for Children	Welfare System Accountability
				Political Values				
Block Grants	0	0	0	0	0	0	7	0
Time Limits	0	1	0	0	0	1	3	0
Workfare	4	2	0	1	1	0	9	1
Teen Mother Policies	0	1	0	1	0	0	2	0
Family Caps	0	2	0	2	0	0	4	0
Paternal Solutions	0	0	0	0	0	0	4	0
Immigrant Benefits	0	1	0	0	0	0	5	0
Medicaid Denial	0	0	0	0	0	0	2	0
State Programs	2	4	0	0	0	2	34	0
Food Stamp Reform	0	0	0	1	0	0	5	0

policy design. Comparing the use of *Industry* (only 4 units of overlap) as a **Political Value** and *Care for Children* demonstrates that one is cited as a causal catalyst and the other as a possible outcome. Consider how welfare reform policy is discussed in light of the *Industry* value in an editorial published in the *Washington Post*:

> Advocates of this bill's deep cuts in programs for the poor and its ending of welfare's "entitlement" status like to cast themselves as true friends of the poor and foes of "dependency." Their hardheadedness, they insist, grows from warmheartedness and a desire to promote work. (Appendix A, 57)

This text unit is emblematic of the four that share coding at *Industry* and *Workfare*. Four units of text overlap is indeed small. But for illustration the qualitative interpretation is more important here. The "desire to promote work" is the justification that is given for advocacy of two specific policy options: spending cuts and ending welfare's "entitlement" status. Contrast that with the intersection of the *Care for Children* political value and the *State Programs* text overlap seen in the below excerpt from an article in the *Los Angeles Times* that comprises 17 of the 26 units focusing on impact:

> Q: What impact will welfare reform have on the children you serve?
> A: Inevitably, no matter how it comes out, over the course of anywhere from immediately to five years, millions and millions of children are going to be dropped because they hit the time limits, either two years or five years. Secondly, children are going to be dropped because they are not able to have a paternity determination on the father. Third, many will be dropped because they are legal immigrants. (Appendix A, 67)

In this excerpt we see the exact opposite relationship between **Political Values** and **Policy Options**. The **Policy Options** of *Time Limits* and *Ending Benefits to Legal Immigrants*, for example, *will produce* terrible outcomes for children. For this qualitative reason, the comparatively large degree of overlap of *Care for Children* does not challenge the overall argument that **Public Identity**, not **Political Values**, serves as the justification for various policy options. Moreover, from a more quantitative perspective, half of the 34 text units sharing coding are from a single article in the sample. This further reinforces my suspicion of **Political Values** as a legitimate competing explanation for the welfare reform *Policy Options* discussed.

Thus overall, the results of the qualitative and quantitative content analyses indicate that *Political Values* is not a driving force of policy discussion in the media data set. Table 3.5 reveals further that *Political Values* and *Public Identity* tap different aspects of the data set, and Table 3.6 indicates that the discussions of *Policy Options* were not particularly value-laden; even the value of *Caring for Children* overlapped in coding on only 34 (2.6%) text units of the 1,280 coded for various *Policy Options*. It appears that *Public Identity* remains an important consideration in welfare reform discourse, independent of *Political Values* such as *Industry, Economic Individualism, Care for Children, Small Government,* and *Personal Responsibility.*

As I mentioned at the start of this section, scholars and journalists alike were well aware that 1996 was a presidential election year, and polls demonstrated that American public opinion was largely in favor of welfare reform (Gilens 2001). Indeed, this chapter's epigraph further supports the idea that Americans want welfare reform—and importantly, welfare reform that emphasizes work (Appendix A, 31). So perhaps the discussion of policy options with regard to welfare reform is not in fact associated with the public identity of the "welfare queen" but instead is merely reflective of the majoritarian democratic theory presumed to undergird all public policy making. Do codes for *Consensus for Welfare Reform* supplant codes for *Public Identity* in welfare politics?

To find out, I conducted an analysis similar to that comparing *Political Values, Public Identity,* and *Policy Options.* First, I sought to determine whether *Public Identity* and *Consensus for Welfare Reform* share an inordinate level of overlapping codes. This test is more than an idle exercise because part of my overall argument rests on the idea that Americans of all races, classes, party identifications, and ideologies share in their susceptibility to the public identity of the "welfare queen."

Evidence of *Consensus for Welfare Reform* in the news media is somewhat scant (48 text units) compared to other variables such as *Public Identity* (621), *Policy Options* (1,280), and *Political Values* (173). Two dimensions, *Among the American Public* and *Bipartisan Support,* represent three-quarters of the text units coded at this node. The small number of units and their skewed distribution render this competing explanation suspect almost from the start.

Table 3.7 reveals the degree of overlap between dimensions of *Public*

TABLE 3.7
Text Code Overlap: **Public Identity** *and* **Consensus for Welfare Reform**

	Consensus for Welfare Reform			
Public Identity	Among American Public	Among Taxpayers	Bipartisan	Among Branches of Government
Drain on National Resources	1	0	0	0
Overly Fertile	0	0	0	0
Don't Work	3	0	2	1
Lazy	1	0	0	0
Cross-Generation Dependency	1	0	0	0
Single-Parent Family	0	0	1	0
Drug Users	0	0	1	0
Crime	2	0	0	0
Teen Mothers	0	0	0	0
Duration on Welfare	0	0	0	0
Culture of Poverty	1	0	0	0
Illegitimacy	1	0	0	0
System Abusers	2	0	2	0
Inner-City Resident	0	0	0	0

Identity and dimensions of **Consensus for Welfare Reform**. Due to the skewed nature of the **Consensus for Welfare Reform** frequencies, the most important dimensions for the analysis are *Among the American Public* and *Bipartisan Support*, where 36 of 48 units are coded. The highest degree of overlap is three units of text between *Consensus Among the American Public* and *Don't Work*. This represents 1.9% of the text units in the *Don't Work* category, and all three units are from the *Christian Science Monitor* article (see chapter epigraph). From this analysis, I am convinced that results regarding **Public Identity** are not conflated with more general findings of **Consensus for Welfare Reform** in the media data set.

Next, I tested Tyson's point regarding the relationship between **Consensus for Welfare Reform** and the **Policy Options** discussed. Again, it is logical to postulate that the welfare reform policy options were closely associated with or were products of **Consensus** rather than the **Public Identity** of the "welfare queen." Table 3.8 displays the results of an index search documenting overlapping codes between **Consensus** and **Policy Options**. Again, the numbers remain small. Tyson's *Christian Science Monitor* article contains all three of the text units jointly coded at *Workfare* and **Consensus**.[7] Among the five units coded at *State Programs* and *Bipartisan Support* are three from an article by former Massachusetts

TABLE 3.8
Text Code Overlap: **Consensus for Welfare Reform** *and* **Policy Options**

	Consensus for Welfare Reform			
Policy Options	Among American Public	Among Taxpayers	Bipartisan	Among Branches of Government
Block Grants	0	0	0	0
Time Limits	1	0	0	1
Workfare	3	0	2	0
Teen Mother Policies	0	0	0	0
Family Caps	0	0	0	0
Paternal Solutions	0	0	2	0
Immigrant Benefits	0	0	3	0
Medicaid Denial	0	0	1	0
State Programs	0	0	5	1
Food Stamp Reform	0	0	2	0

governor William Weld that discusses a bipartisan agreement among governors for welfare reform. It is therefore easy to conclude that **Consensus for Welfare Reform** is not strongly associated with specific **Policy Options** in welfare reform discourse.

Overall, the results from the data set indicate that there is indeed a link between dimensions of **Public Identity** and the **Policy Options** discussed. Moreover, the striking level of overlapping text codes far exceeds the competing variables of either **Political Values** or **Consensus for Welfare Reform**. The results of the empirical content analysis confirm the socio-historical argument of chapter 2.

Conclusion

The national media data set provides convincing quantitative and qualitative evidence of the public identity of the "welfare queen." The content analysis reveals that the "welfare queen" public identity is a coherent construct of stereotypes and moral judgments based on the perceived social construction of welfare recipients as single, poor African American mothers. The strong presence of this public identity and its association with policy options dominates the discourse; of the 149 articles and thousands of text units coded for this project, only one text unit in one document characterized welfare mothers as *Good Mothers*. Clearly, the 1995–1996 welfare reform debate was marked by the second characteristic of the politics of disgust: a communicative context of gross inequality.

Part of the challenge in contesting public identities resides in the grossly inegalitarian communicative context. Working welfare recipients, for example, are profiled as individual exceptions, and though their appearance combats the stereotypes and moral judgments associated with public identity, these text units occurred in 8 of 149 documents (5%), compared with the 109 of 149 (73%) previously noted as evidence of public identity. Further, as I note in chapter 2 and document here, the public identity of the "welfare queen" is an intersectional social construction that includes elements of race, class, and gender when portrayed in welfare politics discourse. I take up profiles of welfare recipients and their experiences with the politics of disgust in chapter 5.

Quantitative and qualitative evidence related to the four questions I asked at the start of this chapter confirmed that the coherent construct of *Public Identity* captures stereotypes and moral judgments associated with the intersectional identity assigned to welfare recipients. Defining the stereotypes and moral judgments within the social construction of welfare policy's target population allows rigorous testing of preexisting assumptions and their relationship to substantive policy outcomes. By qualitatively and quantitatively analyzing a specific case and following up with additional cases, a typology more manipulable than the empirically unwieldy (Schroedel and Jordan 1998) typology proposed by Schneider and Ingram (1993) can develop to explain and eventually predict which policies emerge in light of which target populations.

Public Identity does not serve as a proxy for either *Political Values* or *Consensus for Welfare Reform* in its relationship to *Policy Options*. The relationship between *Public Identity* and *Policy Options* is unmediated by either variable, and therefore any role *Public Identity* plays in the policy discussion is attributable to it and not other competing variables.

Thus the "welfare queen's" long shadow had not yet gone gently into the night in 1996. Its presence in the news media serves as a cognitive resource underlying the debate about policy options in 1995 and 1996. The news media, by either intent or neglect, played a role in linking the social construction of the welfare population to public policy options. I next turn to the role of the "welfare queen" public identity among members of Congress as they deliberated in the summer of 1996.

4

Public Discourse in Congress

Haunted by Ghosts of "Welfare Queens" Past

> We don't define compassion by how many people are on welfare, or AFDC, or living in public housing. We define compassion by how FEW people are on welfare, AFDC, and public housing because we have given them the means to climb the ladder of success. (Representative J. C. Watts [R-OK], speech delivered at Republican National Convention, 1996)

The words of J. C. Watts, an African American congressman from Oklahoma, filled the halls of the Republican National Convention less than two weeks after passage of the Personal Responsibility and Work Opportunity Act of 1996 (PRWA). This chapter looks at how political elites defined and debated welfare reform in 1996.

Analyses of national debates like that on welfare reform are critical because a long tradition of empirical research asserts the importance of elites to public discourse and ultimately to public policy decisions. Defining the terms of debate, as Watts attempted to do in the above statement, is a common practice in elite discourse (VanDijk 1993) and an important method of shaping political outcomes. In this chapter, I reprise the questions tested in chapter 3, using another independent, randomly obtained data set to determine whether the socially constructed elite definitions of "the people on welfare, AFDC, and [in] public housing" were associated with the policy options discussed.

Chapters 2 and 3 present historical and empirical evidence to demonstrate that public identity is indeed a contributor to the national welfare reform debate, but in the final analysis, the media could not cast a single vote for or against HR 3734/S 1795. To best decipher the "welfare queen's" reach in public policy decision making, we must journey down the halls of Congress.

In analyzing a second data set, I intend to comprehensively explore my theory (King et al. 1994) that the public identity of the "welfare queen" empirically embodies the role of a socially constructed target population in the discussion of welfare reform in 1996. As with the media data set, the data were obtained from publicly available archives of information in order to enhance explanatory power (Johnson and Joslyn 1991, 124) and to address further the issue of generalizability among qualitative and quantitative results (see Yin 1994, 122). Interested readers are reminded that Appendix C provides additional detail regarding research design and methodology.

I analyze 82 randomly selected documents from the floor debate concerning HR 3734/S 1795, the PRWA of 1996.[1] Despite the fact that a great deal of work and deal making occurs prior to the full-body deliberations, the floor debates are most often broadcast and cited for public consumption. Although many argue that roll call votes (e.g., Schroedel and Jordan 1998) or personal interviews (e.g., Dodson et al. 1995) may provide better insight into elites' "true beliefs" about the target population at issue, public identity is first and foremost a social cognition, "the product of thinking about things, forming object-specific impressions and communicating about them with other people." Political psychologists who study psychological characteristics "at a distance" argue that the best way to assess the social cognitions of the state and the elites populating it is through formal, prepared speeches (Schafer 2000, 515). I follow in their path, for a member's remarks furnish not only his or her stance (pro or anti) on proposed legislation but the arguments and ideological justifications for their positions. It is in these justifications that the unacknowledged social meaning of public identity lurks.

The context in which the floor debates occur further shapes the data analyzed herein. The number of documents is significantly smaller than that of the media data set, with many characteristics that potentially have an impact on the results, further highlighting the need for multiple data sources and triangulation methods. Generally, the *Congressional Record* data set differs with regard to communicative norms. First, members of Congress at the podium are not expected to be neutral, as the authors of the news reports in the media sample are. Hence, legislators bring their opinions to the podium, backed by whatever political, statistical, or constituent support they can muster.

Second, members of Congress were operating in the political context of an election year, which increases the salience of David Mayhew's celebrated finding: members' top goal throughout their career is to be re-elected. That the political context included both a presidential and a congressional election for all but two-thirds of the senators potentially heightened the importance of going on record with one's stand on welfare reform. Third, the number of speakers, their party identification, and duration of remarks are all regulated by the distinct rules of the House and Senate. Finally, it is a well-established fact that the demographic composition of Congress in no way approaches the racial, gender, or class composition of the country. Some variation from the media data set with regard to empirical results is therefore to be expected.

Yet one cannot completely ignore legislators in an analysis of legislative policy making. How members of political elites define various buzzwords helps in discerning their approach to public policy. For example, if "compassionate welfare reform" involves getting people off the welfare rolls and out of public housing, where do they go and what do they do? Congressional debate of the various policy options shows that the answer lies in a close linkage to the two content areas of the "welfare queen" public identity: getting them into a job—any job—and out of the maternity wards. White U.S. Representative Clay Shaw (R-FL) echoes Watts in this excerpt from the House floor debate:

> The answer to welfare reform very clearly is to get people out of poverty, to get them jobs, to give them incentives, to give them child care, which we do, to give the States greater flexibility in order to craft these programs, the welfare programs, in order to help the people. We are at last going to be measured by the number of people we get out of poverty, not the number of people that we pay while they are in poverty. We are going to give the bureaucrats a vested interest in the solution to poverty, not the question of just how many people they keep in welfare. This is a new day. I think yesterday we saw the action that was taken by the other body as a quantum leap forward in bipartisan cooperation. I can say that I am looking forward to a bipartisan solution in this body also. (Appendix B, 80A)

Shaw shares Watts's definition of successful poverty programs when he says, "We are at last going to be measured by the number of people we get out of poverty, not the number of people that we pay while they are in poverty." Chapter 3 demonstrates a consensus beyond Watts and Shaw, subscribers to the "Republican revolution," about the social construction of welfare recipients. In particular, widespread subscription to the public identity of the "welfare queen" reflected one important aspect of the politics of disgust: a communicative context marked by gross inequality.

The absolute absence of mothers' voices in the *Congressional Record* is also an important replication of the media data set finding. The cueing of public identity in this communicative context has additional strength because it lacks any contestation by those most affected by the public identity of the "welfare queen" and welfare policy: the welfare recipients. Based on this replication of results and the demographic composition of Congress, it is critical that those depended upon to speak for the "welfare queens"—liberal Democrats, women, and African Americans who are members of Congress—*not* perpetuate the use of the public identity. This chapter focuses instead upon two additional features of the politics of disgust: the crumbling of solidarity among previous allies and the failure of representative thinking.

It is important to note again that although the politics of disgust provided much of the political context and that the public identity of the "welfare queen" played a role in the passage of the PRWA of 1996, in no way do I intend to argue that public identity is the sole explanatory variable. However, the rigorous testing of the propositions that conclude chapter 2 indicates that public identity played a significant role that cannot be dismissed when compared to competing explanations. With that caveat, I return to my first question: Is there really a public identity of the "welfare queen"?

The Public Identity of the "Welfare Queen"

Chapter 3 provides strong evidence that the public identity of the "welfare queen" is a coherent construct of stereotypes and moral judgments collected around content areas of work and reproduction. Table 4.1 shows the frequency with which each dimension of the four variables tested earlier occurred in the 82 documents from the *Congressional Record* of the 104th Congress: *Public Identity, Political Values, Consensus for Welfare Reform,* and *Policy Options*. Because multiple codes are permitted in the content analysis, the sum of the dimensions is again greater than the total number of text units coded per variable. Some key

differences and similarities to the media data set emerge from an a qualitative and quantitative content analysis.

One major similarity between the media results and the congressional
results is the failure to represent welfare recipients as *Good Mothers*. This
dimension received *no* coding *in any* document in the entire data set. The
closest thing to compassion for welfare mothers was displayed by Representative Charles Rangel (D-NY):

> We are going even further, not as far as the gentleman would like, but I
> think even the President agrees with the gentleman's posture, that if after
> 5 years or 4 or 3 or 2 or whatever the Governors decide, I think the min-
> imum is 2 years, that if for any reason at all, there are no jobs available,
> and if the mother played by the rules, signed up, went into training, did
> all of the American things in order to show that she wanted to maintain
> her dignity, she wanted her family not to stay on welfare, she wanted to
> go into the private sector and contribute, if all of those things are estab-
> lished, it is my understanding it really does not make any difference.
> Playing by the rules does not make a difference, in election years, be-
> cause we said it does not make any difference what the heck you have
> tried to do; the question is, are you working. (Appendix B, 74A)

This moderately compassionate excerpt from the House floor debate on
the PRWA Conference Report provides one note acknowledging the situation welfare mothers might face, given the bill's passage. It is, however,
only a passing reference; in the very next text unit, Representative Rangel
goes back to the children as the truly legitimate victims:

> Quite frankly, I believe that the mother could vote with her feet if she
> does not like the situation employment-wise. I am mean enough to be
> with you. I am a politician, too. My problem is the child. What did the
> child have to do with the fact that the mother wanted to work, did not
> want to work, jobs were there, jobs were not there? Do Members know
> what the political question is? The Republicans will throw 2 million
> people, children, into poverty, and my President will only throw 1 mil-
> lion into poverty. (Appendix B, 74A)

He later goes further, stating, "Do not ask the child, whether, by choice,
the mother is a bum" (ibid.). Again, with thousands of text units in 82
documents, only the one text unit in the one document quoted above

TABLE 4.1
Key Variables in Congressional Record,
104th Congress, Frequency

Variables/Dimensions	Coded Text Units
Public Identity of the "Welfare Queen"	153
Drain National Resources	6
Overly Fertile	17
Don't Work	39
Lazy	8
Cross-Generation Dependency	26
Single-Parent Family	32
Drug Users	1
Crime	19
Teen Mothers	21
Duration of Welfare	6
Culture of Poverty	60
Illegitimacy	28
System Abusers	6
Inner-City Resident	6
Policy Options	390
Block Grants	14
Time Limits	33
Workfare	112
Teen Mother Policies	13
Family Caps	12
Paternal Solutions	26
Immigrant Benefits	36
Medicaid Denial	101
State Programs	160
Food Stamp Reform	34
Political Values	193
Care for Children	80
Welfare System Accountability	64
Small Government	55
Industry	53
Economic Individualism	35
Parental Responsibility	32
Heterosexual Marriage	16
Christianity	11
Good Mothers	0
Consensus for Welfare Reform	89
Bipartisan Support	36
Among American Public	29
Among Executive and Congress	12
Among Taxpayers	4

alluded to even a modicum of positive attention toward welfare recipients. The replication of this result from the media data set leads me to conclude that despite any efforts to the contrary, the public identity of the "welfare queen" is a profoundly negative social construction.

Is there a coherent construct that underlies the negative social construction of welfare recipients? The results of this content analysis show that, in fact, there is significant replication of the media data set findings. Seven of the ten most frequent dimensions of the "welfare queen" public identity appear in like manner in both data sets: *Don't Work, Overly Fertile, Teen Mothers, Illegitimacy, Single-Parent Family, Crime,* and *Culture of Poverty.* The public identity of the welfare recipient in the 104th Congress thus mirrors the public identity of the welfare recipient in the media: stereotypes and moral judgments abound in policy discussions of welfare reform.

One key difference between the two data sets lies in the internal organization of the public identity construct. In Congress, the buzz term "culture of poverty" is used frequently (60 text units) as a rhetorical cue for the public identity of the "welfare queen." This dimension, which also occurred frequently in the media data set (47 text units), argued that the behavior of people receiving welfare creates a self-fulfilling prophecy that will never help them achieve self-sufficiency. Such behavior, learned by socialization into a welfare family or neighborhood, is also often termed "culture of dependency" or "welfare as a way of life." The following excerpt from the *Congressional Record* illustrates this dimension:

> Mr. Speaker, I was raised to treat the less fortunate in our society with compassion, as most Americans are. The way to effect change for those who suffer in poverty is certainly not additional handouts and entrapment in the current cycle of dependency that has bred second- and third- and now fourth-generation welfare recipients. Rather, we should emphasize welfare as a temporary boost from despair to the sense of self-worth inherent in work. (Appendix B, 74A)

This commentary by Representative Gerald Solomon (R-NY) contrasts the socialization he received, concerning compassion for the "less fortunate," with what he considers the proper route to self-sufficiency for those who have been "bred" into "second- and third- and now fourth-generation welfare recipients." The presence of *Public Identity* as a coherent psychological construct was indicated by text units that are multiply coded, clearly revealing an identity woven together rather than a laundry list of stereotypes.

This *"culture of poverty"* buzz word is correlated to a number of other dimensions in the **Public Identity** variable, providing additional evidence that public identity is indeed a coherent construct. Table 4.2 displays the degree of overlapping text unit codes among dimensions of **Public Identity**. The links between *Culture of Poverty* and other dimensions of **Public Identity** are clear across both content areas. *Culture of Poverty* is most frequently associated with *Cross-Generation Dependency* (10 text units), as the above example illustrates, followed by *Don't Work* (9 text units) and *Illegitimacy* (7 text units). The results are not surprising, given our earlier findings from the media data set.

A brief look at the reproductive content area further confirms the suggested intersecting race- and gender-based organization of the public identity of the "welfare queen." The overlap of dimensions such as *Overly Fertile, Illegitimacy,* and *Single-Parent Family* again suggests that the intersection of race, gender, and class oppressions influences how we think about welfare recipients. The comments of Senator John Breaux (D-LA) are illustrative:

> Mr. President, it is clear, and we all know that about half of all welfare recipients in our country have their first child as a teenager. If we are really talking about true welfare reform, we have to encourage good behavior, staying in school, or living with an adult family, a mother and father, or a mother, or adult supervisor, to help provide the training for that person. (Appendix B, 40A)

In this excerpt Senator Breaux also focuses on the *Teen Mother* dimension of public identity, matching the results from the media data set nearly identically. The association of several dimensions here in the *Congressional Record* confirm the finding in chapter 3 that public identity was indeed a coherent construct with specific dimensions based upon attribution of stereotypical traits and behaviors as well as moral judgments. Having confirmed chapter 3's answer to the question of public identity as a coherent construct, I test the argument that the public identity of the "welfare queen" serves as an ideological justification for specific welfare reform **Policy Options**.

TABLE 4.2
Text Code Overlap: Dimensions of *Public Identity*

	Dimensions of *Public Identity*												
	Overly Fertile	Don't Work	Lazy	Cross-Generation Dependency	Single-Parent Family	Drug Users	Crime	Teen Mothers	Duration on Welfare	Culture of Poverty	Illegitimacy	System Abusers	Inner-City Resident
Overly Fertile	—												
Don't Work	6	—											
Lazy	0	5	—										
Cross-Generation Dependency	8	7	0	—									
Single-Parent Family	2	5	1	6	—								
Drug Users	0	0	0	0	1	—							
Crime	2	4	0	10	8	1	—						
Teen Mothers	3	2	0	1	6	0	5	—					
Duration on Welfare	0	3	0	1	1	0	2	0	—				
Culture of Poverty	3	9	1	10	5	1	3	1	1	—			
Illegitimacy	6	7	2	7	18	1	9	5	5	7	—		
System Abusers	1	0	1	0	2	0	0	1	1	1	2	—	
Inner-City Resident	2	1	0	3	2	0	2	0	0	0	2	0	—

The Relationship between **Public Identity** and **Policy Options**

The qualitative and quantitative content analyses in chapters 3 and 4 aim to ascertain the relationship between the public identity of the "welfare queen" and welfare reform policy options. Though the data collected are nominal-level data from a quantitative standpoint, the qualitative content analysis makes a strong case for public identity's role in identifying and justifying welfare reform policy options in 1996.

The trends found here are similar to the findings in the national media data set. *State Programs* and *Workfare* were again the most numerous dimensions, with 160 and 112 text units, respectively. One significant difference, however, was the greater importance of *Medicaid Denial* in conjunction with termination of cash welfare benefits. This point was a key bone of contention between Democrats and Republicans; while they agreed on welfare reform, they disagreed as to whether children whose parents lose cash benefits either through work or welfare termination should remain eligible for Medicaid. Thus, this category produced a great deal of debate not present in the media sample, and it was often linked to the aforementioned *Political Value* of *Care for Children*.

An index search cross-referencing codes for **Public Identity** and **Policy Options** produced a list of 28 common documents and 61 text units. The list represents 34.6% of all documents in the sample and 50% of the *Policy Options* documents. Table 4.3 displays the number of text units with overlapping codes among specific dimensions of each variable. Overall, the cell contents indicate that the **Public Identity** of the "welfare queen" shares coding with three of the four **Policy Options** specified in chapter 3: *Workfare, Family Caps,* and *State Programs*. Overlap between *Workfare* and the **Public Identity** dimensions of *Don't Work* and *Culture of Poverty* produced the greatest numbers of text units. Representative Thomas Ewing (R-IL) made comments that reflected the overlapping codes:

> Mr. EWING: Mr. Speaker, the Republican plan for welfare reform has five pillars: Welfare reform should not be a way of life; we should have work, not welfare; we should not pay welfare to noncitizens and felons; we should return power and money to the States; and we should restore personal responsibility. (Appendix B, 26A)

Ewing outlines the **Policy Options** and cues the **Public Identity** of the "welfare queen" in the process when he states, "Welfare reform should

TABLE 4.3
Text Code Overlap: *Public Identity and Policy Options*

Public Identity	Policy Option									
	Block Grants	Time Limits	Workfare	Teen Mother Policies	Family Caps	Paternal Solutions	Immigrant Benefits	Medicaid Denial	State Programs	Food Stamp Reform
Drain on National Resources	0	1	0	0	0	0	0	1	2	0
Overly Fertile	0	2	7	4	8	5	1	0	4	0
Don't Work	0	4	19	3	5	1	3	2	9	0
Lazy	0	0	2	0	0	0	0	0	0	0
Cross-Generation Dependency	0	0	0	1	1	0	1	1	2	0
Single-Parent Family	0	1	6	4	4	3	0	1	4	0
Drug Users	0	0	0	0	0	0	0	0	0	0
Crime	0	1	3	2	3	1	2	0	2	0
Teen Mothers	0	0	5	9	4	4	0	0	2	0
Duration on Welfare	0	2	2	0	0	0	0	0	0	0
Culture of Poverty	1	3	8	0	1	1	4	1	7	0
Illegitimacy	0	1	3	3	5	3	1	1	3	0
System Abuses	0	0	0	0	1	0	0	0	2	0
Inner-City Resident	0	1	1	0	0	0	0	0	0	0

not be a way of life; we should have work not welfare. . . ." This kind of association was present, as the quotations in this chapter demonstrate, among Democrats and Republicans, liberals, conservatives, and moderates from a variety of states.

Similarly, overlapping codes of *Public Identity* dimensions and *Policy Option* dimensions in the reproduction content area also emerged. Consider the remarks of Representative George Radanovich (R-CA):

> In July 1994, California passed common-sense "family cap" welfare reform legislation to end the perverse practice of increasing payments to welfare recipients who have additional children. This practice usurps the role of husbands and drives men away from their families. But officials at the federal Department of Health and Human Services have denied the necessary federal waiver that would allow California to implement its law. (Appendix B, 41A)

In this text unit Radanovich discusses the *Policy Option* of a *Family Cap* while cueing an image of welfare recipients that includes the dimensions *Overly Fertile, Single-Parent Family,* and *Illegitimacy.* He is also discussing California's experience with the policy, leading to another overlapping code: *State Programs.* Again, just as in the media data set, *Public Identity* is cued directly in association with proposed *Policy Options.* The repeated examples that occur in both the national news media and the *Congressional Record* lead me to conclude that there is a strong relationship between how target populations are socially constructed and the specific policies that are discussed.

Considering Competing Explanations

The media data set in chapter 3 provides ample, convincing evidence that (1) *Public Identity* is not a proxy for *Political Values* and (2) *Political Values* are not as frequently associated with welfare reform *Policy Options* as are dimensions of *Public Identity.* The *Congressional Record* data set provides a much more challenging test because of the role of political rhetoric and the electoral context of 1996. Journalists generally make stringent efforts to produce news texts that are considered "value free." Members of Congress, particularly when in candidate mode, do the exact opposite by injecting discussions of values in policy debates.

TABLE 4.4
Text Code Overlap: *Public Identity and Political Values*

Public Identity	Industry	Economic Individualism	Heterosexual Marriage	Christianity	Parental Responsibility	Small Government	Care for Children	Welfare System Accountability
Overly Fertile	2	1	4	0	5	2	0	2
Don't Work	8	5	4	0	4	4	3	9
Lazy	2	0	0	0	1	0	1	2
Cross-Generation Dependency	4	2	2	0	1	3	3	11
Single-Parent Family	3	1	7	0	5	2	2	7
Drug Users	0	0	0	0	0	1	0	1
Crime	1	1	2	0	3	3	2	3
Teen Mothers	0	1	2	0	5	1	2	2
Duration on Welfare	0	0	0	0	0	0	0	0
Culture of Poverty	9	13	0	0	5	4	5	28
Illegitimacy	3	0	4	0	4	2	0	7
System Abusers	1	1	1	0	3	1	1	0
Inner-City Resident	0	0	0	0	0	0	0	1

Ideological justifications often occur in floor speeches as well because the floor is the most publicly accessible venue for policy making and deliberation prior to the actual vote.

In light of the specialized context and the heightened role of value-laden rhetoric in congressional floor debates, it is unsurprising that *Political Values* has a greater number of coded text units (193) than *Public Identity* (159). The level of dual codes provides a more reliable test as to whether *Public Identity* and *Political Values* serve as proxies for each other. Table 4.4 displays the results of an index search for the number of text units with overlapping codes of *Public Identity* and *Political Values*. As happened in the media data set, the majority (74%) of cells document no units or 1 or 2 units of overlapping codes. Though this is a drop from 94% of low/empty cells in the media data set (see Table 3.5), a robust majority of the dimensions of *Political Values* and *Public Identity* still display little or no overlap in qualitative coding.

The precipitous jump in overlapping codes along the *Culture of Poverty, Don't Work,* and *Single-Parent Family* dimensions of *Public Identity* merits deeper attention. *Culture of Poverty,* as an umbrella buzz word that cues both content areas of *Public Identity,* is also the most frequently occurring dimension of *Public Identity* in the data set; *Don't Work* and *Single-Parent Family* have the second and third greatest frequencies, respectively. *Culture of Poverty* (or dependency) is used as a specific rhetorical device to talk about welfare recipients in conjunction with the welfare system. This result points to another use of *Political Values* distinct from that found in the media data set: improving the *Welfare System's Accountability* for persistent poverty.

Just as *Care for Children* emerged as unique in its relationship to policy options in the media data set, *Welfare System Accountability*—the idea that the system, not the individual, bears the burden of transformation, gained currency in a Congress that sought to mitigate perceptions of the system as harsh and uncharitable, particularly toward children. The comments of Representative Bill Camp (R-TN) highlight this relationship:

> First, it requires work in exchange for benefits. It encourages independence and self-reliance for able-bodied people. To help those that work, the bill provides more child care funding than current law and more than the President's proposal for working families. We have a moral obligation to improve the lives of our children, and we must do all we

TABLE 4.5

Text Code Overlap: **Political Values and Policy Options**

Policy Options		Political Values						
	Industry	Economic Individualism	Heterosexual Marriage	Christianity	Parental Responsibility	Small Government	Care for Children	Welfare System Accountability
Block Grants	0	0	0	0	0	1	2	0
Time Limits	1	4	1	0	2	1	8	0
Workfare	10	10	3	2	13	5	21	4
Teen Mother Policies	0	0	2	0	2	1	1	0
Family Caps	1	0	3	0	5	1	1	1
Paternal Solutions	0	0	2	0	6	2	5	0
Immigrant Benefits	1	1	0	0	3	4	2	0
Medicaid Denial	1	1	1	0	1	19	4	2
State Programs	7	5	4	0	7	12	13	5
Food Stamp Reform	0	0	0	0	1	0	4	0

can to change the culture of poverty that our current welfare laws have created. (Appendix B, 65A)

Cueing *Welfare System Accountability* potentially counteracts the democratic dilemma caused by the *Public Identity* of the "welfare queen's" association with *Policy Options*. Unfortunately, the content analysis does not support this interpretation. First, the *Welfare System Accountability* category codes 64 text units, compared with 159 for *Public Identity*. Second, despite its high degree of overlap with the *Culture of Poverty* dimension of *Public Identity*, it overlaps with a very small number of text units that also feature discussions of *Policy Options* (see Table 4.5).

Therefore, despite the small jump in overlap between *Political Values* and *Public Identity*, the two variables still do not serve as proxies for each other. Table 4.5 also confirms that the more general relationship between *Political Values* and *Policy Options* is also limited: their association is concentrated in two specific areas: *Workfare* and *State Programs*. A strong, value-laden explanation for workfare is evident in comments made by Senator Jesse Helms (R-NC):

> This legislation will help those on welfare because it restores the American work ethic which once was one of the cornerstones of this Nation. In addition, this bill takes a step in the right direction in helping reduce the rising illegitimacy rates by providing funds for abstinence education, and by allowing States the option of denying benefits to welfare recipients who already have children living on the public dole. (Appendix B, 13A)

Helms's comments are emblematic of the text units that code *Political Values* and *Policy Options* simultaneously. What remains critical to note here is that within the same text unit, dimensions of *Political Values* and dimensions of *Public Identity* do not serve as proxies for each other. Although the American work ethic is cued at the start relative to legislation, a separate sentence cues the *Public Identity* of the "welfare queen" through a reference to "rising illegitimacy rates" and a suggested policy solution of "the option [to deny] benefits to welfare recipients who already have children living on the public dole" (*Family Cap*). Although the numbers suggest that *Policy Options* and *Political Values* share a stronger relationship than in the media data set, it is still one that includes strong cues of the *Public Identity* of the "welfare queen."

Despite the stronger predisposition to a preponderance of *Political*

Values such as *Industry, Economic Individualism,* and *Care for Children* in the *Congressional Record* data set, the argument that *Political Values* supplants the role of *Public Identity* in congressional debate fails. First, *Public Identity* and *Political Values* do not serve as proxies for each other, despite the elevated frequency of *Industry* and *Parental Responsibility* joining evidence of *Care for Children* first acknowledged in chapter 3's media analysis. Second, even though the quantitative measures suggest a possible supercession of *Public Identity* at first glance, a qualitative analysis of the text units comprising the higher numbers indicates that this is instead due to the overall increased frequency of units coded for *Political Values.* Looking more deeply at the association of *Political Values* and *Policy Options* reaffirms this interpretation.

Breaking the dimension of *State Programs* into the three categories enumerated in chapter 3, we see that the concentration of value-inclusive text units discuss preexisting *State Programs* that have been successful. The proportion of value-inclusive text units in discussions of creative programs remains fairly small: 9 units concerning *Care for Children* of 97 creative state program text units is the high-water mark (9%), with *Small Government* (6 units, 6%) and *Industry* (5 units, 5%) trailing. Thus, from either a qualitative perspective of *Industry* or a quantitative perspective of *State Programs, Political Values* are more frequent but only marginally more frequently associated with *Policy Options* than in the news media data set.

The electoral context of 1996 may plausibly stimulate an even greater role for the second competing explanation I analyze. In an era of poll-driven campaigns, it seems logical to examine whether members of Congress are jumping on a public-opinion-driven bandwagon. In some ways, the boundaries of the data set would perhaps predict a greater role for *Consensus* in a manner similar to the role of political rhetoric in enhancing the chance for political values to ingratiate themselves in the debate. The world of Congress is a unique system with numerous rules and restrictions placed on floor debates. To preserve conceptual clarity, the *Congressional Record* database was limited so as to isolate the one piece of welfare reform legislation signed into law from previously vetoed congressional efforts. In a presidential election year, with the desire to claim credit for "ending welfare as we know it," there were strong incentives for *Consensus for Welfare Reform*—from a bipartisan perspective as well as among the branches of government. References to the *Consensus for Welfare Reform* appeared much more frequently in the *Congressional*

TABLE 4.6
Text Code Overlap: **Public Identity** *and* **Consensus for Welfare Reform**

Public Identity	Consensus for Welfare Reform			
	Among American Public	Among Taxpayers	Bipartisan	Among Branches of Government
Drain on National Resources	0	0	0	0
Overly Fertile	2	0	0	0
Don't Work	3	0	1	0
Lazy	3	1	0	0
Cross-Generation Dependency	0	0	0	0
Single-Parent Family	2	0	0	1
Drug Users	0	0	0	0
Crime	0	0	0	0
Teen Mothers	0	0	0	1
Duration on Welfare	0	0	0	0
Culture of Poverty	3	0	5	1
Illegitimacy	2	0	0	0
System Abusers	1	1	0	0
Inner-City Resident	1	0	0	0

Record (89 text units) than in the media data set (48 text units). Its increased prevalence dictated serious consideration of *Consensus for Welfare Reform* as a primary theoretical and contextual explanation of the 1996 welfare reform bill. Ironically, the analysis of this explanation more obviously replicated the results of chapter 3 than the *Political Values* explanation.

We begin again with the notion that *Public Identity* (and the widespread, if unintentional, subscription to its tenets) is really a proxy for *Consensus for Welfare Reform*. Table 4.6 examines this proposition and, as with the media data set, overlapping codes between the dimensions of each variable are nearly nonexistent, despite the increased number of text units coded at *Consensus for Welfare Reform*. The five units of overlap between *Culture of Poverty* and *Bipartisan Support* represents 6% of the total units coded at *Consensus for Welfare Reform* and 3% of those coded at *Public Identity*. Thus, though the five units appear to stand out in Table 4.6, they are a very small percentage of either variable's total text units.

Similarly, the amount of overlap between *Consensus for Welfare Reform* and *Policy Options* is very small; only 40% of the cells have any text units at all, with the largest concentration collecting on the policy option of *Workfare* (see Table 4.7). The *Consensus for Welfare Reform*

TABLE 4.7
*Text Code Overlap: **Consensus for Welfare Reform** and **Policy Options***

	Consensus for Welfare Reform			
Policy Options	Among American Public	Among Taxpayers	Bipartisan	Among Branches of Government
Block Grants	0	0	0	0
Time Limits	2	1	1	0
Workfare	9	1	5	1
Teen Mother Policies	0	0	0	0
Family Caps	1	0	0	0
Paternal Solutions	1	0	1	0
Immigrant Benefits	0	0	1	0
Medicaid Denial	0	0	2	3
State Programs	2	1	3	0
Food Stamp Reform	0	0	0	0

among the American Public supports the idea that welfare reform policy follows the logic of direct representation, but again the 9 text units represent a very small percentage of the 390 total text units coded for *Policy Options* (2%). This is a miniscule level of overlap, as is the association (of the same 9 units) with the 112 total text units coded for workfare (8%). For the five text units coded at *Bipartisan Support*, the proportions are even smaller. Following nearly identical results in two different data sets, the competing explanation of *Consensus for Welfare Reform* can be dismissed. Qualitative and quantitative content analyses of two random-sample data sets indicate that *Consensus for Welfare Reform* is neither a proxy for *Public Identity* nor substantially related to the *Policy Options* discussed for reforming welfare in 1996.

What makes the evidence that a relationship exists between *Public Identity* and *Policy Options* so troubling politically? The politics of disgust warps social constructions and ultimately prevents democratic outcomes. As the next section demonstrates, members of Congress are no less susceptible than their journalist counterparts to various aspects of the politics of disgust.

Members of Congress and the Politics of Disgust

Chapter 1 describes four distinguishing features of the politics of disgust: a perversion of democratic attention; a communicative context marked by gross inequality; the breakdown of political solidarity among those who traditionally serve as champions of the underrepresented; and the failure of representative thinking. Chapters 2 and 3 highlight the role of the first two components—perverted democratic attention and mono-logic communicative contexts, respectively. Using the qualitative content analysis of the *Congressional Record* data set, I explore evidence of the remaining features of the politics of disgust: the lack of political solidarity and the failure of representative thinking.

Despite the failure of representative thinking as a competing explanation for the exact policy options, most scholars agree that members of Congress favoring welfare reform were a diverse group: Democrats and Republicans, liberals and conservatives, patriarchalists and feminists (Mink 1999, 174). African American and White American members supported many of the welfare reform proposals that were discussed and that ultimately became statutes, regardless of their final vote on the Personal Responsibility and Work Opportunities Act of 1996.

Considering the vote from a gender perspective, men and women in Congress similarly supported the PRWA. Despite the anti–HR 3734 lobbying of the National Organization for Women, the American Association of University Women, and prominent feminists such as Gloria Steinem, many congresswomen voted with their male counterparts (Mink 1999, 174; Mink 1998). Twenty-seven women in the House of Representatives, over one-third Democrats, voted for HR 3734.[2] Five female senators, including several who identify strongly as advocates of women's empowerment, voted for the PRWA.

Scholars of women in politics note that while they represent the interests of their districts first, women also take special interest in and responsibility for addressing the concerns of women (Dodson et al. 1995; Burrell 1994). Representative Nancy Johnson (R-CT), expressed this perspective in an interview:

> Now, whenever something comes up, we automatically think, "Gee, how will this affect the environment? How will this affect the working people at the work site?" But we don't really think, "How is this going to affect women who work at home? Women in the workplace with home responsibilities? Women who are single parents?" And so I do feel a special responsibility to participate in the public policy process in a way that assures that where something is going to affect women as well as men, that I think through how this will affect women. . . . (Dodson et al. 1995, 15)

In a press conference hosted by Republican congresswomen to support HR 3734, Johnson responded in this manner to a question concerning drastic cuts in cash benefits to welfare mothers:

> Rep. Nancy Johnson (R-Conn.) said that such mothers could clothe their children without cash support, "It's not hard to clothe your kid, folks," she said. "Go to the secondhand shops." (Appendix A, 124)

The juxtaposition of Johnson's two quotations lends support to both scholarly arguments mentioned above. Johnson clearly views herself as someone uniquely positioned to make a difference on issues that affect women. She also clearly expresses a compassion for women as a general category in the first quotation that is lacking in the second quotation, where the discrete category of women on welfare is the subject.

Feminist activists and scholars have argued that the divergence on the welfare issue among female legislators is linked to a lack of personal experience with the welfare issue; it does not fundamentally influence their lives in a manner similar to that of abortion rights or equal opportunity legislation (Mink 1999, 176). What explains the support of female members of Congress for varying planks of welfare reform policy characterized as antiwoman by the major feminist organizations?

One explanation for the support focuses on congresswomen as members whose primary goal is reelection. Based on citizen support for welfare reform within their districts, they vote their districts' interests. However, the earlier empirical analysis indicates that *Consensus for Welfare Reform* was not considered a justification for specific policy options. Moreover, congresswomen have often taken principled stands in contrast to the interests of their districts in support of issues concerning women. One particularly vivid moment occurred in 1991, when female members of Congress stormed the Senate in support of Anita Hill as she made her accusations against Clarence Thomas, who had been nominated for the Supreme Court. The dramatic action did not change the outcome of the hearings, but it prioritized the importance of making a statement over the political fallout. Why was the political fallout deemed too risky in the case of welfare reform in 1996?

The words of Senator Barbara Mikulski (D-MD), one of those congresswomen known for her march up the Senate steps in support of Anita Hill, reflect a lack of political solidarity with welfare recipients as *women*.

The avowed feminist used her time on the podium to announce her vote in favor of S 1795 and tell of her leadership role in its creation:

> I'm particularly proud of my role in fighting for child abuse programs, for child care health and safety standards and for the health care safety net. I offered amendments on these issues and fought for their adoption.
>
> From day one, I insisted that we could not do anything in this bill to lessen our commitment to fighting child abuse. I am pleased that this bill no longer includes provisions which would have replaced Federal child abuse and protection programs with an inadequate block grant. As a former child protection worker, I know how vital these programs are for taking care of children who have suffered from abuse or neglect.
>
> I fought to keep current Federal child care health and safety standards. Along with Senator [Christopher] Dodd, I offered an amendment to restore those standards which the other party was prepared to abandon. I fought to maintain those standards because I believe strongly that parents should have every assurance that when they place their children in child care, they will be protected from infectious diseases, from unsafe buildings and playground hazards, and that the child care worker will know basic first aid. This is a significant improvement in the bill. (Appendix B, 13A)

Here, Mikulski first puts her role in the current welfare reform process front and center. She positions herself as an expert in child protection with the words "As a former child protection worker" and claims credit for the preservation of child abuse programs, child care health and safety standards, and the health care safety net, speaking in the first person most forcefully with phrases such as "I insisted," "I fought," and "I believe strongly." She completes this part of her statement with the satisfied conclusion "This is a significant improvement in the bill." Indeed, perhaps it is.

Yet Mikulski is a liberal Democrat voting for a Republican welfare reform plan that her compatriots in the Children's Defense Fund declare will throw one million children into poverty. Her support for S 1795 is not an unqualified vote of confidence. While recognizing the potential pitfalls of this bill, she uses strong language for the political benefit of one population, children. Nowhere does Mikulski acknowledge that the children she wants to protect have mothers with any kinds of needs, rights, or interests. In this sense, Mikulski follows a long-established pattern of gendered welfare policy making; these programs were never designed to empower women as independent human beings. Rather, federal programs were focused instead on facilitating the raising of productive children-citizens (see Sapiro 1990).

This trend continued across the aisle and across the chambers in the comments of Representative Marge Roukema (R-NJ), who discusses a traditionally feminist issue with no mention of women:

> Child support evasion is a national disgrace. Each year millions of families are denied billions of dollars to which they are legally and morally entitled. First the children are the victims and, second, the taxpayers. Let us pass this legislation. (Appendix B, 55A).

Roukema, a strong advocate of the child support enforcement provisions inserted by members of the Women's Caucus in the House of Representatives, asserts that compassion should be allocated to two groups: "First the children are the victims, and, second, the taxpayers." Improved child support enforcement has long been a political goal of feminist organizations such as the National Organization for Women (NOW) and the Feminist Majority, who argue that lack of child support is a key contributor to the feminization of poverty. In chapter 1, I explain how this emphasis on child support in a class-biased manner resulted in a failure of representative thinking. Here, however, we see further evidence of the politics of disgust: lack of solidarity among women. But in the context of a welfare reform debate, the importance or even the existence of either a woman or mother simply drops out of the equation. Roukema's obligations, according to the above excerpt, are to children and taxpayers only.

To further illustrate the lack of solidarity between welfare recipients and their traditional champions, consider the words of Sanford Bishop (D-GA), who joined J. C. Watts and Gary Franks as Black members of Congress who voted in favor of the PRWA. Bishop broke ranks with many members of the Congressional Black Caucus (CBC) and voted in favor of HR 3734, in part because he faced a significantly transformed constituency following the resolution of redistricting disputes in Georgia.[3] Regardless of the electoral context, he chose to cue aspects of *Public Identity* in justifying his vote:

This is the beginning of a process that can transform welfare into an opportunity rather than a way of life. It is about requiring and rewarding work while providing access to job skills and expanded job opportunities. (Appendix B, 10A)

In the above units Bishop alludes to a *Culture of Poverty* dimension of *Public Identity* when he provides a twist on the expression "welfare as a way of life." This also obliquely refers to the dimension of *Duration of Welfare* by implying that receipt of welfare occurs for long stretches over a recipient's life span. Both dimensions are linked in the previous section's analysis to *Policy Options* discussed during this floor debate. Facing a tight race for reelection may have sparked a path of political expediency for Sanford Bishop, or, as did J. C. Watts, Bishop may have constructed the issue in a way that was fundamentally different from the way chosen by many members of the CBC. The more important point is that Bishop, an African American Democratic male member of Congress, cued part of the *Public Identity* of the "welfare queen" to justify his vote as one that shows *Care for Children*. In a startling shift from the founding of ADC, mothers are no longer considered a help to their children; they are now considered a hindrance.

The examples of Barbara Mikulski, Marge Roukema, and Sanford Bishop are instructive in that they illustrate the lack of solidarity that traditional allies of welfare recipients' interests—women legislators and African American legislators—displayed during the floor debate of the 1996 PRWA. All three ignore completely any needs or interests of welfare mothers in favor of children and taxpayers.

Even though the political context of an election year may serve as a potential explanation of the lack of solidarity, it is an incomplete one. As I noted above, the debate may also have been influenced by the historical factors regarding gendered policy design (see Sapiro 1990). This explanation is also plausible, but again it does not explain completely the cues of the "welfare queen" public identity because this racialized, gendered, and classed identity emerged after 1935.

All of the above examples—Bishop, Mikulski, Roukema—come from supporters of the PRWA. Yet Bishop's fellow CBC members also cued the "welfare queen" public identity as they argued *against* passage of HR 3734. All four of the documents containing comments by Black representatives contained text units coded at dimensions of *Public Identity*.[4]

These units reiterate a point made from an historical perspective in chapter 2: welfare recipients, including those who are single, poor African American mothers, today experience marginalization similar to that experienced by NWRO and ADC applicants at the hands of Black elites.

In addition to Bishop and Charles Rangel, two African American congresswomen made statements included in the data set. Eva Clayton (D-NC) and Sheila Jackson-Lee (D-TX) joined Rangel in opposing HR 3734. Of the entire sample, Jackson-Lee comes closest to actually verbalizing the claims of mothers receiving public assistance:

> All of us have tried to work to respond to those who would come in good faith. But I want to simply appeal to the women of America, the families of America. This Republican bill cuts some almost $60 billion from individuals across this Nation who, each time we ask them, they say I would like to work, I would like to get off welfare, and yes, as an American I want to contribute to what America has to offer. (Appendix B, 65A)

Although she includes their opinions, Jackson-Lee only goes so far in humanizing "individuals across this Nation who . . . say I would like to work, I would like to get off welfare, and yes, as an American I want to contribute to what America has to offer." She includes them in the citizenry—a far cry from being a "bum," in Rangel's earlier locution, or an "abuser of the system," to paraphrase Bishop's words. Even so, Jackson-Lee shows little sign of any overt compassion or care for these "individuals," as she reveals in the text unit below, discussing children of welfare:

> But these children are the ones that we are speaking about, children who may not have the child care necessary for their parents to transition from welfare to work because we lessen the opportunity for those families to have transitional child care. If the money runs out in the State, folks, if the bucket is empty, then they do not have an opportunity to go to work if the children are not cared for. (Appendix B, 65A)

The focus again is almost immediately diverted from welfare parents to their children and the child care subsidies at issue in the bill.

Representative Eva Clayton (D-NC) stood with Rangel, Jackson-Lee, and other members of the CBC in voting against HR 3734. Unlike the other African American members included in this data set, Clayton focused on the conceptual area of reproduction in the "welfare queen" *Public Identity* rather than the area of work. She focused one text unit on compassion for welfare mothers—the only text unit found in the entire data set. This lone voice in the rush toward welfare reform, in her quest to inspire compassion unfortunately also perpetuated a conflation of teen mothers and welfare recipients common in the public identity of the "welfare queen":

> Mrs. CLAYTON: Mr. Speaker, some in Congress have demonized the poor, that they have become the poster children for all that is wrong in America. They have convinced the American people that the welfare mothers and their children have caused a great debt that our Nation has acquired. They have now made the new JOAN OF ARC out of the teenaged mothers. (Appendix B, 82A; emphasis in original)

Clayton seeks to engender some emotional support for welfare mothers. The use of words and images associated with religion—including "demonization" and "Joan of Arc"—provides an alternative construction of compassion to that of ordained minister J. C. Watts or Clayton's Women's Caucus colleague Marge Roukema. Clayton's employment of Christian values attempts to wrest the emotion of compassion away from the Republican definition that commenced this chapter. The analogy between the treatment of a familiar Christian female martyr and the treatment of welfare mothers, however, did not compensate for the lack of compassion for welfare mothers evident throughout the rest of the data set.

The Clayton excerpt's chastisement of fellow representatives for their bashing of welfare mothers unfortunately dwelt exclusively on certain dimensions of *Public Identity* and their policy solutions in a way that encourages individual-level solutions, albeit government-funded ones.

> At this time, when so many of our children are at their lowest and worst point, we need to call on the very highest and best efforts of this country. Thirty percent of all out-of-wedlock births are to teenagers below the age of 20. Every 1 minute a child is born to a teen mother. We have a national campaign whose goal is to reduce teenage pregnancy by one-third by the year 2005. This is a goal that is essential. This is a goal within our reach. (Appendix B, 79A)

Clayton's focus on teen pregnancy serves to cue the *Teen Mothers* and *Overly Fertile* dimensions of the "welfare queen" public identity. Within the context of a welfare reform debate, she speaks of women under 18, perhaps as an expression of care for children, perhaps not. In doing so, however, she moves away from all welfare mothers to teen welfare mothers, who she acknowledges constitute only 30 percent of the entire single-mother population.[5] This excerpt is one of 28 units in her speech about *Teen Mother Policies*, a dimension of **Policy Options**. She presents a more sympathetic view than do many of her congressional counterparts, but the most important statistic is missing from her speech: the percentage of unwed mothers who are both teenagers and recipients of public assistance. Absent this piece of information, the conflation of welfare mother with *Teen Mothers* remains part of the influence of **Public Identity**.

Neither Clayton nor Jackson-Lee exhibit Rangel's kind of hostility toward welfare mothers, but all three exhibit a clear disconnect between their public utterances and accurate representation of welfare mothers' views. For the single, poor African American mothers among the welfare population, whether these representatives "sold out" on purpose or as a consequence of benign neglect matters little in terms of the result: lack of representation by those most likely to provide any representation at all, liberal African American Democrats in Congress.

These very same African American members of Congress have long prided themselves on giving voice to the silenced. The attacks on welfare mothers and exclusive focus on the children indicate that only some of the silenced can expect to have their voices represented. Both findings indicate the presence of secondary marginalization among the African American community. To the degree that African Americans in Congress fall into lockstep with their non-Black counterparts, the public identity of the "welfare queen" persists with little challenge in political discourse. The failure of representative thinking and the lack of solidarity evident among traditional champions of the underrepresented conflated the reality of welfare recipients' lives unintentionally with the stereotypes and moral judgments of the "welfare queen" public identity.

Conclusion

The analysis of congressional discourse surrounding welfare reform in 1996 provided a more rigorous empirical test of public identity as a construct and influence in the policy option discussion than that of the news media data set due to many discursive characteristics that are well beyond the author's control. Nevertheless, the data from the *Congressional Record* replicate *all* of the general findings in chapter 3's analysis of the news media. The "welfare queen" public identity is a coherent construct that conditioned the 1996 welfare reform debate, particularly with regard to proposed policy options. Chapters 2, 3, and 4 thus provide ample support for the argument that public identity serves as an unconscious filter through which Americans receive the policy options presented in public discourse about welfare reform.

In both data sets, policy options were discussed across political parties and across policy positions without attention to this common filter. Unlike the media data set, which included at least passing acknowledgment of individual welfare recipients, the *Congressional Record* data set featured no significant inclusion of welfare recipients' voices in the final debate, reinforcing the power of public identity as an influence upon policy options. Care or compassion for mothers lacking child support or other forms of income was nearly nonexistent within this set of congressional documents. Policy options were discussed, selected, and implemented with no effective contributions from those affected most (see also Sparks 2003). These oversights effectively prevented welfare recipients' empowered participation in the political sphere.

These findings reflect more than just the role of public identity. The politics of disgust, as the context within which the 1996 PRWA was shaped and passed, was revealed at the congressional level through the failure of two critical safeguards for our democracy. In the absence of one's personal participation in politics, representatives in the form of allies or champions of one's causes should make the case for us. Allies and champions attempt to represent the unrepresented. The data in this chapter provided ample evidence of the lack of solidarity and failure of representative thinking among the longtime champions of the poor, African Americans and women in both the House and Senate. Again, the point is clear: everyone, no matter race, gender, party identification, or class, is susceptible to the power of public identity under the conditions of the politics of disgust.

Chapters 3 and 4 reveal a stunning lack of unmediated participation in the public sphere by and for welfare mothers themselves. In 1996, no NWRO stepped forward to effectively galvanize the welfare population into an interventionary force with which Congress and the media would be forced to contend. Who were the welfare recipients of the 1990s, where were they, and what were they doing? Chapter 5 presents portraits of welfare mothers, often in their own words, as they struggled against public identity and politics of disgust.

5

Contending with the Politics of Disgust
Public Identity through Welfare Recipients' Eyes

Lost are the voices of mothers who receive welfare, yet speak with pride and strength. (L. Williams 1995, 1194)

I began this book with a portrait of Bertha Bridges, a Detroit welfare recipient whose life was "a nightmare"—her words. Congressman Scott McInnis (R-CO) used her story as an ideological justification for his ideas regarding welfare reform, not Bertha's ideas about improving her life. I characterized this behavior as a perversion of democratic attention: employing the story of a less-empowered citizen to advance one's own political purposes. Absent a strong and effective National Welfare Rights Organization (NWRO) in 1996, what was the response of recent welfare recipients to the persistent misconceptions about them?

Chapters 2, 3, and 4 provide ample evidence of the public identity of the "welfare queen" in historical context, media discourse, and congressional debate. They document how cues of the "welfare queen" public identity undergirded both sides of the 1996 welfare reform debate. The discursive hegemony of this public identity prevents accurate information about welfare recipients from being integrated into citizens' preexisting beliefs about the identities of welfare recipients. It also bombards welfare recipients themselves with "demeaning imagery of who society says she is" (L. Williams 1995, 1193; see also Steele and Sherman, 1999). To this point, I have emphasized how the public identity of the "welfare queen" played a role in shaping the Personal Responsibility and Work Opportunity Act of 1996. In this chapter, I want to focus on the more personal political outcomes for mothers receiving public assistance just before and after 1996.

Two former welfare recipients have emphasized welfare mothers' response to the distorted images found in the media and Congress about them. Wahneema Lubiano writes:

> The cumulative totality, circulation and effect of these meanings in a time of scarce resources among the working class and the lower class is devastatingly intense. The "welfare queen" represents moral aberration and an economic drain, but the figure's problematic status becomes all the more threatening once responsibility for the destruction of the "American way of life" is attributed to it. (Lubiano 1992, 339)

Sandy Smith Madsen, another former welfare mother, concurs: "[M]ost welfare mothers know their precarious places and wisely, question nothing" (Madsen 1998, A44). Madsen's article discussed the welfare agency experiences of welfare recipients who pursue higher education, to which I will attend later in this chapter. Recent empirical evidence reveals that many welfare clients would not challenge a situation unless it constituted a predicament extremely detrimental to their children (Soss 1999, 366).

My purpose in this chapter is to explore how welfare recipients contend with the politics of disgust in 1996 and beyond. Instead of exclusively using media and legislative documents, I seek a richer treatment of the complex reality of their lives by including the results of seven in-depth interviews and other quotations from welfare recipients themselves.[1] In addition to illustrating the four aspects of the politics of disgust—perversion of democratic attention; an inegalitarian communicative context; the failure of representative thinking; and lack of solidarity—I will again distinguish between the stereotypes and moral judgments of public identity and the facts regarding welfare recipients, despite decades of scholars' previous attempts to do just that (Jennings 1994, 26).

The Perversion of Democratic Attention

Chapters 2, 3, and 4 show how our attention is drawn in very specific ways to the need for welfare reform through cues of the "welfare queen" public identity. The perversion of democratic attention emerges not simply in the story about Bertha Bridges or in the profile in this chapter of any welfare recipient. Another disturbing manifestation of democratic attention gone awry was the association of welfare recipients with animals, particularly animals with detrimental characteristics. These metaphorical associations again take the multivaried realities of welfare recipients' lives and reduce them to their most base common denominator. In this sense, such allusions are very closely related to psychological findings regarding cues of disgust as an emotion (Rozin, Haidt, et al. 1999, 332; Keltner and Haidt 1999, 513; Rozin, Lowery, et al. 1999, 575).

The reduction of women on welfare, and the women of color who are assumed to be, to animals is not a new phenomenon (White, 1985; Giddings, 1984). In chapter 2, I noted Senator Russell Long's term "brood mares," used to refer to the Black and Puerto Rican welfare recipients testifying before the Senate Finance Committee he chaired (West 1981; L. Williams 1995). This then turned into his ideological justification for workfare: "If they can find the time to march in the streets, picket and sit all day in committee hearing rooms, they can find the time to do some useful work" (quoted in L. Williams, 1995, 1184). By reducing welfare recipients to animals, Long first strips them of citizenship, then humanity. He goes further to propose a policy solution—"useful work"—defined on his terms, of course, not the terms of welfare mother activists. The abstraction of mothers from their respective political contexts for use as an ideological justification of the speaker's own imposed policy solution is a hallmark manifestation of the perversion of democratic attention.

The actions of Senator Long in 1970 were echoed by Representative John Mica (R-FL) in the 1996 welfare reform debate, as these text units from a *New York Times* article included in the media data set documents:

Today's debate featured a veritable menagerie of animal imagery. Representative John L. Mica, Republican of Florida, held up a sign that said, "Don't Feed the Alligators" and he explained: "We post these warnings because unnatural feeding and artificial care create dependency.

"When dependency sets in, these otherwise able alligators can no longer survive on their own. Now I know that people are not alligators, but I submit to you that with our current handout, non-work welfare system, we've upset the natural order. We've created a system of dependency. The author of our Declaration of Independence, Thomas Jefferson, said it best in three words: 'Dependence begets servitude.'" (Appendix A, 17)

The evocative image of an alligator, commonly thought to be a rapacious animal, was conveyed both visually by Representative Mica's use of a sign, as well as verbally. Despite Mica's assertion that he knows "people are not alligators" and Representative Barney Frank's (D-MA) verbal protest (without a counter visual), the image still serves as an ideological justification for a specific piece of legislation. As is the case with the "welfare queen" more generally, such animal allusions were raised by both sexes, as is evident from the words of Representative Barbara Cubin (R-WY):

> Representative Barbara Cubin, Republican of Wyoming, drew a similar lesson from experience in her state. "The Federal Government introduced wolves into the State of Wyoming, and they put them in pens, and they brought elk and venison to them every day," she said. "This is what I call the wolf welfare program.
>
> "The Federal Government provided everything that the wolves need for their existence. But guess what? They opened the gates and let the wolves out, and now the wolves won't go. Just like any animal in the species, any mammal, when you take away their freedom and their dignity and their ability, they can't provide for themselves, and that is what the Democrats' proposal does on welfare." (Ibid.)

In this case wolves—another animal culturally constructed in our society as rapacious, is used to communicate the same point.

In addition to their metaphorically associating welfare recipients with predatory creatures, members of Congress also emphasized a "tough love" approach to presumably recalcitrant welfare mothers: "Earlier, House Ways and Means Chairman Rep. Clay Shaw Jr., who shepherded welfare repeal legislation through the House, stated, 'It may be like hitting a mule with a two by four but you've got to get their attention" (quoted in Polakow 1997, 7). Such repeated insults provide qualitative evidence of the perversion of democratic attention, a primary feature of the politics of disgust. Crocker, Major, and Steele, in their comprehensive review of social stigma, point out: "Many of the predicaments of being stigmatized involve awareness of how one is viewed by others, and construals of the meaning and causes of others' behavior" (1998, 543). How do welfare recipients react to the problems of perversion?

Recent findings by Joe Soss (1999) confirm that many welfare recipients react just as Sandy Smith Madsen predicted: most do nothing, politically speaking, in response to this first aspect of the politics of disgust (367). Their immediate response to the media dissemination of the "welfare queen" public identity and the politics of disgust focuses on an aspect of their life that they can control their children: "On several occasions, women recalled turning off the television because they did not want their children to hear what was being said about them" (Soss 1999, 368).

My interviews further support Soss's finding that welfare recipients know very well what is believed about them. Lapis, a 20-year-old mother of one infant who was also a new Temporary Assistance to Needy Families (TANF) recipient provides one example. Here, I've asked her what Congress would say about people who receive AFDC/TANF benefits:

> They, 'cause pretty much a lot of the Congress people, they really don't care too much about welfare because they are not the ones who need it. So they probably would, you know, say cut it off or something like that. Because they feel like it's too many taxpayers paying money for women who don't want to get a job and don't want to take care of themselves or their kids. But once again it is not always that easy. When you are pregnant or you have a new baby, you can't work all the time. You got to be cautious of your health from being pregnant and cautious of your baby's health when your baby is first born and things like that. So, it's not like you just want to sit back and collect the check that is not much.

Another interview with a former welfare recipient echoes Lapis's comments. Isis was able to leave welfare and public housing following the death of a parent; she inherited a house with no mortgage and now works for a cable company:

> *Interviewer:* What do you think Congress would say about women on welfare?
>
> *Isis:* They don't want nobody on welfare, they want to cut it completely. They don't want to give them any incentives to go back to work, like child care, probably want to cut the child care, subsidized child care, too.
>
> *Interviewer:* What do you think [former mayor of San Francisco] Willie Brown would say about women on welfare?
>
> *Isis:* I think Willie Brown feels that we should be able to support ourselves, than welfare. I think to keep himself in office he's saying

that he's for it. I don't believe he really believes that. So he's just trying to stay in office with subsidized housing and welfare.

Steele and Sherman (1999) have also documented the psychological responses of women on welfare. In concurrence with Soss, these authors focus on responses to behavioral stimuli—such as treatment at the social services office or by the police. Yet as the above quotations from the media data, Congress, and interviews show, discriminatory treatment is not the sole debilitating factor in the lives of welfare recipients. Many are also aware of the discursive distortions that exist as part of the politics of disgust.

A Communicative Context Marked by Gross Inequality

The very large microphones possessed by those who subscribe to the public identity of the "welfare queen" most clearly exemplify the problem posed by this second aspect of the politics of disgust. As I acknowledged in chapter 3, the media data set did not produce a unanimous stereotype that welfare recipients do not work. In fact, 26 text units presented welfare mothers who were either working or in job training programs. Yet a quantitative and qualitative evaluation of these units again reiterates the overwhelming deafening power of the large microphones.

The 26 text units portraying mothers as workers represent 4 percent of all the text units coded at *Public Identity,* occurring in 8 documents, or 5 percent of the 149-article sample. The emphasis in news media coverage centered on working a job—any job—in order to develop a work ethic believed to be lacking in the welfare population. The portraits of Desiree Stewart, Octavia Cavalier, and Rhonda Small, however, reflect a preexisting work ethic and the political value of economic individualism. In an article about microlending as a structural solution to poverty, the *Christian Science Monitor* presents two entrepreneurs, one of whom is Desiree Stewart:

> Desiree Stewart's hair salon is just over one year old. The equipment is used, the pipes are bad, and there are no mirrors on the walls—yet. But the growing Chicago business is making a profit and, if things go as planned, the single mother will soon be able to get off welfare for the first time in seven years. (Appendix A, 54)

Although Stewart has spent seven years in the welfare system, it is unlikely that she was forced to begin her business as part of state or local welfare reform efforts, which center on finding a job—any job. Contrary to the notion of work-ethic atrophy attributed to welfare mothers who are long-term recipients, these excerpts demonstrate that change is possible with the right policies.

The focus of the *Monitor* article, however, is not on the journey of self-transformation that an individualist explanation of poverty would produce. Rather, it is on microlending as a potential structural resource for economically empowering women in pursuit of financial independence, not a rehabilitated work ethic in each woman. In this sense, Stewart is no different from many in the United States who seek a better life through a small business or education. The importance of structural assistance was likewise not lost on the second welfare mother entrepreneur portrayed in the article:

> For someone like Octavia Cavalier in Alexandria, Va., $250 was all she needed to buy a vacuum cleaner, gas for her car and some flyers to advertise her cleaning service. (Ibid.)

In keeping with the individualist nature of American political culture, however, the microlending program through which both Stewart and Cavalier obtained funding for a small business is considered unworkable in the United States for individualist reasons, including the behaviors of the American poor—specifically violence and distrust in inner cities.[2] Thus, many welfare mothers who follow the system and hope to get out from under with the quintessential American dream of owning a business must wait.

Rhonda Small is another welfare recipient portrayed as working and receiving benefits—a clear contradiction of the *Don't Work* stereotype:

> Small, 22, says she opts to work because she believes it will give her financial independence. But battling long hours for low wages and job experience has, in turn, pitted her against the web of AFDC restrictions that tightly dictate how much she may earn and how she should seek work. Her waitress earnings alone would have caused her $420 monthly AFDC check to be reduced according to a complex formula. But because Small delayed telling the District about her job, the cut went deeper than usual, to $378. (Appendix A, 90)

The above paragraphs clearly portray welfare recipients as being willing to work, contrary to the idea that they are *Lazy* and want something for nothing. Elena Roman and others at her job-attainment program Future Works simply seek a wage that will keep them out of the system:

> Several women at Future Works who were interviewed after the Governor [Christine Todd Whitman (R-NJ)] left said they agreed with limiting benefits, as long as decent-paying jobs—and training to qualify for them—were available. (Appendix A, 45)

The consensus for welfare reform as expressed by welfare recipients themselves could not be more apparent. Yet two key differences between these policy solutions and those in the dominant discourse emerge. First, Desiree Stewart and Octavia Cavalier reflect a very tiny percentage of the welfare population: recipients with access to small-business capital. Second, Rhonda Small and Elena Roman seek jobs that will keep them out of the system. This means, essentially, a job with a living wage.

Figures from the 2000 U.S. Census indicate that a woman without a high school diploma makes an average of $11,432. The poverty threshold for a family of three (one parent, two children) in 2000 was $13,874 (U.S. Department of Commerce, *Current Population Reports,* 2000). The poverty guideline used by the U.S. Department of Health and Human Services to determine welfare program eligibility, was $14,150 in 2000. Obviously, it is not just *any* job that will bring a family out of welfare need. Prior to passage of the PRWA (1993), more than 40 percent of mothers on AFDC worked approximately 900 hours a year, closely mirroring the overall labor force participation of working mothers (Polakow 1994, 11), facts ignored by both the media and Congress. Working AFDC mothers were in 4 percent of the media text units and did not appear at all in the *Congressional Record* data set. *More than ten times that percentage actually worked prior to the 1996 welfare reform.*

The critical implication of this ongoing quantitative distortion speaks directly to the silencing of mothers receiving AFDC. Having scarcely a voice does not meet the standard for democratic participation, an argument I take up in chapter 6. Here, the inequality of access to mass communication unmistakably reveals the presence of the politics of disgust. From a qualitative level, the mothers who work are cited by name, age, location, and other general information of their lives—just enough detail for readers or viewers to dismiss their individual stories of hard work and striving as exceptional (see L. Williams 1995, 1167) instead of being representative of the 70 percent of welfare recipients who work (Appendix A, 122). Thus the in-depth coverage of individual welfare mothers does very little to challenge the conventional beliefs of many Americans regarding the work habits of women receiving AFDC/TANF, largely due to a communicative context in which the portrayal of their lives hardly reflects their reality.

The Failure of Representative Thinking

The paucity of media portraits of working welfare recipients is a glut compared to the counterstereotypical portraits of welfare recipients in the content domain of reproduction. In chapters 1 and 4, I note the failure of representative thinking among members of Congress and its relationship to the problematic policy formulations concerning paternal identification and child support. Two examples from the media dataset articulate the clash of these policies with the reality of welfare recipients' complex lives and choices:

> One night seven years ago, the ninth-grade dropout with a pretty smile went to a bar and met a man named Mark. "To put is bluntly," the shy, 32-year-old woman says now, "it was a one-night stand." She never knew Mark's last name, but their encounter led to the birth of her son. A few months later, the baby got sick, and his mother—who asked not to be identified because she's afraid of what her neighbors might think— quit work to stay home with him. Then she went on welfare. (Appendix A, 92)

Christiansburg—one town over from Blacksburg on the way to Charleston, West Virginia, to the northwest, or Roanoke, Virginia, to the east—was one of the first areas to feel the complexity of paternal identification policies under Virginia's new welfare reform programs. The woman with a pretty smile and a shy demeanor worried about a future on welfare in a small rural town—far from any inner city—because of the threat of "noncompliance" with paternal identification policies and the subsequent ramifications for her child.

The 1996 PRWA had no mandated exception to the termination of benefits based on incapacity to name the father for child support enforcement. Congress left the decision to create exemptions in cases of rape or other extenuating circumstances up to the states. The Christiansburg mother may not perhaps present a sympathetic figure, given her admitted "one-night stand," but similar cases abound. One woman in such circumstances is Mary Wilson, an Alexandria, Virginia, grandmother:

> PHOTO [caption]: Mary F. Wilson, of Alexandria, receives assistance to care for six grandchildren, including Patrick, 11, far left, Chris, 3, and Rol, 4. She is unable to name the children's fathers. (Ibid.)

Forty-eight-year-old Wilson faces the threat of benefit reduction because she is able to name only *some* of the fathers of her six grandchildren under her care. She remains resolved to address the situation by any means necessary:

> There is Mary F. Wilson, a 48-year-old Alexandria woman raising her six grandchildren, who was told last fall that the family would lose some of the $518 it received each month if she could not identify the father of 11-year-old Patrick. Wilson's reply: Six men had fathered her daughter's children, and her daughter was now in a mental hospital and incapable of cooperating.
>
> "I will make it. I will do it any way to make ends meet," Wilson said. "But you know, the kids shouldn't have to suffer. . . . It wasn't they that willed to be born here." (Ibid.)

Former welfare mother and congresswoman Lynn Woolsey worked diligently to improve child support laws tied to welfare reform, a necessary component of poverty alleviation. Yet as most experts note, the fathers required to pay child support are often poor or unemployed themselves, thus pursuit of child support, although commendable, does not serve to completely eradicate poverty from the lives of many welfare mothers.

> Had that plan [the PRWA] been the law when Woolsey found herself the sole support of her children, ages 1, 3 and 5, she might not have made it. Even with a couple of years of college, good health and a job as office manager at a small electronics firm, it took her three years to get off welfare. (Appendix A, 134)

Woolsey is not the average or typical welfare mother in terms of her skill or education level, though the article correctly cites her as typical in terms of race and marital status ("husband gone"). The article argues that as a former welfare recipient, she has a special insight into welfare reform. Yet regardless of Woolsey's typicality, her statement reads no differently based on her welfare experience:

> "When some people sit at home getting a check while other people have to work two or three jobs to make ends meet, of course working people are furious," she says. "But I have faith in the American public that they will invest in welfare if it puts people back to work." (Ibid.)

Yet the facts about welfare recipients reveal that the "feminization of poverty" for women considered part of the "persistently poor" is explained primarily by low wages paid to them, not the lack of a husband (Jennings 1994, 20; see also Martin and Giannaros 1990). Woolsey used her personal middle-class-based experience as a lens to analyze the lives of most welfare recipients, who lack her level of education or her previous economic status. Woolsey's education—two years of college—empowered her to land a job paying a living wage as an office manager. However, postsecondary education was not the primary arena in which she sought to have effective influence in the welfare reform bill.

The representative elected to throw her efforts behind adequate child support rather than pushing for educational allowances that would encourage economic independence by facilitating welfare recipients' ability to earn living wages for themselves. As I note in chapter 4, Woolsey, despite her unique status as the only former welfare mother in Congress, joined other women representatives in the fight for adequate child support, binding women to another source of financial support instead of encouraging education as a path to improved job opportunities for women on welfare.

Welfare recipients such as Sheryl Brisco consistently demonstrated an interest in pursuing an education. She challenged the welfare system's right to ruin her life by terminating benefits for lack of work:

> "I don't think the welfare department should have the right to tell me when I have to drop out of school!" Brisco shouted in anger, then in tears. "I'm doing what I'm supposed to do. And on top of that, now you

all are telling me there's a possibility I won't be able to receive that check long enough for me to get my education?" (Appendix A, 117)

Brisco's dreams were also on hold in the era of welfare reform. At the age of twenty-two, she was studying office systems technology at Reynolds Community College in Virginia and receiving public assistance for two pre-school-aged children. Sheryl Brisco is not alone. Consider these similar experiences of four women from around the United States who pursued education despite the penalties they suffered for doing so:

First they gave me a hard time about my major. They saw that I was doing secretarial work for my father and told me they wanted me to get further training in that line of work because it was something I already had experience at. I told them that I was interested in child development and working with the deaf. But they told me I should forget those things, threatening that if I didn't change my major they would take away my childcare subsidy. . . . By the end of my second year of classes, I had an offer to work at a Montessori school. All I needed to get the job was my AA degree. That was when the welfare department decided to pull my childcare. They said they would continue to help with childcare while I was at work but not during the hours that I was at school. I was forced to drop out of school to go to work. [Salt Lake City, Utah—White female] (GROWL 2002, 6)

When I first spoke with my caseworker about going to school, she said she didn't think that I could enroll in school and remain on welfare. It was clear she was not willing to help me. I enrolled in college without even asking. In one year, I graduated with my A.A. degree in business administration. I wanted to continue towards a B.A. degree. That's where the problems started. My caseworker told me that I could not transfer. I informed her that I had two other friends who had transferred and were doing just fine. She said that she couldn't imagine it working out for me. . . . She told me I could make good enough money with an A.A., and that if I pursued the idea of transferring, my benefits would be stopped. When fall came and school began, I began submitting my school hours as part of my work hours. My benefits were cut off for four months. I filed an appeal and they had to back pay me for everything. But the hassles have continued. [Oakland, Calif.—Black female] (GROWL 2002, 7)

When my youngest child was five months old, I enrolled in a GED program, but my caseworker made me quit. She said I would need a babysitter, and welfare wouldn't pay for that, so I'd have to wait until all my kids had started school. . . . In 1999 I tried again with a computer program that had a contract with the Human Resources Administration. The welfare office approved it but six weeks later the office called me back and told me that I must leave the program. My caseworker said that I had to drop out and work wherever they sent me. They wanted me to work cleaning a park. I said no and walked out. After a month they cut off my transportation money. I couldn't afford bus fare, so I began walking from Brooklyn to the middle of Manhattan. For four months I walked six hours a day just to stay in the computer training program. Everything was going really well. I was really advanced; I knew how to type 65 words per minute, I was learning everything about Microsoft Word. I had one year left until graduation. I was really excited about the opportunity to become self-sufficient. The last four months of the program was an internship where they would have sent me to work for a company, on the payroll. If the company liked my work, they would hire me permanently, with benefits. But then welfare took away my child care money. For all these months, I had been walking, and here I was almost through the program, but now my babysitter quit because I couldn't pay her, and I couldn't leave my children alone for fear of them being taken away from me. So I had to leave the program. [Brooklyn, N.Y.—Latina] (GROWL 2002, 10)

Once I got a job, I was going to school two days a week and working three days a week at Cobble Hill Nursing Home. I worked in exchange for my welfare benefits—$150 every two weeks. So I was working for 77 cents an hour. Cobble Hill liked me. The director of volunteers told me they were willing to send me to a college for training to get my CAN certificate and that they would be interested in hiring me on after that. The director was a beautiful person and saw my potential. This was the only time I can remember that I had been offered an opportunity like that. When I took the paperwork to BEGIN, they told me that I couldn't do it, that it was against regulations for me to leave their program and go to another one and that they would terminate my benefits if I tried. I cried like a baby. . . . I finally left the BEGIN school and found a better GED program elsewhere. Now I go to school and do an internship to fulfill my 35 hours a week work requirement. But they are now hassling me about childcare and carfare. I had no problem when I was doing their slave work in WEP. Now that I have taken the initiative and am going to another school, the hassles have begun. They stopped paying the babysitter and asked me to fill out another set of forms before they will resume payment. I have done it but have yet to see the money. . . . [Brooklyn, N.Y.—Black female] (GROWL 2002, 14)

Sheryl Brisco and the women profiled above are choosing the proven path out of poverty for every racial and ethnic group in the United States since its founding: education. This path follows for the poor as well. According to the U.S. Department of Commerce, the duration of welfare receipt drops 37 percent between recipients without a high school diploma and those with some college (Tin 1996, 3). At the time of the PRWA debate, 81.8 percent of welfare recipients did not have the education credentials to obtain jobs that would provide them with a wage and benefit package that would lift them above the U.S. Department of Health and Human Services guidelines for social welfare program (AFDC/TANF, food stamps, Medicaid, WIC) need. Yet postsecondary education was not discussed as a viable option. Only teen mothers—0.5 percent of the 1995–1996 welfare caseload (Sparks 2003, 180) were encouraged to finish high school.

Yet according to U.S. Census statistics, having a two-year associate's degree gains women more than double the average salary of a woman without a high school diploma. A bachelor's degree would nearly triple a woman's average salary. The 1996 PRWA eradicated the federal guarantee of an exemption from work requirements to pursue an education. Women like Sheryl Brisco were really forced to drop out of school. In the City University of New York system alone, welfare recipient enrollment after 1995 has declined by 82 percent (GROWL 2002, 3).

Women members of Congress chose to fight for a decidedly feminist issue, child support enforcement. This choice abandoned a more efficient poverty-reduction mechanism, postsecondary education. Seeing gender but being blind to class, the representatives failed to use an intersectional analysis and instead were susceptible to correspondence bias. The decades-old welfare situation of partially typical Lynn Woolsey does not correspond to the overwhelming majority of most contemporary welfare recipients' lives. This failure of representative thinking has linked women to another entity for financial support—men—rather than encouraging their personal economic independence through productive education and living wages. How feminist is that?

Replicating the results of the congressional content analysis, welfare recipients also get conflated with teen mothers, even among the best-intentioned advocates. The most vocal responses among welfare recipients to the politics of disgust arise from former recipients like Lynn Woolsey, Wahneema Lubiano, and Sandy Smith Madsen—women who have an education that provided a path out of poverty rather than just a wage-earning opportunity. Similarly, in an "Open Letter on Single Parenting," former welfare recipient and now law professor Vernellia Randall responds to former president George H. W. Bush and former vice president Dan Quayle's attacks on single mothers with a rhetorical argument that both resists and embraces the public identity of the "welfare queen," leading to very narrow policy options:

> I have worked hard to provide my sons with a stable family and I think that you should know more about the type of family you are insulting. Let me tell you a little about my background: I became pregnant with Tshaka (age 21) in 1970 my junior year in college. I was 22 years old, poor and had to apply for welfare. I myself had been raised in a foster home. If I quit school because of pregnancy I was looking at going to work as a maid or a nurses aide. That was the best that I, an African-American without a college degree, could hope for. In fact, I had to lie to get welfare because at the time Texas would not provide welfare payments to college students. So I lied and told them I was unemployed. I am not proud of having lied. But a welfare system which refused to encourage and reward self-sufficiency is the worst of two evils. I can remember being advised to either have an abortion, get married or quit school. I did none of these. (Randall, 1992)

We see above that her description of her background justifies some aspects of the "welfare queen" public identity while resisting others. The writer is reinforcing two parts of the public identity: *System Abuse,* in her lies to the welfare office, and *Single-Parent Family,* in her refusal to marry. However, she also resists the stereotypes of laziness, refusal to work, and dependency, through her determination to complete a college degree. The open letter continues later to reinforce the image that most welfare mothers are teenage mothers, despite the fact that her own experiences began at age twenty-two. She argues specifically for increases in funding to combat teenage pregnancy and to strengthen parenting skills and family support programs:

> Teenage pregnancy is a problem precisely because the pregnancy interrupts the girl's education and thus her opportunity to make a decent income. Welfare does not provide a decent income, neither does minimum wages [*sic*]. At best they provide only a subsistence living. In a country with such an abundance of wealth it's incredible that we give many of our youth nothing more to look forward to than a third class education and a subsistence lifestyle.
>
> If you, Mr. Bush and Mr. Quayle, want to strengthen families then you should support funding programs to prevent teenage pregnancies. You should support adequate funding for education so that every child in this country gets an education which is second to none. You should support programs that assure a job for every adult at an income which provides more than a subsistence lifestyle. You should support the funding of programs that provide for quality, inexpensive child care. You should support the revision of the tax code to allow unlimited deductions for child care through the age sixteen. . . . (Randall 1992)

Like Representative Eva Clayton (D-NC), Randall is not interested in lambasting welfare recipients. Yet she repeats the problem of Eva Clayton and Lynn Woolsey: she displays correspondence bias by conflating welfare recipients with teen mothers. As I have noted, in 1995–1996 teen mothers were 0.5 percent of the AFDC caseload—clearly *welfare recipient* should not be synonymous with *teen mother*! Moreover, like Randall, the median age of welfare recipients at the time of having the first child was 20.3 years (Tin 1996, 1). The average age of women receiving AFDC during the PRWA debate was *30 years*.

Though I focus in chapters 4 and 5 upon the irony of female members of Congress with a commitment to feminism as failures in representative thinking, male representatives are of course no less responsible for designing a policy that only re-tethers poor women to a patriarchal system. Yet in a democracy such as the United States, where descriptive representation is often the only hope for any representation of the underrepresented, the failure of representative thinking among women—be they members of Congress or former welfare mothers with a college education (or both)—is extremely disappointing.

Lack of Solidarity among Traditional Allies

African American and feminist political elites more frequently stand in solidarity with the poor. Yet as the content analyses of chapter 4 reveal, many African American members of Congress distanced themselves from adult welfare recipients and/or perpetuated the distortions of welfare recipients' identities. Interviews with Lapis, Chavi, and Neith all suggest their awareness that Black political elites do not necessarily represent the interests of the Black poor. Like Isis, they share a similar opinion of former mayor of San Francisco Willie Brown, an African American male who is also a liberal Democrat:

> *Interviewer:* What do you think Mayor Brown says or has said about women on welfare?
> *Chavi:* Um, that some, some people give their money to their men instead of taking care of their kids and they're just lazy and don't want to work and stuff like that.

Chavi clearly communicates her belief that Brown is no different from other political elites who may be less inclined to stand in solidarity due to their race.

Neith uses her personal experience with the mayor's office as an anchor for her beliefs about the former mayor's welfare attitudes:

> *Interviewer:* Yeah, do you think anything ever changes?
> *Neith:* No because I voted and different things for Mayor Willie Brown and things he was supposed to get done he never got done. The only thing he really got done was the Treasure Island thing, because where is the other part of the housing, there are only so many women who can go in that area. And they always get the good one; it is good to have good people living in those areas but the ones who really need it the most. Things are tricked too.
> *Interviewer:* How do they pick and choose, they say, you said only the good ones?
> *Neith:* I know a lot of people suffer from substance abuse yes, just like I went to Mayor Willie Brown with different things concerning my issues and he sent other people letters without sending me a letter, I had to fight for my housing.

Neith, who is not a substance abuser or one of the "good ones," asserts that the mayor plays favorites and does not respond equally to all of his constituents, even when they meet directly with him, as Neith did.

Lapis's comments speak to a broader lack of solidarity among Black political elites with welfare recipients:

> *Lapis:* Mayor Brown [*laugh*] he . . . I think he's pretty nonchalant about it too. 'Cause like I have heard him and his good friend, um, supervisor Amos Brown they, I heard them say things like we need to get all the poor people out of San Francisco and they consider people on welfare poor. So they care less about [it] really because they don't need it.
>
> *Interviewer:* So those two aren't related they just have the same last name, right?
>
> *Lapis:* I don't know. To me it seems, well, they are good friends. I know that because Supervisor Brown is my pastor too.

Lapis's comments regarding the Reverend Amos Brown (who, she correctly states, is *not* related to Mayor Willie Brown) also prove interesting. Amos Brown, pastor of Third Baptist Church in San Francisco, is also a longtime civil rights activist and until 2000 was also a member of the San Francisco Board of Supervisors. The tension between the Black church–led mainstream civil rights movement and welfare recipients that I first identify historically in chapter 2 appears to continue today, judging from Lapis's comments.

Public opinion polls further display the lack of solidarity of the mass public with welfare recipients. A 1997 poll by the Joint Center for

TABLE 5.1
Cross-Racial Consensus Regarding Welfare System Problems

Welfare System Problem	Blacks (%)	Whites (%)	Hispanics (any race) (%)
Fraud and abuse by welfare recipients	72	70	79
Encouraging poor women to have babies out of wedlock by giving cash assistance for children	70	74	70
Providing benefits so generous that recipients have no incentive to work	51	60	55

Data source: 1997 National Opinion Poll, Joint Center for Political and Economic Studies.

TABLE 5.2
Consensus Regarding Community Service Work
Requirements, Selected Populations

Q: In your view, should mothers on welfare be required to do community
service work in return for their welfare benefits?

| Population | Consensus | |
	For (%)	Against (%)
Blacks	72	26
Hispanics	73	22
Whites	80	14
Men	78	18
Women	79	15
Democrat	75	18
Independent	75	13
Republican	83	13

Data source: 1997 National Opinion Poll, Joint Center for Political and
Economic Studies.

Political and Economic Studies, a think tank that specializes in African
American issues, noted the ongoing consensus regarding both public
identity and policy responses. Despite decades of research documenting
the differences between Blacks and Whites on issues that cue race, the
politics of disgust breaks down racial solidarity among Blacks who might
be predicted to favor social welfare programs for a variety of reasons. For
example, in responses to a national survey regarding an evaluation of the
welfare system and its biggest problems, the cross-racial consensus was
undeniable (see Tables 5.1 and 5.2).

The prevalent beliefs about the behaviors of welfare recipients—which
have been disproven in this chapter, as well as by decades of scientific research—lead to a strong consensus regarding the policy solution of requiring community service work in exchange for welfare benefits across
race, gender, and party identification (see Table 5.2).

The political isolation of welfare recipients, who express many of the
same political values (Steele and Sherman 1999) and dreams for their
children as do many Americans, is clear. Little solidarity with traditional
allies exists despite welfare recipients' desire to live and work independently. Consider the response of Neith:

Interviewer: The next question I have is what do you want your chil-
    dren to do when they grow up? Do you have any particular dreams
    for them?

Neith: Um, basically I want them to get a career, go to school, go to college, and be what they want to be.

We see in this chapter the ways that welfare recipients are exactly like us *and* not like us. In other words, a diversity of experiences and complexity of lives emerge that are not reducible to unemployment and giving birth. Yet, the politics of disgust obscures the similarities and differences between welfare recipients and nonrecipients that are most relevant to their chances to escape poverty. Whether they have lofty dreams of a college education, a thriving business, or simply a living wage, welfare mothers face the conundrum of being required to work without structural supports for economic independence such as a college education or small business funding. Such supports are readily available to most American citizens; the only condition required is a modicum of financial standing, most often produced when workers are paid a living wage. Most of us assume, as Sheryl Brisco did, that if we play by the rules, we will reach the goal we have set for ourselves. The key difference is, unlike Brisco, usually we are right.

Conclusion

Confronting the politics of disgust—the perversion of democratic attention; the gross inequality of the communicative context; the failure of representative thinking; and the lack of solidarity among traditional allies—can be devastatingly intense, to use Wahneema Lubiano's summation. The discussion in this chapter focuses upon clearing away the politics of disgust in order to present the words of welfare mothers themselves as they speak for themselves about the multifaceted realities of their lives, their political awareness, and the policy solutions they pursue to end their poverty. This chapter is designed to be an intervention in a discourse that largely silences them. Although they speak in mediated voices for themselves a certain percentage of the time, they are spoken *about* much more frequently.

The primary policy solutions emerging from welfare recipients' words are the pursuit of postsecondary education and living-wage jobs, as well as dramatic increases in attention to the role of domestic violence in their lives. Since passage of the PRWA, many states have passed domestic-violence exemptions from paternal identification requirements, but the federal government has not yet mandated that all states do so. Similarly, only some states permit welfare recipients to count postsecondary education toward their work requirement.

The most recent renewal process, initiated by the administration of President George W. Bush, has focused on neither of these policy prescriptions. Instead, it has sought to promote and strengthen the incentives for marriage, an extension of using fathers as proxies for government support. The alternative path, encouraging women's economic independence, remains ignored. I discuss the Bush plan for the renewal of the PRWA in the epilogue. Yet it seems clear from even this brief recapitulation that the politics of disgust rolls on.

The personal snapshots featured in this section are admittedly and understandably sympathetic. Yet even the wealth of portraits and public opinion surveys enumerated in this chapter fail to consistently articulate any structural critiques. The mothers are characterized as fighting with a "bad" social welfare system that is portrayed as isolated from the country's other economic and political structures, particularly a changing labor market that requires low-wage service workers for growth and profit.

The ongoing evidence of the politics of disgust highlights a troubling problem for our democracy overall, not simply for the women saddled with the public identity of the "welfare queen." The emotion of disgust and its political manifestations continue to marginalize a significant percentage of an already disadvantaged population. We must consider where to draw the line, theoretically. Democratic theorists have long wrestled with the nature of participation in the polity. Feminist theorists have often argued for the inclusion of emotions in political rhetoric. In the case of the politics of disgust, can emotions really serve a liberatory, participatory purpose? Or must we, as a community, think carefully about which emotions are "democratic" and which are "antidemocratic? I take up this dilemma in chapter 6.

6

The Dual Threat

The Impact of Public Identity and the Politics of Disgust on Democratic Deliberation

The above comic strip[1] presents one of the central political moments susceptible to the influence of public identity and the politics of disgust: the clash of citizens' claims in the public sphere. Luther, the African American protagonist of Brumsic Brandon Jr.'s strip, voices a claim—that he was unable to get money from his mother—which is challenged by his White friend. The clash of claims is highlighted in the second and third panels, as each boy is brought out of a shadowed conversation onto center stage.

The competition between the boys' rationales is unmistakable, as are their racial identities. Luther and his friend are clearly drawn to represent different races, and a gender distinction also emerges: Luther quotes his mother; his friend quotes his father; each attempts to represent the words of his respective parent to the best of his ability.

Yet despite what is said by each boy (the boys are presumably friends), the most interesting aspect of the clash of claims is the filter through which each claim is heard. Despite Luther's own words and his friend's willingness to hear them, the reason that the money is not forthcoming is vastly different, based on the speaker. Luther's friend relates it to an individualist behavioral trait: the inability to live on a budget. Luther elaborates on his mother's logic and gives a structural explanation: having more income. Such disparate diagnoses of the problem could lead to vastly different policies for change.

Chapter 5 concludes the empirical portion of the 1996 welfare reform case study by pointing to the disjuncture created between the public identity of the "welfare queen" and the complex reality of many welfare recipients' lives. The politics of disgust, as the mechanism that preserves the discursive hegemony of the "welfare queen," was revealed as the political context within which the national print media (chapter 3), political elites (chapter 4), the mass public and welfare recipients (chapter 5) all found themselves deliberating about "what is to be done next" regarding social welfare policy. Here in chapter 6, I broaden the discussion beyond welfare reform as a case study to consider the impact of public identity and the politics of disgust upon democratic deliberation.

The public identity of the "welfare queen" and the politics of disgust force us to ask tough questions about our democracy. Can we Americans overcome the threats these phenomena pose to our democratic ideals? Can we operate outside the politics of disgust?

Perhaps the most alarming (though not surprising) finding of this project was the absolute silence of welfare mothers within the floor debate of HR 3734/S 1795. Their lack of representation, even among their allies, reflects just how far we have to go in attaining fully inclusive democracy.

Chapter 2 traces the extent of single, poor African American mothers' political marginalization from the time of the women's club movement to the 1980s. As I review the history, I find two long-standing inaccurate beliefs about those mothers that dated to slavery: their laziness and hyperfertility.

Despite the galvanizing events of the 2000 election and the terrorist attacks on the World Trade Center and Pentagon, most Americans remain passive consumers of politics. Their exposure to the media and to political elites (mostly through the media) serves as the primary method by which they gain information and, more importantly, cues about how to interpret that information. Chapter 3 provides emphatic support for the argument that welfare recipients are tagged with the public identity of the "welfare queen," and that image is posited as having been a catalyst for policy options discussed during the welfare reform discussion of 1996.

Chapter 4 provides the most systematic evidence of the class divide among those assigned the public identity of the "welfare queen" and Black political elites. Regardless of their stand on HR 3734 at the time, all of the African American representatives whose statements were part of the sample reflected some aspect of the politics of disgust concerning "welfare queens." Often, the focus on caring for children completely obscured the predicament of "our" children's mothers. At times, it went beyond neglect or omission to outright embrace of the public identity of the "welfare queen." In either case, the link between public identity and policy options was clear. Together, the public identity of the "welfare queen" and the politics of disgust thwarted the process of democratic deliberation concerning welfare reform in 1996.

This historical and empirical evidence strengthens my argument for intersectionality in two ways. First, it recognizes the importance of class as an increasingly large cleavage within the African American community, a circumstance that refutes the revisionist argument of Black nationalists, who assume that at some point in history an essential, uniform racial experience existed. Chapter 2 shows the importance of class from the dawn of welfare politics. Yet the persistence and growth of the cleavage, although disheartening, cannot surprise us when we use a framework attentive to race, class, and gender.

Second, the argument for intersectional approaches encourages us to go deeper within the data, beyond superficial interracial or cross-gender analyses. On the face of it, the votes of most Congressional Black Caucus members against HR 3734 indicate some amount of political support for single, poor African American mothers. However, analysis of the *Congressional Record* reveals chinks in their unity: evidence of the politics of disgust already displayed by legislators of another party, race, and gender (or at times, all of the above). Moreover, the content analysis indicates their complicity in perpetuating, however unintentionally, the public identity of the "welfare queen." All three are indicators that superficial interracial or intraracial comparisons are insufficient. Intersectional approaches provide the most comprehensive method of analyzing the data for more nuanced questions of democratic representation and deliberation.

Acknowledgment and pursuit of intersectionality as more than an annex to the study of African American or gender politics attacks some of the unspoken power that unquestioned norms such as public identity gain in public discourse. Intersectionality also emphasizes the importance of context as well as voice. In this sense, it is a tool for those who suffer inequality based on the prejudice of fellow group members in addition to out-group members. It is a way, in fact, of remedying secondary marginalization. The more we focus the spotlight on such phenomena, the greater the opportunity for contestation.

Participatory Democracy and the Process of Public Judgment

Researchers have long argued that the democratic values and practices we share as American citizens are key contributors to the preservation of our democracy (Almond and Verba 1963; McCloskey and Zaller 1984). Yet the shortcomings of liberal democracy in providing "liberty and justice for all" is well documented in the theoretical works of Benjamin Barber (1984, 1998), Michael Sandel (1992), and Rogers Smith (1993), as well as more social scientific approaches like that of Lani Guinier (1994), Michael Dawson (1994), and Katherine Tate (1994). Formal participation, such as the legal right to vote, has now been guaranteed to most segments of the population previously excluded from the public sphere. Still, scholars note that theoretical questions of voice and speech—of participation in the public discourse—are less about the fact of participatory opportunities than the quality of tangible participation.

Often the most public acts of political participation are also conditioned by the filters that we as citizens carry in our heads and use as rhetorical resources in the process of public judgment. The empirical case study demonstrates that the "welfare queen" public identity was an important factor in deliberation about the range of policy options deemed legitimate. The politics of disgust ensured that alternative policy options considered important by many welfare mothers, such as postsecondary educational opportunities, services for survivors of domestic violence, and sustainable wages, were generally ignored within the marketplace of ideas. The lack of substantive participation by those most affected by changes in AFDC policy illustrates the challenge to democracy that public identity and the politics of disgust—in tandem—pose.

To return to the democratic dilemmas I pose in chapter 1, in this chapter I want to consider the implications of the "welfare queen" and the politics of disgust for democratic theory. To no one's surprise, I argue that both factors have a deleterious effect on democracy. My argument proceeds on several levels.

First, I assert that the public identity of the "welfare queen" and the politics of disgust distort the political legitimacy of welfare recipients as citizens. Here I note the role of public identity and two aspects of the politics of disgust—the perversion of democratic attention and the failure of representative thinking—as contributing factors to the delegitimization process. The distortion of political legitimacy for welfare recipients provides a justification for denying welfare recipients any empowered participation in the process. The exclusion of welfare recipients from deliberations that have a critical impact on their lives is reinforced by the two remaining features of the politics of disgust: a grossly unequal communicative context and the lack of solidarity from traditional allies.

I then explain that the exclusion of welfare recipients contradicts the democratic standard of participation on two levels. The results of this empirical case study are troubling for democratic theorists who believe in the power of deliberative or participatory democracy, as well as for feminist theorists who argue for the appropriateness of emotion-laden political communication in the public sphere.

The participatory strain of democratic theory rests on the normative premise that citizen participation in the polity is good, choosing as its springboard Aristotle's discussion of citizen involvement in the just state. Contesting the Madisonian fear of the "tyranny of the majority," participatory democrats assert that politics is a necessary realm of public action by most, preferably all, citizens. Indeed, acting in this fashion represents a very basic expression of one's humanity (Arendt 1958, 22). Beyond its importance as an example of humans' faculties, participation in the political realm is also critical because of its purpose: the authoritative allocation of resources. In theory, citizens who participate in politics vary widely in their opinions about such allocation. Because few agree completely on just how resources should be allocated, participation by the broadest, most diverse number of citizens is crucial because none remain impartial in the process (Rosenstone and Hansen 1993, 235; see also Arendt 1968, 49). Thus, it is critical that public deliberation be an inclusive process.

For participatory democrats, public deliberation loses its meaning without all citizens' involvement in the process. In addition to the pursuit of democracy, participatory democratic theory retains republican aspirations of citizen development and enhancement of individuals' capacities (see Young, 1990; Barber 1984). Both Benjamin Barber and Hannah Arendt agree that women and men distinguish themselves as individuals through their actions in the arena where public judgment occurs (Barber 1984, xv; Arendt, 1958).

By defining public judgment as an activity conducted in common by citizens (Barber 1998, 25), democratic theory combats inequalities in participation because it recognizes that such inequalities lead to overall inequality in political outcomes (Rosenstone and Hansen 1993, 243; Verba et al. 1995). The public identity of the "welfare queen" and the politics of disgust both shape the deliberative process, something I also refer to as the process of public judgment. All stages of the public judgment process are susceptible to public identity and the politics of disgust.

Choosing or Enforcing Common Conduct?

According to participatory democrats, even the terms of democratic debate must be contestable through reasonable dialogue and discourse. It is this faculty for public communication that all citizens share. It must be supported by institutional devices to protect all citizens' fair utilization of their communicative capacity in the public sphere of politics (Fraser 1989). Yet this step in public deliberation is also the primary point of entry for the public identity of the "welfare queen."

In a participatory framework, the deliberative step of articulating political values and choosing common conduct are vulnerable to the public identity of the "welfare queen" as citizens continue to ignore the facts and realities of welfare recipients' lives and use the identity as a touchstone for political thinking. Chapters 2, 3, and 4 provide multiple layers of evidence to demonstrate that the public identity of the "welfare queen" represents a fundamental assumption underlying the entire contemporary debate concerning welfare. In essence, it has become an unchallenged term of the debate, held in a privileged position as fact (despite its falsity) by the politics of disgust.

In the domain of welfare politics, the underlying assumption called the public identity of the "welfare queen" enters into discussions of common conduct—the process by which citizens distinguish between permissible and sanctioned behavior. The moral judgments of laziness and hyperfertility, though incorrect, represent violations of both cherished political values and permissible behavior, according to most citizens.

The faulty evaluation of welfare recipients' behavior is sparked by the politics of disgust. For example, the associating of welfare recipients with animals—be they the brood mares of chapter 2 or the alligators, wolves, or mules of chapter 5—cues the emotion of disgust. Again, as welfare recipients' actions are judged worthy of sanction, they were *talked about* rather than *listened to*. Political elites and the media directed our attention to Bertha Bridges and her compatriot welfare mothers for their own purposes. This perversion of democratic attention cues the emotion of disgust primarily because humans do not wish to acknowledge that they are animals (Rozin, Haidt, et al. 1999, 332). Pointing out the animal-like qualities in our fellow citizens who happen to receive public assistance cues the disgust reaction, sharpening the boundaries between publicly identified welfare recipients and the "rest of us." The collective response of disgust has two antidemocratic outcomes: practically, it increases the political marginalization of welfare recipients. More troubling from a theoretical point of view, it also closes off the possibility of an inclusive deliberative process.

Evaluating the Legitimacy of Citizens Who Make Political Claims

The act of public judgment has a long history in democratic theory,[2] but the more recent contributions of contemporary theorists such as Fraser (1989), Collins (1990), Taylor (1994), and Cohen (1996) demonstrate the importance of identity to the political outcomes produced by supposedly democratic processes of public judgment. The central argument of this book hinges on the link between the collection of misperceptions known now as the public identity of the "welfare queen" and public discourse of welfare reform policy options considered viable in a political context of disgust.

A just democracy, according to most deliberative democracy theorists, would include practices that facilitate the maximum feasible participation of all citizens as a supplement to representative institutions (Bickford 1999, 96; see also Sparks 2003, 174). Chapters 3, 4, and 5, however, empirically demonstrate the absence of an important set of voices—those of welfare recipients—in public discourse about welfare reform in 1996. Given this disappointing evaluation of recent welfare discourse, can we say that the United States has achieved its democratic ideal of liberty and justice for all?

Those who would argue that the current democratic process of public judgment works effectively and efficiently fail to note the role of macro-level factors such as the state in facilitating conditions conducive to the development and exercise of citizens' capacities and expression of their experience (Young 1990, 37; Pateman 1970; Barber 1984; Arendt 1958) and, I would argue, social constructs like public identity in the pursuit of participatory democracy. It is a daunting conundrum. While expressing one's experience implies a public presentation of the self, the significance/interpretation given to such experience in the public arena is in "the eye of the beholder" (Arendt, 1982, 46). In chapter 6, we see a perfect example of this in Luther's conversation with his friend. Luther has the last word in the strip's final panel, but is it granted legitimacy?

When a citizen makes a political claim, the claim is judged not merely on the basis of reason but on the legitimacy invested in the citizen making the claim. As a part of the interpretive process, such legitimacy is within the control of the listener rather than the speaker. If the person making the claim is deemed an illegitimate claimant, the claim will logically suffer a similar fate. The dissemination of the public identity of the "welfare queen" delegitimizes welfare recipients' claims and often incites the politics of disgust. Elites are then free to devise a policy remedy in their own interests, or based on their own misdiagnosis of the claimants' situation. Within the legislative process, legitimacy can be awarded only through the exercise of power by those who are listening to the political claim.[3]

Chapter 5 most clearly delineates the disjuncture among the public identity of the "welfare queen," the politics of disgust, and the reality of welfare recipients' lives and policy preferences. The interviews and profiles illustrate welfare recipients' familiarity with the public identity of the "welfare queen" and the politics of disgust. In particular, Neith, Isis, and Lapis all note the lack of substantive representation among local African

American political elites, revealing the presence of one prong of the politics of disgust: lack of solidarity with traditional allies. Combined with the challenge of intervening in a grossly unequal communicative context, the politics of disgust unquestionably interfered with the potential for an inclusive process of public judgment regarding welfare reform in 1996.

Cueing the emotion of disgust at the sociocultural level "motivates the avoidance and shunning of people" deemed disgusting (Keltner and Haidt 1999, 513). The interviews and extensive quotations of current and former welfare recipients replicate the findings of Soss (1999) as well as of Steele and Sherman (1999) but add new information about welfare recipients' perceptions of their own political isolation. Exposure to the news media and its oversimplified coverage of their complex lives, as noted in chapters 3 and 5, make the entry of qualifying and contradictory information into the public discourse extraordinarily difficult and, consequently, rare.

Using the public identity of the "welfare queen" as a heuristic for all welfare recipients enables elites and citizens to deny them the political legitimacy that should be conferred simply by their status as human beings, much less citizens. As I note in chapters 1 and 3, the denial of welfare recipients' political legitimacy eases the erosion of their rights by diverting attention to more "legitimate" claimants, children. In a political context of disgust, doing what's best for the presumably legitimate claimants, children, was separated analytically from doing what is best for illegitimate claimants, adult welfare recipients. Chapters 4 and 5 provide extensive evidence of the fourth aspect of the politics of disgust: the failure of representative thinking in this vein. Women lawmakers emphasized the pursuit of child support as a policy option designed to lift families out of poverty, despite the research reviewed in chapter 5 demonstrating the greater efficacy of a college education and livable wages in achieving a *permanent* departure from the welfare rolls.

Members of Congress who thought they were taking the woman-friendly position by supporting paternal solutions such as enforced paternal identification and salary garnishment did not anticipate the hardships they created for grandmother Mary Wilson or the majority of welfare recipients fleeing domestic violence. The failure of representative thinking also granted political cover for misrepresenting policy options designed to economically empower welfare recipients.

In this sense, the public identity of the "welfare queen" and the politics of disgust preempt a democratic outcome for any process of public judgment because all claimants are not perceived as equally legitimate prior to making their claim. Any listening that follows postdelegitimization is almost hopelessly tainted. The focus upon claims of citizens in the process of deliberation involves an exercise of power among those who must listen to the claimant. This power is nearly absolute. In appealing to one's fellow citizens, a claimant can only "'woo' or 'court' the agreement of everyone else" (Arendt 1982, 72). Regardless of the listener's identity, the power to interpret the claim of another, to grant it legitimacy, is nearly omnipotent. For example, in the political arena, a rational, measured, masculine voice making a political claim is more likely to be awarded legitimacy than a voice that is feminine and filled with emotion. As citizens come to consensus about political values, practices, and frames thereof, they do so in a particular cultural context that privileges specific communication patterns and identities with a lower burden of proof for some claimants' legitimacy rather than others (Young 1998). Yet emotional cues can enter the discourse from the words of either men or women. Thus, such cues of emotion in democratic deliberation, even when delivered in a masculinist, rational voice, can have deleterious effects on our process of public judgment. Democratic theorists may wish to carefully consider not simply the delivery of the message but whether the message itself cues emotions dangerous to democracy.

It is clear from this review that public identity and the politics of disgust condition the process of public judgment through its impact on choice of common conduct, evaluations of the legitimacy of those making claims, and citizens' subsequent listening power. These artifacts of inequality curtail the democratic potential of legislative policy making by infusing the process with misperceptions, misrepresentations, and emotional miscues that reinforce the marginalization of welfare recipients. The need for expanded participation alone cannot address the intransigence of public identity because the politics of disgust keeps the identity in place.

The lack of political legitimacy granted to welfare recipients also prevents those who would normally be inclined to stand in solidarity from doing so. Despite our desire that American democracy function as an objective, unbiased, marketplace of ideas, politics by its very nature is local and specialized. Dependence upon representation in the hopes that any citizen may rise above a situation and exercise impartial judgment is contested by the evidence demonstrating the roles of public identity and the politics of disgust.

Public Identity and Democracy

The American political culture claims to support democratic processes that disregard a citizen's identity as irrelevant for political representation and participation, but citizens possessing multiple marginal identities, even when granted the power of speech, find their voices devalued or disrespected, increasing their isolation and alienation from the public sphere (Taylor 1994, 70; Young 1997, 64). The "double consciousness" comprising two simultaneous group identities once enumerated by such writers as W. E. B. Du Bois, Frantz Fanon, and Paulo Freire has given way to identities of exponential complexity. To be at once African and American, or other combinations of ethnic identities, now includes categorizations of race, gender, class, and sexual orientation (Conover 1999, 1, 26; Appiah and Gutmann 1996; Cohen 1999). The work of social movements such as the modern civil rights movement and the first and second waves of the women's movement have in many ways produced public policy that is somewhat sensitive to such discrete identities as race *or* gender (M. Williams 1998). Importantly, intersectional approaches addressing distinct problems of individuals with a specific race and gender in public policy remain a distant goal (Crenshaw 1991).

The process of democratic deliberation in a participatory democracy requires the abandonment of preconceived notions of other citizens and the accurate interpretation of individuals' varying experiences. Citizens' evaluations of their experiences with government, for example, have serious ramifications for how people see themselves as citizens and members of groups simultaneously. This further shapes individuals' perceptions of their groups' relative status in society (Tyler 1990, 164; see also Soss 1999; Steele and Sherman 1999) and their approach to participation in the public sphere.

The constructive utilization of individuals' experiences may, in fact, prove fruitful in redefining important aspects of our democracy. Yet this does not speak to the concerns of those experiencing ongoing political isolation. How do marginalized individuals express their experiences in a public sphere conditioned by a political context and public identity designed to alienate them? Individually, members must find a way to adequately express their experiences and address them at the same time. Truly a challenging task!

They must also, as Luther does, contend with opposing and—more disturbingly—discriminatory counterclaims from their fellow citizens.

This may occur not once or twice but frequently. Conditions conducive to such frequent reactions occur in public policy decision making if one is a member of what Lani Guinier (1994) terms "a permanent minority."

Individual citizens expressing their opinions in this process who are members of marginal groups face the same threat of marginalization, which potentially results in disengagement from the political system. Disengagement, a fundamentally "normal, non-pathological, adaptive response" to repeated discriminatory experiences (Crocker et al. 1998, 528), is not the only alternative. The NWRO reacted differently, by remaining engaged with the situation. The words of NWRO members (see chapter 2) revealed their efforts to reinterpret and contest the identity assigned to them by their fellow American citizens. The lack of a similarly successful response in 1996 reflects the importance of the political context, which also plays a critical role in political outcomes by influencing windows of opportunity for such interventions.

Public Identities in Political Context

The political context[4] in which legislative deliberations occur interacts critically with public identities to challenge our democracy. Throughout this book, I define the political context surrounding the 1996 welfare reform process as a politics of disgust. As I argue above, exposure to the public identity of the "welfare queen" leads to the overall devaluation of welfare recipients' claims to resources and their policy ideas regarding welfare reform.

As demonstrated in chapters 3 and 4, in this sense both public identity and the politics of disgust shape the public policy options considered in the legislative process. Chapter 5 reveals at least two alternative policy options that never received serious attention but were clearly viable, given the current facts about welfare recipients and the words of welfare mothers themselves. The roles played by public identity and the politics of disgust represent serious obstacles in terms of democratic deliberation and democratic political outcomes because they bias the process of public judgment.

The political context of disgust shapes all citizens' capacities to act in the public sphere by constraining three conditions for democratic public judgment: (1) the development and exercise of citizens' capacities, particularly to express their experiences; (2) the degree to which the expressions of such experiences are accurately perceived by others; and (3) the extent to which self-determination is facilitated while individuals interact. To the extent that a group of citizens experiences constraints in the expression or accurate representation of themselves, their interactions with other citizens will serve to silence them, regardless of their formal inclusion in the process. Scholars have historically conceptualized lack of participation as a citizen-centered pathology (e.g., alienation or lack of efficacy). Ignoring the debilitating effects of sociocultural phenomena such as public identities and a politics of disgust further compounds subgroups' silence in the deliberative process.

Ultimately, the four aspects of the politics of disgust—the perversion of democratic attention; the unequal communicative context; the failure of representative thinking; and the lack of solidarity from traditional allies—contributes to what democratic theorists have previously defined as misrecognition. Misrecognition, a distortion of a marginal group's voice(s) due to culturally embedded interaction predispositions, prevents effective communication and thus effective political participation (Taylor 1994, 25; Bickford 1996, 130). The use of public identities also leads to misrecognition not simply because of the stereotypes and moral judgments from which it is constructed but because by cueing public identities, marginalized groups are more often rendered salient in the discourse by other citizens pursuing political interests rather than by their own accord and for their own interests.

Conclusion

I have argued that democracy's ambitious project of citizen self-government is derailed by the continued marginalization of some groups from political discourse. This marginalization persists in part due to the lingering effects of public identities and a political context of disgust that affect the process of democratic deliberation regarding welfare reform in 1996. Both phenomena obstruct the path toward effective participation by marginalized group members by having created a political context that prevents them from playing a role in the public judgment process as their authentic selves. In a political context of disgust, genuine democratic deliberation falters as public identities long debunked by empirical research persist in the memories of elites and citizens. Although the challenges for marginal individuals seem daunting, thankfully marginalized individuals live in a world in which all agency is not lost.

Can we speak? Can we act? Of course agency in the public sphere is possible. In the comic strip's final panel, Luther presents a "counter counterclaim" to his friend's counterclaim. But as I've argued throughout this chapter, the legitimacy granted to Luther's claim (and to that of his friend) depends crucially on the filters through which we the audience interpret them.

If we disregard Luther's claims or deem them less legitimate than his friend's claim based on Luther's race, or his mother's gender, or their common poverty (or all three in concert), the ramifications are as dire as the absence of Luther's voice altogether. The material results of such misrecognition include oppressive experiences that subgroup members have with non-group members (particularly government officials) and, ultimately, public policy that is ineffective due to its misdiagnosis of the problem. For Sheryl Brisco, the material cost was an associate's degree in office systems technology; in its place was a minimum-wage job. For Brisco and others like her who took "a job—any job," the costs are now surfacing as the U.S. economy slouches along in a recession.

As the analysis of Luther's conversation reveals, the mere presence of a voice does not guarantee accurate interpretation. Inclusion is not the panacea many hoped it would be, largely because of the obstacles that public identities like that of the "welfare queen" and a political context of disgust present to democratic deliberation. The clash of claims presented by Luther and his friend in 1970 still confront us today, and our ability to address them democratically remains constrained by the public identity of the "welfare queen" and the politics of disgust, as the epilogue confirms.

7

Epilogue
Public Identity and the Politics of Disgust in the New Millennium

In the context of this book, public identity limits and controls welfare recipients' ability to develop the capacities cherished by "small-d" democrats who embrace the idea that political participation is both necessary for democracy and good for citizens. The results of stereotyping and judging people in a particular political context include control and limitation of a person's self-determination as well as antidemocratic political outcomes. The public identity of the "welfare queen" and the politics of disgust that emerge from this comprehensive examination of macrolevel welfare politics in 1996 reinforced the silence and invisibility of those saddled with "welfare queen" as a label. Since 1996, welfare reform has proceeded unevenly in all fifty states, with many of the stories from chapter 5 illustrating the fallout.

The PRWA came up for renewal in 2002. After a lengthy delay, the House of Representatives passed the Bush administration's renewal package in February 2003. The Senate continues to debate the bill. A comprehensive content analysis of the final political outcome must await actions of the Senate and President George W. Bush, but there are many indications that the public identity of the "welfare queen" and the politics of disgust continue to threaten democratic deliberation.

The Bush Administration Changes

President Bush's plan to "improve" the PRWA falls squarely into the 1996 framework emphasizing work requirements and managing welfare recipients' intimate relationships. First, the administration proposes to close a "loophole" that allows a limited number of welfare recipients in every state to receive work exemptions. Instead of requiring that each state force half its caseload to work thirty or more hours per week, the administration favors a 70 percent caseload requirement and that each beneficiary work forty or more hours per week. The restriction against counting educational time toward the work-hour total is retained, and hours in job training would no longer count either. This mandated increase in workers and work hours is not accompanied by additional allocations for child care or job transportation; many states are balking at what they see as an unfunded mandate (Waller 2003, A21).

The welfare caseload increased for the first time since 1994 during the last quarter of 2002. As many predicted, an economic downturn stopped the welfare reform "success" in its tracks. However, a sputtering economy did not serve as an impetus for changed thinking about welfare. Within the domain of work, the renewal proposal remains focused on ever-higher work requirements, again under the assumption that recipients must be made to work, yet there is no regard given to related expenses, such as child care or job transportation, *and* no regard given to the rising level of unemployment over the past two years.

Even so, stiffer work requirements have received far less public attention than the administration's proposed incentives for marriage and for faith-based, marriage-strengthening programs (see McClain 2003; Rogers-Dillon 2003). The current proposal would allocate $300 million in federal funds to be spent by states in partnership with faith-based and other nonprofit groups to encourage "traditional" marriage and marital roles for welfare recipients (McClain 2003). This proposal continues to ignore the role of domestic violence in the lives of women receiving public assistance. One current welfare mother, a survivor of domestic violence, had this response to the idea of "marriage incentives":

> I was married to my ex-husband for thirteen years, and we have four children together. . . . When things escalated and it became unsafe for my children too, I found the strength to leave him. . . . I can't imagine what I would have done if, at the time I left my husband, the welfare office had been full of messages praising marriage. There is so much emotional trauma involved in being abused and then leaving. . . . A welfare system that holds up marriage as the "right thing to do" just reinforces the shame you feel and, if you are dealing with abuse, it weakens your resolve to leave. People glorify marriage, but when they talk about

fatherhood and marriage initiatives, I think of real people I know. I think of the woman who is married and has had a gun held to her head, a knife held to her throat. Do we want to be a society that supports that, that encourages her to stick with it just because she is married and in a two-parent family? (GROWL 2002, 18)

As is manifest in these proposals, the public identity of the "welfare queen" and the politics of disgust loom ever large in an ongoing discussion of policy options that continue along the path of the 1996 PRWA, with no attention given to the voices documented in chapter 5 or above. In fact, a third policy proposal most clearly reflects the politics of disgust regarding the level of political isolation experienced by welfare recipients. The Bush administration proposes to codify the exclusion of welfare beneficiaries' voices purported in 1996 by dramatically expanding the waiver process first introduced by the Clinton administration.

Under the terms of this policy option, a state would negotiate its waiver for welfare-program experimentation directly with the relevant cabinet secretary, who would have the power to waive any federal regulation standing in the way of the requirement (Rogers-Dillon 2003). The politics of disgust turned against welfare recipients threatens democratic processes of legislative oversight and public hearings, directly in this instance, for the ostensible purpose of encouraging state program creativity. Realization of this attempted expansion of executive branch power is conceivable because of the target population at issue (welfare recipients) and the politics of disgust.

Eradicating the Politics of Disgust

The public identity of the "welfare queen." The politics of disgust. Are we doomed to contend with these two phenomena of the political culture forever? The goals of American democracy require us to integrate groups that are marginalized based on the inaccurate stereotypes and moral judgments *we* carry around in our heads. Public identity, when used in a political context of disgust, does the heavy lifting for us by offering facile methods of identifying the problem at hand, misattributing causes, and circumscribing the range of possible policy solutions. Knowing what we know now, when we close our eyes and picture Bertha Bridges, or

Rhonda Small, or Lapis or Neith, do we see a complicated image or do we still see the one designed for us?

Often remedies to inequality focus on one part of the problem—boiling down a complex problem to one small aspect targeted for change. Yet "just as oppression is complex, so must resistance aimed at fostering empowerment demonstrate a similar complexity" (Collins 2000, 289). Patricia Hill Collins concludes her anniversary edition of *Black Feminist Thought* by proposing four domains of power within which political struggles for equality must occur. I want to use similar logic in arguing that attention to any *one* aspect of the politics of disgust is insufficient. Moving toward a more egalitarian democracy in practice (as opposed to one on paper) has never been successful when one single avenue was taken. Thus, we must confront all four aspects of the politics of disgust simultaneously to create a space for the eradication of the "welfare queen" public identity once and for all.

Mendelberg (2001) has argued that the best approach to addressing implicit racial messages in campaign communication is to direct attention toward the racialism explicitly. Addressing the perversion of democratic attention, especially the comparison of welfare recipients to rapacious animals, may work in a similar fashion. I diverge from Mendelberg, however, by expanding the norms cued to *simultaneously* include gender equality and class equality. In 2003, a strong norm of gender equality and a somewhat latent form of class equality coexist with the norm of racial equality. Cueing animalistic images of welfare recipients presents an intersectional identity of welfare recipients who are presumed to be a specific race, gender, and class. Identifying all of the norm violations potentially taps citizens' beliefs in gender and class equality in addition to race.

In chapter 5, I note that Representative Barney Frank (D-MA) did challenge the animalistic images used by Representatives John Mica (R-FL) and Barbara Cubin (R-WI). But Frank did not have the large microphone required to combat the hegemony of such ideas about welfare recipients. His comments in a single newspaper article, flanked on either side by the comments of Mica and Cubin, could not overcome a grossly unequal communicative context found in both the news media and the political discourse. Typically, regulation of the news media is considered a completely separate policy issue from welfare reform. Yet the work of Martin Gilens (1995, 2001) and Frank Gilliam (1999) indicates that media coverage of welfare shapes public opinion. Chapter 3 clearly demonstrates the mainstream print media's exclusion of alternative constructions of welfare recipients and alternative policy options (such as, for example, encouraging postsecondary education). Despite his prominent position as a legislator, Frank was no match for a news media ownership concentrated in an ever-shrinking number of hands.

The decline of a truly independent fourth estate produces homogenous news coverage that is often dependent on government for most of its information. To confront the politics of disgust, addressing the perversion of democratic attention is also dependent in an important way upon improving equal access to the media through diversification of ownership and/or greater public access to modes of media dissemination.

Similarly, the failure of representative thinking and the lack of solidarity with traditional allies also present battles to be fought in the eradication of the politics of disgust and ultimately, the public identity of the "welfare queen." Opening media spaces for welfare recipients to publicly present themselves in a complex, non-sound-bite format can challenge the correspondence bias plaguing members of Congress prone to think along a single axis of oppression (e.g., gender *or* race) instead of intersecting axes of oppression (race × gender × class). For example, seeing class distinctions among women who are single parents will perhaps finally turn Congress's attention toward the underserved population of domestic-violence survivors[1] among the welfare population and away from father-based solutions as a panacea for the poverty of single-female-headed families.

Last but not least, the self-presentation of welfare recipients as complex human beings facing multiple yet ultimately surmountable challenges, the revelation of perversions of democratic attention, and the curing of correspondence bias will ideally lead to a return of solidarity with traditional allies and, it is hoped, new allies. Attending to norm violations of racial, gender, and class inequality may increase the number of Americans who recognize that persistent poverty in the United States goes well beyond the limitations or capabilities of any one impoverished individual or aggregate thereof. Building coalitions by emphasizing the links between seemingly separate issues like TANF and FCC ownership regulations may provide an important opportunity for multicultural, egalitarian coalition building. Black feminism brought the world an egalitarian form of standing in solidarity (see Hancock 2003), among other things. Turning this aspect of the politics of disgust on its head may be the best tribute to the aspirations of the NWRO still possible.

Psychologists argue that we must believe another person is wrong to inspire confidence in our own worldviews. Part of the enduring strength of the public identity of the "welfare queen" and the politics of disgust emerges from the idea that most Americans do not identify with welfare recipients. The remedies to the politics of disgust outlined above are designed to foster that identification in a way that retains welfare recipients' humanity and citizenship, as well as our own. Although hearing about the tribulations of welfare recipients inspires gratitude that we are not in their shoes, we do have one critical common identity: our humanity.

There have been plenty of practical policy solutions proposed by welfare recipients and their nongovernmental allies that have been dismissed out of hand when recipients were denied a seat at the table. I share Arendt's (1958) conviction that tangible political participation is somehow emblematic of our humanity. At the heart of this book is the conviction that our denial of the right to empowered political participation for all Americans regardless of their relationship with the welfare state is downright inhumane.

Appendix A
Citations for News Media Data Set
Analyzed in Chapter 3

1. Georges, Christopher, and Dana Milbank. "A Shot at Reform: Sweeping Overhaul of Welfare Would Put Onus on the States," *Wall Street Journal* [Eastern Edition], July 31, 1996: C5.

2. Scheer, Robert. "Terrorism in the Guise of Reform," *Los Angeles Times* [Home Edition], July 30, 1996: 7.

3. Balz, Dan. "Looming Choices Will Shape Candidacies," *Washington Post*, July 29, 1996: C53.

4. Melloan, George. "Global View: The Welfare State Is Being Altered, Not Scrapped," *Wall Street Journal* [Eastern Edition], July 29, 1996: C53.

5. King, Colbert I. "Trashed by the Welfare Bill," *Washington Post* [Final Edition], July 27, 1996: A23.

6. Shogren, Elizabeth. "Study Warns of Welfare Reform Impact; Policy," *Los Angeles Times* [Home Edition], July 26, 1996: 16.

7. Sawhill, Isabel. "A Million More Poor Children," *Washington Post* [Final Edition], July 26, 1996: A27.

8. Sneider, Daniel. "Who Feels Welfare Overhaul," *Christian Science Monitor*, July 25, 1996: 1.

9. Georges, Christopher. "Senate Approves Welfare-Overhaul Bill," *Wall Street Journal* [Eastern Edition], July 24, 1996: A3.

10. Hanson, Cynthia, and Suman Badrapalli. "The News in Brief," *Christian Science Monitor*, July 22, 1996: 2.

11. Herbert, Bob. "The Mouths of Babes," *New York Times* [East Coast Late Edition], July 22, 1996: C59.

12. Pear, Robert. "Senators Vote to Cut Off Benefits for Legal Aliens," *New York Times* [East Coast Late Edition], July 20, 1996: 17.

13. Havermann, Judith. "Advancing Welfare Bill Holds Compromises, Radical Changes," *Washington Post* [Final Edition], July 17, 1996: A6.

14. Hook, Janet. "GOP Pares Legislative Wish List in Run-up to Elections," *Los Angeles Times* [Record Edition], July 7, 1996: C5.

15. Besharov, Douglas. "Perspective on Government: Waivers Change the Face of Welfare," *Los Angeles Times* [Home Edition], June 20, 1996: 9.

16. Pear, Robert. "Clinton Wavers after Backing Welfare Plan," *New York Times* [East Coast Late Edition], June 15, 1996: 1.

17. Miller, Martin. "Senate Bill Would Cut Immigrants' College Aid; Education," *Los Angeles Times*, June 14, 1996: 1.

18. Finn, Peter. "In New World of Va. Welfare, Caseworkers Are Team Leaders," *Washington Post* [Final Edition], June 6, 1996: B1.

19. McGrory, Mary. "Minding the Children," *Washington Post,* June 4, 1996: A2.

20. Walker, Sam. "Wisconsin's Thompson Trumpets State Solution on Welfare A GOVERNOR'S VIEW," *Christian Science Monitor,* May 30, 1996: 4.

21. Chen, Edwin. "Dole Campaigns Against Crime in California Visit," *Los Angeles Times* [Home Edition], May 30, 1996: 1.

22. Havermann, Judith. "Governors' Welfare, Medicaid Deal Blows Up Amid Charges of Partisanship," *Washington Post* [Final Edition], May 30, 1996: A7.

23. Hsu, Spencer S. "After 11 Months, Welfare Changes Hard to Gauge," *Washington Post,* May 29, 1996: B1.

24. Offner, Paul. "Wisconsin Shuffle," *New York Times* [East Coast Late Edition], May 28, 1996: C57.

25. Scheer, Robert. "How to Nip Poverty in the Bud," *Los Angeles Times,* May 28, 1996: C58.

26. Goodman, John C. "Welfare privatization," *Wall Street Journal* [Eastern Edition], May 28, 1996: C58.

27. Jeter, Jon. "Firms Line Up in Maryland to Cash In on Welfare Shift," *Washington Post* [Final Edition], May 27, 1996: C.5.

28. Gerth, Jeff. "Republicans Critical of Clinton Welfare Move," *New York Times* [Late Edition], May 20, 1996: B7.

29. Frisby, Michael K. "Clinton's Welfare Move Boosts His Claim of Improving System without GOP Help," *Wall Street Journal* [Eastern Edition], May 6, 1996: C56.

30. Tyson, Ann Scott. "Americans Say Work Is Key to Welfare Reform," *Christian Science Monitor,* April 24, 1996: 4.

31. Lesher, Dave. "Proposed Budget Needs $1.6 Billion Trim, Wilson Says," *Los Angeles Times*, April 17, 1996: 1.

32. Pyatt, Rudolph A., Jr. "Who Will Create the Jobs That Md. Wants Welfare Recipients to Take?" *Washington Post*, April 11, 1996: D11.

33. "Bungling Privatization," *New York Times* [East Coast Late Edition], March 30, 1996: A22.

34. Devroy, Ann. "Clinton Budget Returns '96 Campaign to Capital," *Washington Post* [Final Edition], March 20, 1996: C5.

35. Devroy, Ann. "Clinton's Campaign Fights Complacency," *Washington Post* [Final Edition], March 9, 1996: C5.

36. "Frame for the Campaign," *Washington Post* [Final Edition], March 8, 1996: A20.

37. Herbert, Bob. "Red, Plaid and Nutty," *New York Times* [East Coast Late Edition], February 23, 1996: A31.

38. Preston, Jennifer. "Region's Governors Draw Own Blueprint for Welfare," *New York Times* [East Coast Late Edition], February 17, 1996: C5.

39. "Maryland's Welfare Reform," *Washington Post* [Final Edition], February 10, 1996: A22.

40. Weld, William. "The States Won't Be Cruel," *New York Times* [East Coast Late Edition], February 9, 1996: A29.

41. Havemann, Judith. "Governors' Pact May Spur Budget Deal, Speaker Says," *Washington Post*, February 9, 1996: C56.

42. Richter, Paul. "Clinton Is Urged Not to Sign On to Governors' Plan," *Los Angeles Times* [Home Edition], February 8, 1996: 1.

43. Chen, Edwin. "An Accord Born in State of Civility; Negotiations," *Los Angeles Times* [Home Edition], February 7, 1996: 10.

44. Preston, Jennifer. "Job Trainees Support Whitman on Welfare," *New York Times* [East Coast Late Edition], February 6, 1996: B6.

45. Grier, Peter. "Beneath Washington Civility, Maneuvers for New Round," *Christian Science Monitor*, February 2, 1996:1.

46. "State of the Union: Clinton's Seven Challenges," *Los Angeles Times* [Home Edition], January 24, 1996: 9.

47. McQuiston, John T. "Nassau Chief Recommends Schoolfare for Parents," *New York Times* [East Coast Late Edition], January 23, 1996: B5.

48. Bernstein, Nina. "Under Siege, Lawyers Seek New Tactics to Help Poor," *New York Times* [East Coast Late Edition], January 21, 1996: 13.

49. "Flawed but Promising Welfare Reform," *Los Angeles Times* [Home Edition], January 19, 1996: 8.

50. Dewar, Helen. "GOP Skewers Clinton for Veto of Welfare Bill," *Washington Post*, January 11, 1996: A7.

51. Havemann, Judith. "Clinton Vetoes Welfare Measure That Would Have Shifted Power to the States," *Washington Post* [Final Edition], January 10, 1996: A4.

52. "Wilson to seek Extra Funds for Schools," *Los Angeles Times* [Record Edition], January 8, 1996: A3.

53. "Abusing the Nation's Children," *New York Times* [East Coast Late Edition], January 1, 1996: A30.

54. Burstyn, Linda. "Micro Lending Gains as Way Out of Welfare," *Christian Science Monitor*, December 29, 1995: 1.

55. "Welfare Reform as Steady Work," *Washington Post* [Final Edition], December 28, 1995: A22.

56. "Hard Hearts, Soft Heads," *Washington Post* [Final Edition], December 22, 1995: C58.

57. "Conferees Reach Accord on Welfare Overhaul Bill," *Wall Street Journal* [Eastern Edition], December 21, 1995: C56.

58. Gephardt, Richard A. "Newt Can't Toss Them in the Street," *Wall Street Journal* [Eastern Edition], December 15, 1995: C55.

59. Pear, Robert. "Bill Would Sever Medicaid Benefits from Welfare Aid," *New York Times* [Current Events Edition], December 12, 1995: C5.

60. Mann, Judy. "Welfare Cuts: Making the Children Pay," *Washington Post*, December 6, 1995: C26.

61. Shillinger, Kurt. "Florida Project Shows Cost and Complexity of Welfare 'Caps,'" *Christian Science Monitor*, December 1, 1995: 1.

62. "A Hard-Liner Stirs the Welfare Debate," *Los Angeles Times* [Record Edition], November 26, 1996: M4.

63. Murray, Charles. "Welfare Hysteria," *New York Times* [Current Events Edition], November 14, 1995: A25.

64. Sun, Lena H. "As Effects of Welfare Reform Bills Emerge, So Do Critics," *Washington Post* [Final Edition], November 9, 1995: C5.

65. Kenworthy, Tom. "For the Most Part, Americans Ignore Drama of GOP Revolution," *Washington Post*, October 28, 1995: C50.

66. Terry, Gayle Pollard. "Peter Digre," *Los Angeles Times* [Record Edition], October 22, 1996: M3.

67. "Cross Purposes," *Washington Post* [Final Edition], October 17, 1995: C56.

68. Abramowitz, Michael. "Governors Diverge on U.S. Budget Cuts," *Washington Post*, October 14, 1995: C1.

69. Baker, Peter. "Welfare Reform Also Carries Rewards," *Washington Post* [Final Edition], September 29, 1995: C1.

70. "World-Wide: The House Majority Leader," *Wall Street Journal* [Eastern Edition], September 25, 1995: C5.

71. Wines, Michael. "The Social Engineers Let Welfare Go Unfixed," *New York Times* [Current Events Edition], September 24, 1995: 41.

72. Apple, R. W., Jr. "Republican Blitz Shakes Congress," *New York Times* [Current Events Edition], September 23, 1995: C5.

73. Feldmann, Linda. "Dismantling 60 Years of Aid to Poor Compromise Plan on Welfare Reform Would Halt a Federal Entitlement for the First Time," *Christian Science Monitor*, September 18, 1995: 1.

74. "Contentious Issues Remain," *Washington Post* [Final Edition], September 12, 1995: A4.

75. Broder, John M. "Wilson Aims Double-Barrel on Clinton, Dole for Welfare," *Los Angeles Times* [Home Edition], September 7, 1995: 16.

76. Rosenblatt, Robert A. "View from Washington/Squeeze on Federal Spending," *Los Angeles Times* [Home Edition], August 27, 1995: 2.

77. "Helping Welfare Mothers Get Out from Under," *Washington Post* [Final Edition], August 27, 1995: C10.

78. "Dole's Chance to Show What He's Made Of," *Los Angeles Times* [Home Edition], August 7, 1995: 4.

79. Broder, David S. "Race to the Bottom?" *Washington Post*, August 6, 1995: C9.

80. Vobejda, Barbara, and Judith Havemann. "Conservatives Criticize Dole Welfare Plan," *Washington Post*, August 4, 1995: C57.

81. "Competing Welfare Plans: Is Goodwill Too Much to Ask?" *Los Angeles Times* [Home Edition], August 3, 1995: 8.

82. Broder, David S., and Robert A. Barnes. "Governors Split on Welfare Plans," *Washington Post*, August 1, 1995: A4.

83. Shogren, Elizabeth. "Gramm, 11 Colleagues Propose More Conservative Welfare Plan," *Los Angeles Times* [Home Edition], July 21, 1995: 28.

84. Georges, Christopher. "House Republicans Want More Cuts in Aid Programs," *Wall Street Journal* [Eastern Edition], July 11, 1995: A5.

85. Taylor, Paul. "Hill's GOP Freshmen Poised for Historic Impact," *Washington Post* [Final Edition], July 10, 1995: C5.

86. "A Sign of the Times Series: 1 in 8. Who's to Blame for Teen Pregnancy," *Los Angeles Times* [Home Edition], July 9, 1995: 1.

87. Stolberg, Sheryl. "A World without Welfare?" *Los Angeles Times* [Record Edition], July 9, 1995: Mag6.

88. "Clinton Assails GOP Plan to Cut Child Care Benefits," *Los Angeles Times* [Record Edition], July 2, 1995: C58.

89. Davis, Patricia. "Two Mothers' Tales: Tough Times, Tough System," *Washington Post* [Final Edition], June 29, 1995: C55.

90. Hsu, Spencer S. "Va. Unfazed by Welfare Warnings," *Washington Post* [Final Edition], June 16, 1995: B1.

91. Scherer, Ron. "The Pataki Revolution Is Slowly Taking Hold," *Christian Science Monitor*, June 14, 1995: 4.

92. Stout, Hilary. "Senate Panel Clears Measure Giving Some Antipoverty Funds to the States," *Wall Street Journal* [Eastern Edition], May 30, 1995: C56.

93. Schneider, Howard. "D.C. Council May Vote Today for Welfare Limits, Curfew," *Washington Post* [Final Edition], June 6, 1995: B1.

94. Sack, Kevin. "A Study in Budgetary Realities," *New York Times* [Current Events Edition], June 4, 1995: 144.

95. "Albany's Painful Budget Accord," *New York Times* [Current Events Edition], May 27, 1995: C58.

96. Somoza, Mary. "Broken by the Budget?" *New York Times* [Current Events Edition], May 27, 1995: C59.

97. Shogren, Elizabeth. "Senate Republicans Unveil Welfare Reform Proposal to Congress," *Los Angeles Times* [Home Edition], May 24, 1995: 12.

98. "World-wide: The President Will Veto," *Wall Street Journal* [Eastern Edition], May 24, 1995: C5.

99. Myers, Steven Lee. "Comptroller Says Cuts May Prove Costly," *New York Times* [Current Events Edition], May 17, 1995: B7.

100. Shogren, Elizabeth. "Senate Welfare Plan Would Lessen Mandates for States," *Los Angeles Times* [Record Edition], May 16, 1995: C52.

101. Vise, David A., and Sari Horwitz. "GOP Leaders Seek to Change Face of District," *Washington Post*, May 12, 1995: C5.

102. Havemann, Judith. "Chiles Raps Florida's Cut of Welfare Pie," *Washington Post* [Final Edition], May 2, 1995: C57.

103. Duggar, Celia W. "Exodus over Welfare Cuts? Researchers Say It Isn't So," *New York Times* [Current Events Edition], May 1, 1995: C5.

104. Kuttner, Robert. "Don't Punish the Children," *Washington Post*, April 30, 1995: C7.

105. Deane, Robin Y. "Community Comment Foster Care 'Made Me Believe I Wasn't Worthy of Love,'" *Los Angeles Times* [Home Edition], April 24, 1995: 7.

106. Jehl, Douglas. "Clinton Lays Out Three Priorities for Legislation," *New York Times* [Current Events Edition], April 16, 1995: 11.

107. Vobejda, Barbara. "Clinton Says GOP Governors' Welfare Revisions Fall Short," *Washington Post* [Final Edition], April 14, 1995: C53.

108. Yellin, Jessica. "A Slip Up in the Sisterhood," *Los Angeles Times* [Record Edition], April 12, 1995: B7.

109. Shogren, Elizabeth. "Senators Drafting Milder Welfare Reforms," *Los Angeles Times* [Home Edition], April 12, 1995: 5.

110. "Washington Wire: Clinton Plans," *Wall Street Journal* [Eastern Edition], April 7, 1995: C5.

111. Kaus, Mickey. "The G.O.P.'s Welfare Squeeze," *New York Times* [Current Events Edition], April 6, 1995: A31.

112. Archer, Bill, Bill Goodling, and Pat Roberts. "Ineligible Agricultural Workers," *Washington Post*, April 3, 1995: C58.

113. Vobejda, Barbara. "Yanking the Safety Net," *Washington Post* [Final Edition], April 2, 1995: C5.

114. Mitchell, John L. "U.S. Welfare Cuts Seen as Big Burden for County," *Los Angeles Times* [Record Edition], April 2, 1995: B1.

115. Cimons, Marlene. "Virginia's Tough New Welfare Law Poses Problems in Transportation, Education," *Los Angeles Times* [Record Edition], April 1, 1995: A23.

116. Neal, Terry M. "Md. Parents Behind on Child Support Could Lose Driver's Licenses," *Washington Post* [Final Edition], March 30, 1995: B3.

117. Pear, Robert. "House Backs Bill Undoing Decades of Welfare Policy," *New York Times* [Current Events Edition], March 25, 1995: C5.

118. Shogren, Elizabeth. "House Oks Welfare Overhaul That Cuts Off Aid Guarantees," *Los Angeles Times* [Record Edition], March 25, 1995: C5.

119. "A Blow at Foster Care," *Washington Post*, March 24, 1995: A22.

120. Mann, Judy. "What Welfare Reformers Need to Know," *Washington Post* [Final Edition], March 24, 1995: E3.

121. Shogren, Elizabeth. "House Oks 3 Anti-Abortion Amendments Reform," *Los Angeles Times* [Home Edition], March 23, 1995: 4.

122. Cooper, Kenneth J. "Welfare Overhaul Survives Abortion Dispute," *Washington Post*, March 23, 1995: C52.

123. Pear, Robert. "Catholic Bishops Challenge Pieces of Welfare Bill," *New York Times* [Current Events Edition], March 19, 1995: 11.

124. "Catholics Assail GOP Welfare Reform Plan," *Los Angeles Times* [Home Edition], March 19, 1995: 18.

125. Kenworthy, Tom. "Clinton Urges GOP to Back Child Support Measures," *Washington Post*, March 19, 1995: C51.

126. "Food Stamps in Peril," *New York Times* [Current Events Edition], March 7, 1995: C58.

127. Harris, John F. "Clinton to Push Child-Support Enforcement Idea," *Washington Post* [Final Edition], March 7, 1995: A4.

128. Blank, Rebecca M. "Beyond Social Policy: Unwed Mothers Need Role Models, Not Roll Backs," *Wall Street Journal* [Eastern Edition], March 7, 1995: C58.

129. Cimons, Marlene. "Past Offers Guidance on Welfare Reform Proposals," *Los Angeles Times*, February 27, 1995: 1.

130. Shogren, Elizabeth. "GOP Drops Bid for Lifetime Aid Ban for Teen Mothers, Babies," *Los Angeles Times*, February 25, 1995: 18.

131. Morella, Connie. "Welfare Reform's Silver Bullet," *Christian Science Monitor*, February 24, 1995: 20.

132. Fiore, Faye. "A Woman Who Knows Welfare," *Los Angeles Times* [Home Edition], February 24, 1995: 3.

133. Belsie, Laurent. "Americans See GOP as on Track Midway through Campaign," *Christian Science Monitor*, February 22, 1995: 3.

134. Havemann, Judith, and Barbara Vobejda. "House Panel Approves Restructuring Welfare," *Washington Post*, February 16, 1995: C50.

135. Stout, Hilary. "GOP's Welfare-Overhaul Plan Clears a House Panel Amid Partisan Rancor," *Wall Street Journal* [Eastern Edition], February 16, 1995: A2.

136. "Replacing the Welfare State," *Wall Street Journal* [Eastern Edition], February 16, 1995: C54.

137. Vobejda, Barbara, and Judith Havemann. "Democrats' Welfare Plan Demands Immediate Work," *Washington Post*, February 11, 1995: C5.

138. Havemann, Judith, and John M. Goshko. "Facing Welfare Handoff, States Willing but Some Not Able," *Washington Post*, February 10, 1995: C54.

139. Bleakley, Fred R. "Both Parties' Welfare Plans Are Assailed—Experts Say Proposals Ignore Wide Economic Impact," *Wall Street Journal* [Eastern Edition], February 8, 1995: A2.

140. ". . . And His Retreat," *Washington Post*, February 5, 1995: C6.

141. Raspberry, William. "A Matter of Attitude," *Washington Post*, February 1, 1995: C59.

142. Dillin, John. "Welfare Reform Spurs New Plans to Create Jobs," *Christian Science Monitor*, January 31, 1995: 1.

143. Cimons, Marlene. "GOP Governors Seek More Leeway to Revamp Welfare Funding," *Los Angeles Times*, January 30, 1995: 13.

144. Havemann, Judith, and Kenneth J. Cooper. "States May Get Control of Immigrants' Benefits," *Washington Post* [Final Edition], January 24, 1995: A4.

145. MacDonald, Heather. "SSI Fosters Disabling Dependency," *Wall Street Journal* [Eastern Edition], January 20, 1995: C52.

146. McGrory, Mary. "Tea for Two Who Are Toe to Toe," *Washington Post* [Final Edition], January 15, 1995: C1.

147. Vobejda, Barbara. "Republicans Open Hearings on Welfare; Grants Likely to Come with Strings Attached," *Washington Post* [Final Edition], January 14, 1995: A4.

148. Gorman, Tom. "Riverside Welfare-to-Work Success Touted Benefits," *Los Angeles Times* [Home Edition], January 11, 1995: 3.

149. Vobejda, Barbara, and Spencer Rich. "Medicare Is Barrier to the GOP Miracle," *Washington Post*, June 24, 1995: A1.

Appendix B

Congressional Record *Documents* *Analyzed in Chapter 4*

Document Number	Document Description	Page, Congressional Record	Body of Congress	Date of Remarks[1]
1A	Roth Amendment #4932	S8378	Senate	7-19-96
2A	Conference Report HR3734	H9392	House	7-31-96
3A	Morella Remarks	E1453	House	7-31-96
4A	Chrysler Remarks	H9380	House	7-31-96
5A	Gillmor Remarks	E1454	House	7-31-96
6A	Hastert Remarks	E1451	House	7-31-96
7A	McCarthy Remarks	E1495	House	7-31-96
8A	Roberts Remarks	E1041	House	6-06-96
9A	Roth Remarks	S7171	Senate	6-27-96
10A	Bishop Remarks	E1539	House	6-27-96
11A	Roth Remarks	S3186/87	Senate	5-29-96
12A	Roth Remarks	S4637	Senate	5-02-96
13A	Debate and Floor Vote	S9387	Senate	8-01-96
14A	Torkildsen Remarks	H8109	House	7-23-96
15A	Packard Remarks	E1137	House	6-20-96
16A	Chabot Remarks	H5308	House	5-21-96
17A	Bartlett Remarks	H5385	House	5-22-96
18A	Packard Remarks	E1295/96	House	7-16-96
19A	Hefley Remarks	E1295/96	House	7-16-96
20A	Seastrand Remarks	H5310	House	5-21-96
21A	Cooley Remarks	H5574	House	5-29-96
22A	Jones Remarks	H8382	House	7-25-96
23A	Armey Remarks	H7163	House	7-10-96
24A	Weller Remarks	H8109	House	7-23-96
25A	Bass Remarks	H5386/87	House	5-22-96
26A	Ewing Remarks	H7663	House	7-17-96
27A	Stearns Remarks	H5385	House	5-22-96
28A	Ballenger Remarks	H9382	House	7-31-96
29A	Ballenger Remarks	H7537	House	7-16-96
30A	Duncan Remarks	H9381	House	7-31-96
31A	Knollenberg Remarks	H7663	House	7-17-96
32A	Durbin Remarks	H9709	House	8-01-96
33A	Bereuter Remarks	E1240	House	7-10-96
34A	Knollenberg Remarks	H8253	House	7-24-96
35A	Harkin Remarks	S6671	Senate	6-21-96
36A	Dole Remarks	S5647	Senate	5-24-96

Document Number	Document Description	Page, Congressional Record	Body of Congress	Date of Remarks
37A	Hefley Remarks	H8382	House	7-25-96
38A	Weldon Remarks	H7244/45	House	7-10-96
39A	Boehner Remarks	H7537	House	7-16-96
40A	Breaux Remarks	S4780	Senate	5-07-96
41A	Radanovich Remarks	E337	House	3-13-96
42A	Bartlett Remarks	H9381	House	7-31-96
43A	Lewis (CA) Remarks	H9708	House	8-01-96
44A	Bartlett Remarks	H5310	House	5-21-96
45A	Herger Remarks	H7269	House	7-11-96
46A	Funderburk Remarks	H5311	House	5-21-96
47A	Seastrand Remarks	H9381	House	7-31-96
48A	Gutknecht Remarks	H7266	House	7-11-96
49A	Baker (CA) Remarks	H9382	House	7-31-96
50A	Ballenger Remarks	H5572	House	5-29-96
51A	Lewis (KY) Remarks	H7164	House	7-10-96
52A	Lewis (KY) Remarks	H5653	House	5-30-96
53A	Johnson Remarks	E838	House	5-16-96
54A	Seastrand Remarks	H7664	House	7-17-96
55A	Roukema Remarks	H4441	House	5-07-96
56A	Faircloth Remarks	S5201	Senate	5-16-96
57A	Klug Remarks	H7269	House	7-11-96
58A	Dole Remarks	S4568	Senate	5-01-96
59A	Riggs Remarks	H7243	House	7-10-96
60A	Chabot Remarks	H5940	House	6-06-96
61A	Hamilton Remarks	E1236	House	7-10-96
62A	Chabot Remarks	H5651	House	5-30-96
63A	Lewis (KY) Remarks	H5653	House	5-30-96
64A	Moynihan Remarks	S11044/45	Senate	9-19-96
65A	House Floor Debate	H7745	House	7-17-96
66A	House Rule Report	H7779	House	7-17-96
67A	Eshoo Remarks	E1444	House	8-01-96
68A	Daily Digest	—	—	7-31-96
69A	House Message to Senate	S8865	Senate	7-25-96
70A	House Floor Debate II	H7784	House	7-18-96
71A	Smith (MI) Remarks	H11400	House	9-27-96
72A	House Rule Debate	H9392	House	7-31-96
73A	House Agenda Setting	H7506	House	7-12-96
74A	House Floor Debate III	H9393/94	House	7-31-96
75A	House Rule Debate II	H9388	House	7-31-96
76A	House Rule Report II	H10927	House	9-24-96
77A	House Rule Debate III	H10074	House	9-05-96
78A	House Message to Senate	H8309	House	7-24-96
79A	Clayton Remarks	H7646	House	7-16-96
80A	Floor Debate IV and Conference Committee Appointment	H8319	House	7-24-96
81A	Manzullo Remarks	E1386	House	7-26-96
82A	Clayton Remarks	H7664	House	7-17-96

Appendix C
Data Analysis Procedures

Instrumentation

The measures studied in this project are the product of an extensive literature review and a dialogue with the data that is central to qualitative research.[1] The development of a single underlying concept, *Public Identity*, was the primary goal of this project. Dimensions of this variable, along with dimensions of three other substantive variables are detailed below.

Operational definitions of three primary variables were developed through the review of the literature. One variable emerged from the qualitative and quantitative analysis of the data from the *Congressional Record*. Variables of both information origins were tested for confirmation of the theory put forth throughout the book. I provide the definitions of **Public Identity, Policy Options, Political Values,** and *Key Buzz Words* below.

Public Identity

Public Identity refers to welfare recipients/mothers as a group with specific characteristics, behaviors, and morality. As the central variable of this project, it was defined as a variable with fourteen conceptually distinct dimensions. Many of the dimensions were determined through a review of the academic literature surrounding welfare policy. One or two dimensions were split to better fit with the definition of public identity. For example, the dimension of Don't Work was split from Lazy, to better separate attributions of behaviors and moral judgments, two separate cognitive processes used in the process of public identity assignment. The dimensions of **Public Identity** are listed in Table C.1 with their definitions; additional descriptive analysis of both the news media and the *Congressional Record* data samples are presented later in this appendix.

Policy Options

Policy Options is the variable that intervenes prior to the substantive political outcome, passage of the Personal Responsibility and Work Opportunities Act of 1996 (PRWA). Analyses in chapters 3 and 4 investigate the proposition that *Policy Options* and *Public Identity* are strongly associated. *Policy Options* refers to any proposed solution to reform the welfare system, whether seriously considered or not. Half of the ten dimensions of *Policy Options* were obtained through a review of the literature before the qualitative analysis. The second five dimensions were revealed during the qualitative analysis. Each of the dimensions of *Policy Options* is hypothesized to correspond to one or more aspects of *Public Identity*. The dimensions of *Policy Options* are listed in Table C.2 with their definitions; frequencies and data analysis in the news media and the *Congressional Record* are presented in chapters 3 and 4.

American Political Values

American Political Values has the longest history in the literature among the variables considered for this project. It is defined as values or beliefs that many Americans think are vital to the success and continued prosperity of themselves and of the United States. The majority of dimensions for this variable, surprisingly, arose from the qualitative investigation rather than the literature review. Only three common political values were included in the discussion of welfare reform. Others arose within the context of the welfare reform analysis. The nine dimensions of *American Political Values* are listed in Table C.3 with their definitions; frequencies and data analysis pertaining to the news media and the *Congressional Record* are presented in chapters 3 and 4.

Key Buzz Words

This last variable is a summary variable of words and phrases that arose through the exploration of the data. Its more frequent components likewise have dimensions, including *Consensus for Welfare Reform*, *Compassion,* and *Escape from Poverty.* In this area, *Responsibility* was separated from the *American Political Value* dimension, *Parental Responsibility,* and referred to the concept of personal responsibility contained in the title and preamble of the PRWA. The five terms are listed in Table C.4, with their dimensions and definitions.

The presence of each of these variables within each document analyzed is determined by the presence of the dimensions identified in appendix tables C.1, C.2, C.3, and C.4, respectively. Notably, missing data were left as such and not coded as absent in order to avoid imputing a specific motive to the speaker (Hodson 1999, 27). For example, if a speaker does not refer to block grants in her discussion of welfare reform on the floor of Congress, her reasons for doing so can span from conscious omission, oversight, error, previous mentions not covered by the random sample, and so on. As noted above, the qualitative coding process suggested a number of amendments to the list that extended beyond the scope of this project.

The dimensions contained in Tables C.1, C.2, C.3, and C.4 were confirmed by means of an intercoder reliability test. Two individuals unfamiliar with the goals of this project were trained to code fourteen articles (10 percent of the sample) according to a written protocol focusing on the primary dimensions of each variable. The result of the intercoder comparison between the researcher and the coders is an agreement rate of 63 percent, a figure above the minimum agreement rate of 56 percent for abstract categories (Hodson 1999, 51). Although very concrete categories reach agreement rates of 90 percent and even 100 percent, the nature of the categories—particularly **Public Identity, Political Values,** and **Consensus for Welfare Reform**—contained within this analysis fall on the extremely abstract side of content analysis. Concrete categories tend to seek exact word or phrase matches rather than to interpret meanings. The coding protocol, because it is qualitative as well as quantitative, could not avoid some degree of ambiguity in this regard.

The variability by article of agreements on coding varied widely, from zero to 100 percent; to account for possible outliers, the agreement rate was calibrated by discarding the highest and lowest scores. The rate of 63 percent was virtually unchanged.

Data Analysis Procedures

Chapter 3: News Media Data Set

The data obtained for this content analysis emerged from a computerized search I conducted with the Pro-Quest reference database software of five newspapers selected for their diversity in terms of three factors: geography, ideology, and circulation. The exclusive utilization of newspapers follows in the tradition of most content analyses in the political science literature (Hodson 1999). The *Los Angeles Times* and *Christian Science Monitor* in particular were selected to provide geographical diversity beyond the two business and politics centers of New York and Washington, D.C. Ideologically, the *Christian Science Monitor* and the *Wall Street Journal* were selected to provide a counterbalance to the perceived liberal bias of major news institutions. Both papers share the level of respect accorded the *New York Times* and *Washington Post* by their respective readerships.

Moreover, both the *Christian Science Monitor* and the *Wall Street Journal* have fewer pages of news copy; traditionally one or two sections in each issue, rather than the six to nine sections of the *Los Angeles Times, New York Times,* and *Washington Post.* Thus, there is additional diversity regarding the size as well as the frequency of production among the outlets; both are ramifications of lower circulation figures for the two news outlets. The *Washington Post, New York Times,* and *Los Angeles Times* are published seven days a week; the *Wall Street Journal* and *Christian Science Monitor* are published Monday through Friday only. Table C.5 displays the five publications and their frequency distribution over the 149-article data set. A significant part of the variations in article and text unit frequencies are attributable to these factors.

Data Characteristics

As mentioned above, the sample of 149 media articles was obtained by way of random sampling using SPSS 10.0. All results presented in the remainder of this appendix are subsets of the sample. Text units, the primary measure for the NUD*IST qualitative data software, represent a sentence or group of sentences printed together in a single paragraph in the article. The article sample contains 2,966 units of text—paragraphs as they appeared in each original document. Even though the text unit is a standard measure for qualitative analysis, it is important to note that text units are not of identical size in terms of word count or sentence count, just as they are not identical in content. Variations in text unit size and number within each article were due, of course, to editorial policies, space constraints, and the writing style of the author. Therefore, the size of the unit or article length could not be controlled for the purpose of this study.[2] The only limited control available was five outlets' conformity with the *Associated Press* (AP) *Stylebook,* which may impact word usage, grammar, and syntax in addition to sentence and paragraph construction. However, AP style does not systematically influence content.

Newspaper Article Demographics

The 149-article sample yielded a total of 2,966 units of text, more than enough to consider it representative of the population of 1,477 articles from which it was drawn, statistically speaking. Yet, although the sample was large enough to detect moderate quantitative effects of public identity, the nominal level of measurement prevents such analyses. Accordingly, the frequencies presented and the comparisons among them constitute the quantitative analysis of the data. This information is discussed in chapter 3.

Three types of documents emerged from the original coding of the articles, as noted in Table C.5. Each of the 149 articles fit into one of three categories: news reporting, editorial, or column. *News Reporting,* the largest category (101 documents, 2,344 text units), consists of articles written with the purpose of objective presentation of facts and events. They represented 68 percent of the documents and 79 percent of the text units in the sample. *Editorials,* unsigned articles expressing the opinion of the editorial board of a particular newspaper, were commonly shorter articles written to persuade the reader to share a specific opinion. In this sample, 30 articles comprising 339 text units were classified as editorials. This represented 20.3 percent of the articles and 11.4 percent of the text units in the data set. Last, *Columns* are signed articles written by regular or guest authors who are empowered to select a specific aspect of an issue and to present a specific perspective. This smallest category of media articles, 17 documents and 283 text units, included both regular newspaper columns in any section of the newspaper about welfare reform as well as op-ed pieces written on a one-time basis by public figures or academicians; 11.5 percent of the articles and 9.5 percent of the text units were attributable to newspaper columnists.

In congruence with feminist theory's argument that each person writes from his or her sociopolitically constructed standpoint, I also sorted the documents along the most readily available category: gender. Using the names of the authors, I divided the articles into those written by women, those written by men, and those written by male-female teams. In all, 115 of the 149 articles were so organized; the remaining 33 were placed in an "undetermined" category. The category is relatively large because of the number of editorials in the sample that lack bylines. After I accounted for the thirty unsigned articles, only four were assigned to this category due to a byline that was not readily assimilable into existing gender categories. In particular, first names replaced by initials and some international names were difficult to categorize.

Journalistic coverage of welfare politics reflects some degree of gender parity: 60 articles by male writers or male-male writing teams constituted 40.5 percent of the articles and 42 percent (1,250) of the text units. Female writers or female-female writing teams were responsible for 47 articles: 31.7 percent of the data set and 36.2 percent (1,074) of the text units. Mixed writing teams, one male and one female, produced 8 documents yielding 207 text units, 5.4 percent and 7 percent, respectively. Given this parity, possible bias effects stemming from author gender were assumed to be randomized. The presence of women writers on this topic exceeds their representation in most newsrooms; using a logic based on descriptive representation, patriarchal bias is not expected to skew the data relative to writer identity.

Demographics of Political Elites

Two ways of systematically approaching the data arose from the qualitative analysis of the articles. First, it is important to recognize that the media discourse and political discourse are not mutually exclusive. In covering news events involving the national government, elected officials are considered a primary source and are often consulted, quoted, and discussed as part of the news reporting and editorializing processes. Thus, looking at political elites' role in the media discourse became another way of interacting with the data. While many political elites were featured in the articles—including President Bill Clinton, governors of numerous states, social services officials, mayors and members of the Clinton Administration, I focused on Congress for the purpose of comparing results to the findings presented in chapter four. To do so, I counted the involvement of Congress along four dimensions: party affiliation, race, gender, and congressional body. Table C.6 presents the frequencies along each dimension among the newspaper articles data set.

The counts presented in Table C.6 reflect a particular role for the political elite. Each of the 171 text units coded with this category had to meet the following criterion: the member of Congress must be quoted or used as a resource in the text unit for further information. In other words, the member is characterized as an expert, a person whose opinion and perspective is afforded a privileged position. The mere mention of a member's name was not sufficient to be categorized in this area; thus the numbers are lower than we might expect for news coverage of welfare reform, a national issue in 1995 and 1996.

Political elites of the political parties and congressional bodies were included in the media discourse in generally equal numbers of articles and text units. Democrats and Republicans, as would be expected, monopolized the discussion as they monopolize the government but ended in a virtual tie when set against each other. Of the 44 documents containing this code, 21 feature Democratic and 23 feature Republican members of Congress. The column inches tilted more in favor of the Republicans, but it is possible that this finding is at least partly due to Republican control of Congress (and thus of the political agenda and news information).

Several congresspersons were invested with expert status and repeatedly quoted or cited. Representative E. Clay Shaw (R-FL), chairman of the subcommittee that drafted the welfare reform legislation in the House, was quoted frequently and at length by many members of the press—logically enough. Generally, his comments centered on the progress being made through the legislative process, such as the following:

> "We're pretty much unified in the direction we're going," said Rep. E. Clay Shaw Jr. (R-Fla.), the chairman of the subcommittee that drafted the welfare reform. "I don't anticipate any significant departures from a unified approach." (Appendix A, 132)

While not making an overtly polemical statement, Shaw displayed confidence in the process and in the political outcome. This unit, which concludes the article, provides a reassuring settlement to the partisan bickering covered earlier in the article between Shaw and the ranking minority member on the subcommittee, Harold Ford (D-TN). Ford, though quoted earlier in the article, did not provide a rejoinder in the article to Shaw's assertion concerning consensus on welfare reform legislation.

Similarly, even numbers of articles and text units were attributed to members of the House and Senate: 19 articles featured representatives; 20 featured senators (see Table C.6). Again, the importance of a current position of leadership assisted in the elevation of a member to expert status.

Both Bob Dole (R-KS) and later Trent Lott (R-MS) were cited frequently in light of their position of Senate majority leader.

As several studies of Congress have demonstrated (Mayhew 1974; Fenno 1978), a long-standing interest and prior leadership in debates about an issue can similarly help in attaining a bully pulpit. Consider this quotation from Senator Daniel P. Moynihan (D-NY), the author of *The Moynihan Report* (1965) discussed in chapter 4 and the author of welfare reform legislation passed in 1988:

> This bill would have begun the dismantling of the Social Security Act of 1935, which requires the federal government to match state payments for AFDC, Moynihan said. "We have avoided that but on other hand, the administration appears to be ready to let it happen as part of the bargaining over the budget. This would be devastating." (Appendix A, 52)

Although Moynihan was no longer in the Senate majority and held no critical position in the shaping of welfare legislation capable of supplanting the Republican majority, his nearly forty years of experience in welfare politics similarly granted him the opportunity to be heard repeatedly by Americans on the topic of welfare reform in 1996.

Both types of power analyzed so far are consistent with previous scholars' findings about the operations of Congress. The importance of the committee system as an incubator of political power and the role of expertise developed through extended service on congressional committees both have long been cited as sites of power for members. To these analyses I add the power of the media as a further mechanism for consolidating and wielding political power, especially the power to persuade the American public. Contrary to charges of liberal bias, my findings here note that parity among parties and the houses of Congress exists in terms of coverage by members of the news media.

Gender parity is not so clearly reflected in the media's dance with Congress. From a numbers perspective, women do not serve in Congress at levels anywhere approaching their prevalence in the population. However, one example of power investment is qualitatively different from that of either Representative Shaw or Senator Moynihan. In fact, it implicitly and perhaps unconsciously follows the feminist tradition of privileging lived experience. Note this excerpt from a profile of Representative Lynn Woolsey (D-CA):

As welfare reform becomes the defining issue of this Congress, only Lynn Woolsey has bought groceries with food stamps or paid a doctor with a Medi-Cal card. When angry Republicans rant against that face-less sector of humanity that won't get off the dole, Woolsey can say, "That was me."

Twenty-seven years ago Woolsey was a Bay-area June Cleaver, wife of a stockbroker, mother of three, keeper of the comfortable suburban house. "Good Housekeeping was my Bible," she says now. "I graduated high school in 1955; I was a sorority girl in a cashmere sweater. I did not grow up planning to be on welfare." (Appendix A, 134)

The foregoing two text units are preceded by a physical description of Woolsey before we are informed that she is a former welfare mother: "At 58, Lynn Woolsey is well-spoken and steady in her navy blue suit and graying pageboy. A second-term Democratic congresswoman from Petaluma, she has a weakness for caffe latte, a pair of slippers in her stately office. . . ." Woolsey is thus invested simultaneously with the power of public office as well as the lived experience that is discussed in the remainder of the article, which goes on to specially qualify Woolsey for policy advocacy and information in the domain of welfare politics based on her experience with welfare nearly three decades ago. Here we see a different type of authority granted to a member of Congress.

In the domain of race, parity is again nonexistent. As with gender, the disparity is due in large part to the skewed pattern of political represen-tation in Congress. There simply aren't enough congresspersons of color to approach their racial groups' prevalence in the general population. Un-like the above axis of gender, however, there is no alternative investment of power. Members of racial minorities are quoted far less frequently than their majority counterparts.

Caucasian members of Congress were four times as likely as African American members to be part of a news article and fourteen times as likely as Latino/a officials. Significantly, the Latino/a congressional dele-gation has greater diversity in terms of political party affiliation than the African American delegation. Thus, their lack of appearances in the news media cannot be explained completely by their membership in the mi-nority party.

Chapter 4: *Congressional Record* Data Set

The data obtained for this content analysis was obtained from a computerized search conducted at two government documents archives: the *Thomas* Web site of the Library of Congress and the General Printing Office's *GPO Access*.[3] To briefly summarize, I conducted two searches for documents from the *Congressional Record* relative to welfare reform. Each search produced well over 200 documents, which were winnowed down to 81 based on several criteria.

Two previous attempts at welfare reform were vetoed by President Clinton earlier in the 104th Congress. HR 3734/S 1795 became a last-ditch effort by both parties to gain an edge in a presidential election year. Suddenly, the consensus for welfare reform was met with a political context in which the bill would be passed and signed into law. I specifically narrowed each search to the months when the 104th Congress was debating the actual bill that became law, HR 3734 by design. As I noted earlier, the impact of issue frames and other products of political culture is strongest under conditions of consensus. There was some degree of debate about the strategy to be used to enact welfare reform, but little if any debate occurred around the question of whether to pursue welfare reform.

Documents from both houses of Congress were reviewed for inclusion in the sample, based on identical criteria. First, as with the media articles used in chapter 3, all duplicate citations were deleted, cutting the search results approximately in half. *Thomas* and *GPO Access* contain many documents that overlap, although *GPO Access* provided a broader range of documents on-line—more comprehensive transcription of the *Congressional Record* from 1996 in particular. Second, all remaining documents were reviewed for the context in which the words "welfare reform" or HR 3734/S 1795[4] appeared. Documents merely containing the words "welfare reform" or bill numbers, such as the Daily Digest listings of hearing dates, times, and locations, were excluded. Other documents found to be irrelevant to this research, such as a House rules report summarizing rules passed to date during the second session, were similarly excluded. The purpose of this analysis was not to count how many times the words "welfare reform" or the designations HR 3734 and S 1795 were uttered in Congress but to analyze the substance of the deliberative process. Using these criteria, the searches produced 81 documents for the study.

The 81 documents included substantive floor debate, specifically related rules and parliamentary procedures, and messages between the houses. Again, text unit and document were the measures used within the NUD*IST qualitative software program to analyze data. In all, 10,191 text units[5] were contained in this sample; however, a much smaller subsample was coded at various substantive nodes. For example, the text unit stating, "I yield to the gentlewoman from North Carolina two minutes" was not coded at any substantive node such as **Public Identity, Policy Options, Political Values,** or **Consensus for Welfare Reform.** The estimate of the sample size regarding codes substantively relevant to the qualitative and quantitative exploration of the data was 7,626 text units.

The analysis in this chapter explored the data using the same variables as those discussed at length earlier. To replace the descriptions of the data set based on publications (e.g., publication title, article type, author's gender), a set of codes was used to organize the documents based on the house of Congress and across specific demographic groups within Congress similar to those described in detail above. One additional node was added to the monitoring of the congressional floor debate that arose from interaction with the data. *Independent Documents within the Congressional Record* is designed to measure the relative influence of outside organizations and institutions on the substantive debate that ensues in Congress. This node focused on the contributions of agents within the political culture such as the news media, interest groups, and individual citizens to the recorded debate about welfare reform.

Data Characteristics

The smaller number of documents included in this data set naturally led me to expect a smaller number of documents and text units to appear for each variable. In a manner comparable to that of chapter 3, I focused my attention on summarizing the relevant quantitative aspects of this data set. I pursued tests of the hypotheses and qualitative analyses in chapter 4.

Demographics of Political Elites

Unlike the data contained in the media sample, there is a wide discrepancy between the number of documents and text units available for each house of Congress. Democratic deliberation theoretically involves even and equal exchange, but the rough-and-tumble arena of contemporary politics presents few data to support such exchange. The new Republican majority in 1996 mimicked the behavior of the Democratic majority of earlier generations: it dominated floor debate. Table C.7 displays demographic information regarding the identities of the speakers.

Notable differences from the data set of chapter 3 include the disparity in party affiliation and house of Congress. As I alluded to above, the Democrats were heavily outnumbered in terms of both documents and text units. Documents about welfare reform were four times as likely to be produced by Republicans than Democrats. In particular, speeches of one page or two by Republican members that appeared as single, self-contained documents in the searches rather than as part of a larger floor debate contributed to this result. This domination of the documents category produced 43 percent more Republican text units than Democratic ones. This imbalance confirms the expected Republican control of the deliberation about welfare reform in a Republican-controlled Congress.

Less expected was the overwhelming disparity between the House and Senate. Table C.7 shows that the bulk of the political discourse surrounding welfare reform at this time emanated from the House. The lower body produced approximately 85 percent of the documents and text units in this sample. There are two possible structural explanations for this finding. First, the House simply has more people to speak—335 more—on any topic. Thus, based strictly on membership, the House could be expected to produce four to five times more documentation in the *Congressional Record*. But this explanation accounts for a split of 80 percent to 20 percent at most. What about the other 5 percent?

The second structural explanation derives from the Constitution: all appropriations bills originate in the House of Representatives. HR 3734 fundamentally concerned the appropriation of federal monies for public welfare programs, which potentially accounts for the skewed origins of documents and text units as well. Because of these structural factors, I do not discount this data sample as unrepresentative of congressional deliberation relating to welfare reform.

As would be expected, the data reflect the composition of 104th Congress in 1995 and 1996: heavily Republican, male, and White. In regard to gender and race, the documents and text units attributed to various members include quantitative comparisons that are less surprising than their qualitative counterparts. Males have more than a five-to-one majority over female comments in the sample in terms of both documents and text units. Similarly, Whites are nine times as likely to comment on welfare reform than are African Americans; Latino/a and Asian American opinions barely register on the scale.

TABLE C.1
Dimensions of Public Identity Variable

Drain National Resources: Welfare programs for mothers and children take up too much of the national budget.

Overly Fertile: Welfare mothers have too many children, whom they cannot often afford, often doing so to receive more benefits.

Don't Work: Welfare mothers are unemployed; their sole source of income is the check they receive each month; they don't work and are not looking for work.

Lazy: Welfare recipients do not work because they do not want to (moral judgment).

Cross-Generation Dependency: Welfare recipients are producing children who will grow up to be welfare recipients and re-create all of the same social problems we face today.

Single-Parent Family: Welfare families are single-female households, which prevents their economic self-sufficiency.

Drug Users: Many or most welfare recipients have current problems or a history of problems with substance abuse.

Crime: Welfare recipients live in high-crime neighborhoods and/or contribute to the crime rate.

Teen Mothers: Most welfare recipients are teenagers or teen mothers.

Duration of Welfare: Most welfare recipients receive assistance for a number of years or months that is too long (judgment).

Culture of Poverty: A buzz term that coincides with "culture of dependency" and "welfare as a way of life." It argues that the behavior of people receiving welfare creates a self-fulfilling prophecy that will never get them to a level of self-sufficiency; such behaviors are learned by socialization into a welfare family or neighborhood.

Illegitimacy: Includes the argument that welfare mothers should get married or otherwise reduce "out of wedlock" births (moral judgment). Welfare encourages illegitimacy through additional funds for additional children.

System Abusers: Most welfare recipients are getting something they do not deserve because they are cheating the system (either the welfare system—implying fraud or crime; or the national value system).

Inner-City Resident: Most or all welfare recipients live in the inner cities of the United States.

TABLE C.2
Dimensions of Policy Options Variable

Block Grants: States would receive grants from the national government to spend as they see fit on social welfare programs, with few restrictions.

Time Limits: Welfare eligibility would last for no longer than a set number of years in a person's lifetime, e.g., two or five years; once the time span is exhausted, no more federal guaranteed assistance will be given.

Workfare: Welfare recipients should work or be in job training in order to receive any cash benefits, regardless of the length of time they have received public assistance.

Teen Mother Policies: Funding of programs to encourage abstinence or otherwise prevent teens from becoming pregnant as a solution to welfare problems.

Family Caps: Capping welfare benefits after a woman has a certain number of children; when the number is exceeded, no additional benefits are given regardless of circumstances.

Paternal Solutions: Proposals that advocate the involvement of fathers, including child-support enforcement, encouragement of marriage, and so on.

Immigrant Benefits: Discussions or debates concerning whether legal immigrants should remain eligible for social welfare program assistance.

Medicaid Denial: Discussions about any kind of stricter restrictions to be placed on those who qualify for Medicaid.

State Programs: Discussions or mentions of state programs, as opposed to national-level welfare programs and changes.

Food Stamp Reform: Discussions or mentions of changing the Food Stamp Program, especially in order to end food stamp fraud.

TABLE C.3
Dimensions of Political Values Variable

Industry: Hard work builds character. Also known as the Puritan work ethic.

Economic Individualism: Every American can and should succeed on his or her own. Also known as the Bootstrap Theory or Self-Sufficiency/Self-Reliance.

Heterosexual Marriage: The best way for this country to flourish is to return to the sanctity of marriage between one man and one woman.

Christianity: Traditional evangelical Christian values are the appropriate guide for the government. Also refers to the Judeo-Christian foundation of the United States.

Parental Responsibility: Parents must be responsible for their children, and parents who refuse to be responsible should be forced to be so.

Good Mothers: Good mothers have certain qualities, including a willingness to sacrifice for their children, that bad mothers lack.

Small Government: Small government is better/more efficient than big government.

Care for Children: The United States and its citizens are concerned about, love, and care about kids.

Welfare System Accountability: The welfare system is turning recipients into the irresponsible and parasitic people they are.

TABLE C.4
Key Buzz Words and Dimensions

Consensus for Welfare Reform: Everyone agrees that there must be welfare reform.
    Among American Public: It's what the public wants.
    Among Taxpayers: It's what taxpayers want and deserve as people who pay taxes.
    Bipartisan Support: Members of both parties are in favor of welfare reform.
    Among Executive and Congress: Members of both branches are in favor of welfare reform.

Compassion: Reform that is compassionate should make change on behalf of a specific group.
    Compassion for the Poor: As a unitary group; no race, gender, or welfare references.
    Compassion for the Children: General statements and specific policy statements.
    Compassion for the Mothers: Specifically for welfare mothers.
    Compassion for the Taxpayers: Those who are "footing the bill" for welfare programs.

Escape from Poverty: "The way to escape poverty is through . . ."
    "Hand Up Not a Hand Out": Encouraging welfare recipients to help themselves.
    Hope: Welfare recipients should be inspired to have hope for a specific reason.
    Hope for the Future: That things will get better for them.
    Hope for Their Children: That their children will not be like them.

Long Time Spent Discussing Welfare Reform: Americans and the government have been discussing welfare reform for years with little to no results.

Responsibility: The idea of personal responsibility for one's predicament. Different from parental responsibility for children.

TABLE C.5
*Frequency Table for Data Set of News Media
Articles, 1995–1996*

Publication	Number of Articles	Number of Text Units
Christian Science Monitor	12	273
Los Angeles Times	38	888
New York Times	27	550
Wall Street Journal	17	235
Washington Post	55	1,020
Total	149	2,966

TABLE C.6
Frequencies among Media Articles, Political Elites

	Articles	Text Units
Party Affiliation		
Democrat	21	54
Republican	23	78
Independent	0	0
Total	44	132
Congressional Body		
House	19	89
Senate	20	82
Total	39	171
Gender		
Male	28	82
Female	12	54
Total	40	136
Race		
Caucasian	29	116
African American	7	14
Latino/a	2	3
Asian American	0	0
Total	38	133

TABLE C.7
Relevant Frequencies among
Congressional Record *Documents*

	Documents	Text Units
Party Affiliation		
Democrat	15	461
Republican	63	808
Independent	0	0
Total	78	1,269
Congressional Body		
House	61	8,600
Senate	10	1,529
Total	71	10,129
Gender		
Male	62	1,308
Female	13	238
Total	75	1,546
Race		
Caucasian	69	1,148
African American	6	126
Latino/a	1	3
Asian American	0	0
Total	76	1,277

Notes

NOTES TO CHAPTER 1

1. *Political context* is used here as a commonly understood term rather than the more specialized definition intended by political scientists such as Huckfeldt and Sprague (1995) and Beck et al. (2002), which includes specific attention to state or neighborhood demographics as predictors of political participation.

2. Mountains of data have been collected over three decades to prove this public image false, but it lingers in most Americans' minds (see Gilens 1995, 1996, 2001).

3. The empirical method utilized in the study is content analysis, from both a qualitative and quantitative perspective. Further information about data analysis procedures appears in Appendix C.

4. This shift in the perceived race of many welfare recipients is largely due to structural changes such as the shift of widows to Social Security benefits and out of Aid to Dependent Children (ADC) programs. As well, the New Deal marks an important historical transition in that the creation of Social Security in 1935 was facilitated by the support of southern Democratic congressmen, who wrangled the exclusion of African American–dominated occupations (such as agricultural labor and domestic work) from Social Security eligibility in order to preserve the racial status quo in the southern states (see Giddings 1984 and Quadagno 1994, among others).

5. The psychological transition here is described in Shaver et al. 1999. The political transition is my own extrapolation of that transition.

6. Here I do not mean to suggest that elites simply create the frames and American citizens are tabulae rasa, accepting the frames completely at face value. Rather, I mean to suggest that frames are created to comply with fundamental egalitarian and inegalitarian beliefs that are part of American political culture, with public identities crystallizing in the process.

NOTES TO CHAPTER 2

1. All such quotations are in block format.

2. This is not to say that nationalism operates in universal ways among

women or even among Black women. A theoretically complex account of nationalism as an ideological discourse in all its facets is beyond the scope of this study but will be attended to as necessary within it.

3. Indeed, the highest prices for female slaves were paid for those deemed attractive enough for sale into the "fancy trade" that flourished in New Orleans and had an elaborate system of "octoroon" and "quadroon" balls, where women of mixed racial ancestry (deemed slaves because they were daughters of slave mothers) were presented for male guests' pleasure.

4. I am grateful to Michelle Hardy, M.A., UNC-Chapel Hill, for her excellent presentation on this subject, which has not yet been published.

5. Despite its demographics, the NWRO remained formally and informally committed to racial inclusion. Latinas and White women were included in the leadership via executive committee positions, and several WROs in the southwestern United States were predominantly Latina. Formal leaders urged mobilization outside the inner cities, and published their newsletter in Spanish as well as English.

6. A sense of injustice is a key affective component for building a psychological framework conducive to collective action (W. Gamson 1992, 7).

7. Leaders participating in the meeting included Johnnie Tillmon, Etta Horn, and Beulah Sanders from the NWRO, and Martin Luther King, Jr., Ralph Abernethy, and Andrew Young from SCLC.

8. In particular, debates about policy priorities revealed such cleavages. This included the debate over the top priority: economic independence (favored by the NWRO elected leaders and NWRO members) or reinforcement of intact, traditional, heterosexual families. Such controversies ultimately led to the resignation of George Wiley, the Black middle-class executive director of the NWRO and most of the White middle-class male staff. The outside funding went with them.

9. See, e.g., *Levy v. Louisiana, Marsh v. Alabama, Goldberg v. Kelly* (West 1981; Mink 1998).

10. I use this date to refer to the closing of the NWRO national offices in Washington and the cessation of nationwide organizing. Several state and local chapters continued to work for welfare rights post-1975.

11. I take up the role of the media explicitly in chapter 5.

12. See C. Murray 1986; Herrnstein and Murray 1994 for examples of such frames.

13. Taylor and Lincoln (1998) found that Million Man March attendees had higher levels of income (61 percent had incomes of $30,000 or more), education (73 percent had some education beyond high school), and voter registration (80 percent were registered to vote) than the overall Black male population.

14. See Collins 1990 and hooks 1989, for more general treatments of Black women in this vein.

15. Sanford Schram provides an excellent account of the role of policy dis-

course in perpetuating the marginalization of the poor in *Words of Welfare: The Poverty of Social Science and the Social Science of Poverty* (1995, especially chapter 1).

16. Indeed, as Giddings notes, "In fact, Moynihan was less harsh in his evaluation of the nontraditional family structure than E. Franklin Frazier had been in *The Negro Family in the United States*" (Giddings 1984, 328).

17. Until the work of William Julius Wilson, celebrated by President Bill Clinton, more structural explanations of the problem have received comparatively little attention. The next section will reveal the limits of such explanations in welfare policy discourse.

18. One of the most celebrated and castigated examples of such media portrayals was a special edition of *Bill Moyers' Journal,* which aired on PBS in 1986, chronicling the tangle of pathology rampant in the neighborhoods of Chicago's South Side (Crenshaw 1991, 71).

19. Again, I don't mean to say that no activism exists; it is simply up against a media machine and other obstacles that prevent its effectiveness in forcing policy change.

20. See Collins 1998b for a summary of the nation-as-family-of-contributors argument.

21. See Jill Nelson, *Volunteer Slavery* (1993), for a vivid example of this phenomenon.

NOTES TO CHAPTER 3

1. All excerpts are quoted verbatim, indented and single spaced.

2. Analyzing print media or electronic media is standard operating procedure in political science approaches to media study (Hodson 1999); I analyze print media only.

3. The procedures utilized to analyze this data set both quantitatively and qualitatively are discussed in Appendix C. I present first the central tendencies of the data set, using descriptive statistics such as frequencies, as well as a qualitative discussion of themes revealed through the dynamic process of data immersion. Each of the primary variables defined in Appendix C—*Public Identity, Policy Options, Political Values*, and *Consensus for Welfare Reform*—is discussed at length in this section.

4. I further use the quantitative/qualitative hybrid test of index searches to indicate the level of overlapping codes of various units of text among the articles. All numbers are reported, using the text unit as a standard unit of measurement; a text unit is amenable to both qualitative and quantitative analysis and is defined as the line of text as written in the original computer-generated document. It is important to note that when one counts text units, they do not correspond directly to column inches, the measurement a journalist might use, nor does each

have a standard number of words, the measurement an analyst might employ. The content analyses used in chapters 3 and 4 are more interpretive, in the sense that they focus on the meanings within each text unit, rather than a count of exact words—e.g. how many times the words "welfare queen" appeared in each article of every newspaper. See Appendix C for further details regarding the empirical analysis.

5. A code for working welfare mothers was also part of the analysis; it is discussed in chapter 5 because of its qualitative and quantitative differences from the rest of the data.

6. A reminder: the outlier article for Drug Abuse continues to be deleted from the discussion of the analyses because of its potential to skew the results.

7. The same result occurs regarding the three units of overlap between Consensus and Immigrant Benefits with a different article, that by Lena Sun in the *Washington Post* (Appendix A, 64).

NOTES TO CHAPTER 4

1. The sampling and data analysis procedures used with regard to this data set are contained in Appendix C.

2. Now the Personal Responsibility and Work Opportunity Act, signed into law by President Clinton in August 1996.

3. Although Democrats and Republicans alike advocated welfare reform, most African American members of Congress voted against HR 3734/S 1795 even after President Clinton announced his intention to sign it into law.

4. The sample contained no excerpts attributed to Senator Carol Moseley-Braun (D-IL), the sole African American senator in 1996.

5. The figure is actually much smaller, as I document in chapter 5.

NOTES TO CHAPTER 5

1. To protect the seven interviewees' anonymity, they have been given the names of ancient Egyptian goddesses.

2. The article also mentioned traditions of pride and privacy in rural communities.

NOTES TO CHAPTER 6

1. Reprinted from Milwaukee County Welfare Rights Organization, *Welfare Mothers Speak Out* (1972).

2. Aristotle, Mill, Rousseau, Arendt, and Habermas are but a few of the theorists who have wrangled with public judgment as the quintessential form of democratic decision making.

3. Americans' attitudes about their fellow citizens' legitimacy have been empirically linked to policy opinions concerning the same fellow citizens (Sniderman et al. 1991; Feldman and Zaller 1992; Kinder and Sanders 1996; Peffley et al. 1997).

4. *Political context* is used here as a commonly understood term rather than the more specialized definition intended by political scientists such as Huckfeldt and Sprague (1995) and Beck et al. (2000), which includes specific attention to state or neighborhood demographics as predictors of political participation.

NOTE TO CHAPTER 7

1. I do not mean to imply that poor women are the sole victims of domestic violence. However, they are most likely to lack education or access to services or other elements of social capital such as support networks and families who can provide safe haven.

NOTE TO APPENDIX B

1. Documents with dates after August 1996 did not receive coding, though they were part of the original sample.

NOTES TO APPENDIX C

1. Possible additions and/or changes to the number and content of the dimensions of each variable are an important product of qualitative analysis.

2. This practice is distinct from traditional content analysis strategies of counting single word/phrase repetitions or sentences. It provides the advantage of a more comprehensive analysis that includes qualitative perspectives because each word or sentence is considered in the context of those surrounding it. This requires a more abstract form of coding that does not normally reach the levels of intercoder reliability recommended for traditional counting methods. However, it provides contextual information lacking from narrowly focused quantitative efforts.

3. These two archives are located at http://thomas.loc.gov and http://www.gpoaccess.gov.

4. Each bill in Congress is assigned a tracking number; though the numbers vary between houses; each of the above numbers represent the same bill, the PRWA of 1996.

5. Text units are lines of writing contained in the original document—they are not standardized in word length and so vary in size at random. However, the focus of this study is on substantive content instead of counts of a specific word or word combinations' appearances, the practice of many earlier media studies.

Bibliography

Abramovitz, Mimi. *Under Attack, Fighting Back: Women and Welfare in the United States.* New York: Monthly Review Press, 1996.

Almond, Gabriel, and Sidney Verba. *The Civic Culture: Political Attitudes and Culture in Five Nations.* Princeton: Princeton University Press, 1963.

Amott, Teresa. "Black Women and AFDC: Making Entitlement Out of Necessity." In *Women, the State, and Welfare,* edited by Linda Gordon, 280–298. Madison: University of Wisconsin Press, 1990.

Anderson, Myrna. "Assisting the Poor." *New York Times* (January 26, 2003): 12.

Appiah, Kwame Anthony, and Amy Gutmann. *Color Conscious: The Political Morality of Race.* Princeton: Princeton University Press, 1996.

Arendt, Hannah. *The Human Condition.* Chicago: University of Chicago Press, 1958.

———. *Between Past and Future: Eight Exercises in Political Thought.* New York: Penguin Books, 1968.

———. *The Origins of Totalitarianism.* Revised and expanded edition. New York: Harcourt Brace and Company, 1973.

———. *Lectures on Kant's Political Philosophy.* Chicago: University of Chicago Press, 1982.

Associated Press. "Study: Media Falls for Poverty Stereotype." *New Orleans Times-Picayune* (August 1997): A2.

"Bad News for Charles Murray: Uneducated White Women Give Birth to More Babies than Do Uneducated Black Women." *Journal of Blacks in Higher Education* (1998): 68–69.

Barber, Benjamin. *Strong Democracy: Participatory Politics for a New Age.* Berkeley: University of California Press, 1984.

———. *A Passion for Democracy.* Princeton: Princeton University Press, 1998.

Beck, Paul Allen, Russell J. Dalton, Steven Green, and Robert Huckfeldt. "The Social Calculus of Voting: Media, Organizational, Party and Personal Influences on Presidential Choices." *American Political Science Review* 96 (March 2002): 57–73.

Berry, Deborah Barfield. "Senate Revisits Welfare Reform." *New York Newsday* (March 13, 2003).

Bickford, Susan. *The Dissonance of Democracy: Listening, Conflict and Citizenship*. Ithaca: Cornell University Press, 1996.

———. "Reconfiguring Pluralism: Identity and Institutions in the Inegalitarian Polity." *American Journal of Political Science* 43, no. 1 (1999): 86–108.

Bobo, Lawrence, and Franklin D. Gilliam. "Race, Sociopolitical Participation and Black Empowerment." *American Political Science Review* 84 (1990): 377–393.

Bositis, David. *Joint Center for Political and Economic Studies Public Opinion Poll*. Washington, D.C.: 1997.

Brewer, Paul. "Values, Public Debate and Policy Opinions." Ph.D. diss., University of North Carolina, Chapel Hill, 1999.

Butler, Judith. *Gender Trouble*. New York: Routledge, 1990.

Campbell, Nancy Duff. *Using Women: Gender, Drug Policy, and Social Justice*. New York: Routledge, 2000.

Cohen, Cathy J. "Contested Membership: Black Gay Identities and the Politics of AIDS." In *Queer Theory/Sociology*, edited by Steven Seidman, 362–394. Cambridge: Blackwell Publishers, 1996.

———. "Punks, Bulldaggers, and Welfare Queens: The Radical Potential of Queer Politics." *GLQ* 3, no. 4 (1997): 437–465.

———. *The Boundaries of Blackness: AIDS and the Breakdown of Black Politics*. Chicago: University of Chicago Press, 1999.

Cohn, Jonathan. "Irrational Exuberance: When Did Political Science Forget about Politics?" *The New Republic* (October 1999): 25–34.

Collins, Patricia Hill. *Black Feminist Thought: Knowledge, Consciousness and the Politics of Empowerment*. New York: Routledge, 1990.

———. *Fighting Words: Black Women and the Search for Justice*. Minneapolis: University of Minnesota Press, 1998a.

———. "It's All in the Family: Intersections of Gender, Race and Nation." *Hypatia* 13 (1998b): 62–82.

———. *Black Feminist Thought: Knowledge, Consciousness and the Politics of Empowerment*. Second Edition. New York: Routledge, 2000.

Conover, Pamela Johnston. "The Role of Social Groups in Political Thinking." *British Journal of Political Science* 18 (1988): 51–76.

———. "The Politics of Recognition: Some Social Psychological Considerations." Paper presented at the Ohio State University Institute of Political Psychology, Columbus, August 1999.

———, Donald D. Searing, and Ivor M. Crewe. "The Deliberative Potential of Political Discussion." *British Journal of Political Science* 32 (January 2002): 21–62.

Cose, Ellis, et al. "The Good News about Black America." *Newsweek* 133 (1999): 28–34.

Crenshaw, Kimberle Williams. "Demarginalizing the Intersection of Race and Sex: A Black Feminist Critique of Antidiscrimination Doctrine, Feminist Theory, and Antiracist Politics." In *Feminist Legal Theory: Readings in Law and Gender*, edited by K. T. Bartlett and R. Kennedy, 57–80. San Francisco: Westview Press, 1991.

———. "Mapping the Margins: Intersectionality, Identity Politics and Violence Against Women of Color." In *Critical Race Theory: The Key Writings That Formed the Movement*, edited by K. Crenshaw et al., 357–383. New York: New Press, 1995.

Crocker, Jennifer, Brenda Major, and Claude Steele. "Social Stigma." In *The Handbook of Social Psychology*, edited by Daniel T. Gilbert, Susan Fiske, and Gardner Lindzey, 504–553. New York: McGraw-Hill, 1998.

The Damned. *Lessons from the Damned: Class Struggle in the Black Community*. Ojai, Calif.: Times Change Press, 1990.

Dandridge v. Williams, 397 U.S. 471 (1970).

Dash, Leon. *When Children Want Children: The Urban Crisis of Teenage Childbearing*. New York: William Morrow, 1989.

Davis, Angela. *Women, Race and Class*. New York: Vintage Books, 1981.

Dawson, Michael. *Behind the Mule: Race and Class in African-American Politics*. Princeton: Princeton University Press, 1994.

"Deepening Poverty." *Boston Globe* (May 13, 2003): A14.

Dodson, Debra L., Susan J. Carroll, Ruth B. Mandel, Katherine E. Kleeman, R. Schreiber, and D. Liebowitz. *Voices, Views, Votes: The Impact of Women in the 103rd Congress*. New Brunswick, N.J.: Center for the American Woman in Politics, Rutgers University, 1995.

Edsall, Thomas B., and Mary Edsall. *Chain Reaction: The Impact of Race, Rights and Taxes on American Politics*. New York: Norton, 1991.

Eiser, J. Richard. *Social Judgment*. Milton Keynes, U.K.: Open University Press, 1990.

Feldman, Stanley, and John Zaller. "The Political Culture of Ambivalence: Ideological Responses to the Welfare State." *American Journal of Political Science* 36 (1992): 268–307.

Fenno, Richard F. *Homestyle: House Members in Their Districts*. Boston: Little, Brown, 1978.

Fineman, Martha. "Images of Mothers in Poverty Discourses." *Duke University Law Journal* 2 (1991): 274–295.

Fiske, Susan T. "Stereotyping, Prejudice and Discrimination." In *The Handbook of Social Psychology*, edited by Daniel Gilbert, Susan Fiske, and Gardner Lindzey, 357–411. New York: McGraw-Hill, 1998.

Fiske, Susan T., and Susan Taylor. *Social Cognition*. New York: McGraw-Hill, 1991.

Fraser, Nancy. *Unruly Practices: Power, Discourse and Gender in Contemporary Social Theory*. Minneapolis: University of Minnesota Press, 1989.

———. "Rethinking the Public Sphere: A Contribution to the Critique of Actually Existing Democracy." In *Habermas and the Public Sphere*, edited by Craig Calhoun, 109–142. Cambridge: MIT Press, 1992.

———, and Linda Gordon. "Decoding Dependency." In *Reconstructing Political Theory: Feminist Perspectives*, edited by Mary Lyndon Shanley and Uma Narayan. Cambridge: Polity Press, 1997.

Frazier, E. Franklin. *Black Bourgeoisie*. New York: Free Press, 1965.

Frijda, Nico H., and Batja Mesquita. "The Social Roles and Functions of Emotions." In *Emotion and Culture: Empirical Studies of Mutual Influence*, edited by Shinobu Kitayama and Hazel Rose Markus. Washington, D.C.: American Psychological Association, 1994.

Funicello, Teresa. *Tyranny of Kindness: Dismantling the Welfare System to End Poverty in America*. New York: Atlantic Monthly Press, 1993.

Gaines, Kevin. *Uplifting the Race: Black Leadership, Politics, and Culture in the Twentieth Century*. Chapel Hill: University of North Carolina Press, 1996.

Gamson, Joshua. "Must Identity Movements Self-Destruct? A Queer Dilemma." In *Queer Theory/Sociology*, edited by Steven Seidman. Cambridge: Blackwell Publishers, 1996.

Gamson, William. *Talking Politics*. New York: Cambridge University Press, 1992.

———, and Kathryn Lasch. "The Political Culture of Social Welfare Policy." In *Evaluating the Welfare State: Social and Political Perspectives*, edited by Shimon E. Sapiro and Ephraim Yuchtman-Yaar. New York: Academic Press, 1993.

Giddings, Paula. *When and Where I Enter: The Impact of Black Women on Race and Sex in America*. New York: Bantam Books, 1984.

Gilens, Martin. "Racial Attitudes and Opposition to Welfare." *Journal of Politics* 57 (1995): 994–1014.

———. "Race Coding and White Opposition to Welfare." *American Political Science Review* 90 (1996): 593–604.

———. *Why Americans Hate Welfare: Race, Media and the Politics of Anti-Poverty Policies*. Chicago: University of Chicago Press, 2001.

Gilliam, Franklin D. "The Welfare Queen Experiment." *Nieman Reports* 53 (1999): 112–119.

Gordon, Linda, ed. *Women, the State and Welfare*. Madison: University of Wisconsin Press, 1990.

Greene, Joshua, and Jonathan Haidt. "How (and Where) Does Moral Judgment Work?" *Trends in Cognitive Sciences* 6, no. 12 (2002): 517–523.

GROWL—Grass Roots Organizing for Welfare Leadership. *Welfare Reform as WE Know It.* 2002. Available on-line at www.ctwo.org/growl.

Guinier, Lani. *The Tyranny of the Majority: Fundamental Fairness in Representative Democracy.* New York: Free Press, 1994.

Gutmann, Amy, ed. *Multiculturalism: Examining the Politics of Recognition.* Princeton: Princeton University Press, 1994.

Habermas, Jurgen. *The Theory of Communicative Action: Reason and the Rationalization of Society.* Boston: Beacon Press, 1984.

Haidt, Jonathan, and Jonathan Baron. "Social Roles and the Moral Judgment of Acts and Omissions." *European Journal of Social Psychology* 26 (1996): 201–218.

Haidt, Jonathan, Sylvia Koller, and M. G. Dias. "Affect, Culture, and Morality, or Is It Wrong to Eat Your Dog?" *Journal of Personality and Social Psychology* 65 (1993): 613–628.

Hancock, Ange-Marie. "Overcoming Willful Blindness: Building Egalitarian Multicultural Women's Coalitions." In *African Women and Imperialism: Sisterhood Revisited,* edited by Obioma Nnaemeka. Westport, Conn.: Greenwood Press, 2001a.

———. "Public Identity and Policy Options: 'Welfare Queens' in Democratic Deliberation." Conference Paper, American Political Science Association Annual Meetings, San Francisco, August 29–September 1, 2001b.

———. Review of *Freedom Dreams: The Black Radical Imagination,* by Robin D. G. Kelley. *Peace Review* 15 (2003): 111–116.

Herrnstein, Richard, and Charles Murray. *The Bell Curve: Intelligence and Class Structure in American Life.* New York: Free Press, 1994.

Hoberman, John. *Darwin's Athletes: How Sport Has Damaged Black America and Preserved the Myth of Race.* New York: Houghton Mifflin Books, 1997.

Hodson, Randy. *Analyzing Documentary Accounts.* Thousand Oaks, Calif.: Sage Publications, 1999.

hooks, bell. *Talking Back: Thinking Feminist, Thinking Black.* Boston: South End Press, 1989.

Huckfeldt, Robert, and John Sprague. *Citizens, Politics, and Social Communication.* New York: Cambridge University Press, 1995.

Jennings, James. "Persistent Poverty in the US: Review of Theories and Explanations." *Sage Race Relations Abstracts* 19 (1994): 5–34.

Johnson, Janet Buttolph, and Richard Joslyn. *Political Science Research Methods.* Washington, D.C.: CQ Press, 1991.

Joint Center for Political and Economic Studies. National Opinion Poll. Washington, D.C.: 1997.

Jordan, June. "A New Politics of Sexuality." In *Words of Fire: An Anthology of African-American Feminist Thought,* edited by Beverly Guy-Sheftall, 407–411. New York: New Press, 1995.

Jordan-Zachary, Julia. "Black Womanhood and Social Welfare Policy: The Influence of Her Image on Policy Making." *Sage Race Relations Abstracts* 26 (2001): 5–24.

Kelley, Robin D. G. *Race Rebels: Culture, Politics and the Black Working Class.* New York: Free Press, 1996.

Keltner, Dacher, and Jonathan Haidt. "Social Functions of Emotions at Four Levels of Analysis." *Cognition and Emotion* 13, no. 5 (1999): 505–522.

Kinder, Donald R. "Opinion and Action in the Realm of Politics." In *The Handbook of Social Psychology*, edited by Daniel Gilbert, Susan Fiske, and Gardner Lindzey, 778–867. New York: McGraw-Hill, 1998.

———, and Lynn M. Sanders. *Divided by Color: Racial Politics and Democratic Ideals.* Chicago: University of Chicago Press, 1996.

King, Deborah. "Multiple Jeopardy, Multiple Consciousness: The Context of a Black Feminist Ideology." In *Words of Fire: An Anthology of African-American Feminist Thought*, edited by Beverly Guy-Sheftall, 294–317. New York: New Press, 1995.

King, Gary, Robert Keohane, and Sidney Verba. *Designing Social Inquiry: Scientific Inference in Qualitative Research.* Princeton: Princeton University Press, 1994.

Kitayama, Shinobu, and Hazel Rose Markus, eds. *Emotion and Culture: Empirical Studies of Mutual Influence.* Washington, D.C.: American Psychological Association, 1994.

Landes, Joan. *Visualizing the Nation: Gender, Representation and Revolution in Eighteenth-Century France.* Ithaca: Cornell University Press, 2001.

Lane, Robert. C. "Patterns of Political Belief." In *The Handbook of Political Psychology*, edited by Jeanne N. Knutson, 83–116. San Francisco: Jossey-Bass Publishers, 1973.

L'Engle, Madeleine. *Walking on Water: Reflections on Faith and Art.* New York: North Point Press, 1995.

Lerner, Gerda, ed. *Black Women in White America: A Documentary History.* New York: Vintage Books, 1973.

Lewis, Oscar. *La Vida: A Puerto Rican Family in the Culture of Poverty.* New York: Random House, 1966.

Lieberman, Robert. "Social Construction (Continued): Response (in Controversy)." *American Political Science Review* 89, no. 2 (1995): 441–446.

Link, M. W., and R. W. Oldendick. "Social Construction and White Attitudes Toward Equal Opportunity and Multiculturalism." *Journal of Politics* 56, no. 1 (1996): 149–168.

Lubiano, Wahneema. "Black Ladies, Welfare Queens and State Minstrels: Ideological War by Narrative Means." In *Race-ing Justice, En-gendering Power: Essays on Anita Hill, Clarence Thomas and the Construction of Social Identity*, edited by Toni Morrison, 323–363. New York: Pantheon Books, 1992.

Madsen, Sandy Smith. "Point of View: A Welfare Mother in Academe." *Chronicle of Higher Education* (July 31, 1998).

Manstead, Antony S. R., ed. *Emotion in Social Life.* Hillsdale, N.J.: Lawrence Erlbaum Associates, 1991.

Marcuse, Herbert. "Repressive Tolerance." In *A Critique of Pure Tolerance,* by Robert Paul Wolff, Barrington Moore Jr., and Herbert Marcuse. Boston: Beacon Press, 1965.

Marshall, Catherine, and Gretchen Rossman. *Designing Qualitative Research.* Thousand Oaks, Calif.: Sage Publications, 1995.

Martin, Linda R., and Demetrios Giannoros. "Would a Higher Minimum Wage Help Poor Families Headed by Women?" *Monthly Labor Review* 113, no. 8 (1990): 33–37.

Mayhew, David R. *Congress: The Electoral Connection.* New Haven: Yale University Press, 1974.

McClain, Linda C. "Back to Marriage, or to Servitude?" *New York Newsday* (April 13, 2003): A34.

McClintock, Anne. "Family Feuds: Gender, Nationalism and the Family." *Feminist Review* 44 (1993): 61–80.

McCloskey, Herbert, and John Zaller. "Social Learning and the Acquisition of Political Norms." In *The American Ethos,* by Herbert McCloskey and John Zaller, 234–263. Cambridge: Harvard University Press, 1984.

McClure, Kirstie. "On the Subject of Rights: Pluralism, Plurality and Political Identity." In *Feminists Theorize the Political,* edited by Judith Butler and Joan W. Scott, 341–368. New York: Routledge, 1992.

Mendelberg, Tali. *The Race Card: Campaign Strategy, Implicit Messages, and the Norm of Equality.* Princeton: Princeton University Press, 2001.

Mead, Lawrence. *Beyond Entitlement: The Social Obligations of Citizenship.* New York: Free Press, 1986.

Merelman, Richard M. *Making Something of Ourselves: On Culture and Politics in the United States.* Berkeley: University of California Press, 1984.

Milwaukee County Welfare Rights Organization. *Welfare Mothers Speak Out: We Ain't Gonna Shuffle No More.* New York: Norton, 1972.

Mink, Gwendolyn. *The Wages of Motherhood: Inequality in the Welfare State, 1917–1942.* Ithaca: Cornell University Press, 1995.

———. *Welfare's End.* Ithaca: Cornell University Press, 1998.

———, ed. *Whose Welfare?* Ithaca: Cornell University Press, 1999.

Moyers, Bill. *Bill Moyers' Journal:* "The Vanishing Black Family." New York and Washington, D.C.: Public Broadcasting Service, January 1986.

Moynihan, Daniel Patrick. "The Negro Family: The Case for National Action." In *The Moynihan Report and the Politics of Controversy,* edited by Lee Rainwater and W. L. Yancey. Cambridge: MIT Press, 1967.

Moynihan, Daniel Patrick. *Miles to Go: A Personal History of Social Policy.* Cambridge: Harvard University Press, 1996.

Mullings, Leith. *On Our Own Terms: Race, Class, and Gender in the Lives of African American Women.* New York: Routledge, 1997.

Murray, Charles A. *Losing Ground: American Social Policy 1950–1980.* New York: Basic Books, 1986.

Murray, Pauli. "The Liberation of Black Women." In *Words of Fire: An Anthology of African-American Feminist Thought,* edited by Beverly Guy-Sheftall, 186–197. New York: New Press, 1995.

Mutz, Diana C., Paul Sniderman, and Richard Brody, eds. *Political Persuasion and Attitude Change.* Ann Arbor: University of Michigan Press, 1996.

Nadasen, Premilla. "Expanding the Boundaries of the Women's Movement: Black Feminism and the Struggle for Welfare Rights." *Feminist Studies* 28 (2002): 271–301.

Naples, Nancy. "The 'New Consensus' on the Gendered 'Social Contract': The 1987–1988 U.S. Congressional Hearings on Welfare." *Signs* 22, no. 4 (1997): 907–945.

———. *Grassroots Warriors: Activist Mothering, Community Work, and the War on Poverty.* New York: Routledge, 1998.

Nelson, Jill. *Volunteer Slavery: My Authentic Negro Experience.* Chicago: Noble Press, 1993.

Parker, Star. *Pimps, Whores and Welfare Brats: From Welfare Cheat to Conservative Messenger, the Autobiography of Star Parker.* New York: Pocket Books, 1997.

Pateman, Carole. *Participation and Democracy.* Cambridge: Cambridge University Press, 1970.

Peffley, Mark, Jon Hurwitz, and Paul Sniderman. "Racial Stereotypes and Whites' Political Views of Blacks in the Context of Welfare and Crime." *American Journal of Political Science* 41, no. 1 (1997): 3–60.

Personal Responsibility and Work Opportunity Act of 1996, Pub. L. No. 104-193.

Piven, Frances Fox, and Richard Cloward. *Poor People's Movements: Why They Succeed, How They Fail.* New York: Pantheon Books, 1977.

Polakow, Valerie. "Savage Distributions: Welfare Myths and Daily Lives." *Sage Race Relations Abstracts* 19 (1994): 3–29.

———. "The Shredded Net: The End of Welfare as We Knew It." *Sage Race Relations Abstracts* 22 (1997): 3–23.

Popkin, Samuel. *The Reasoning Voter.* Chicago: University of Chicago Press, 1991.

Quadagno, Jill. *The Color of Welfare: How Racism Undermined the War on Poverty.* New York: Oxford University Press, 1994.

Randall, Vernellia. "Open Letter to President Bush and Vice-President Quayle"

(May 27, 1992). Available on-line at http://academic.udayton.edu/Vernellia Randall/essays/openltr.htm.

Roberts, Dorothy. *Killing the Black Body: Race, Reproduction and the Meaning of Liberty.* New York: Pantheon Books, 1997.

Rogers-Dillon, Robin H. "Welfare Reform Would Subvert Constitution." *New York Newsday* (January 15, 2003): A27.

Rosenberg, Shawn M. "Self-concept Research: A Historical Overview." *Social Forces* 68 (1986): 34–44.

Rosenstone, Stephen J., and John Mark Hansen. *Mobilization, Participation and Democracy in America.* New York: Macmillan, 1993.

Rozin, Paul, Jonathan Haidt, Clark McCauley, Lance Dunlop, and Michelle Ashmore. "Individual Differences in Disgust Sensitivity: Comparisons and Evaluations of Paper-and-Pencil versus Behavioral Measures." *Journal of Research in Personality* 33 (1999): 330–351.

Rozin, Paul, Laura Lowery, Sumio Imada, and Jonathan Haidt. "The CAD Triad Hypothesis: A Mapping between Three Moral Emotions (Contempt, Anger, Disgust) and Three Moral Codes (Community, Autonomy, Divinity)." *Journal of Personality and Social Psychology* 76, no. 4 (1999): 574–586.

Rowley, Stephanie J., et al. "The Relationship between Racial Identity and Self-Esteem in African-American College and High School Students." *Journal of Personality and Social Psychology* 74 (1998): 715–724.

Sandel, Michael. *Democracy's Discontent: America in Search of a Public Philosophy.* Cambridge: Harvard University Press, 1992.

Sapiro, Virginia. "The Gender Basis of American Social Policy." In *Women, the State, and Welfare,* edited by Linda Gordon, 36–54. Madison: University of Wisconsin Press, 1990.

Schafer, M. "Issues in Assessing Psychological Characteristics at a Distance: An Introduction to the Symposium." *Political Psychology* 23, no. 3 (2000): 511–525.

Schlozman, Kay L., Nancy Burns, and Sidney Verba. "Gender and the Pathways to Participation: The Role of Resources." *Journal of Politics* 56 (1994): 963–990.

Schneider, Anne L., and Helen Ingram. "Social Construction of Target Populations: Implications for Politics and Policy." *American Political Science Review* 87, no. 2 (1993): 334–347.

———. "Social Construction (Continued): Response (in Controversy)." *American Political Science Review* 89, no. 2 (1995): 441–446.

Schram, Sanford. *Words of Welfare: The Poverty of Social Science and the Social Science of Poverty.* Minneapolis: University of Minnesota Press, 1995.

Schroedel, J. R., and D. R. Jordan. "Senate Voting and Social Construction of Target Populations: A Study of AIDS Policy Making, 1987–1992." *Journal of Health Politics, Policy and Law* 23, no. 1 (1998): 107–132.

Sellers, Robert M., et al. "Multidimensional Inventory of Black Identity: A Preliminary Investigation of Reliability and Construct Validity." *Journal of Personality and Social Psychology* 73 (1997): 805–815.

Shaver, P. Richard, John P. Robinson, and Lawrence Wrightsman, eds. *Measures of Political Attitudes*. San Diego: Academic Press, 1999.

Simpson, Andrea. *The Tie That Binds: Identity and Political Attitudes in the Post–Civil Rights Generation*. New York: New York University Press, 1998.

Skocpol, Theda. *Social Policy in the United States*. Princeton: Princeton University Press, 1995.

Smith, Rogers M. "Beyond Tocqueville, Myrdal and Hartz: The Multiple Traditions in America." *American Political Science Review* 87 (1993): 549–565.

Sniderman, Paul M., Richard A. Brody, and Philip Tetlock. *Reasoning and Choice: Explorations in Political Psychology*. New York: Cambridge University Press, 1991.

Soss, Joe. "Lessons of Welfare: Policy Design, Political Learning and Political Action." *American Political Science Review* 93 (1999): 363–380.

Sparks, Holloway. "Queens, Teens and Model Mothers: Race, Gender and the Discourse of Welfare Reform." In *Race and the Politics of Welfare Reform*, edited by Sanford Schram, Joe Soss, and Richard C. Fording, 171–195. Ann Arbor: University of Michigan Press, 2003.

Steele, Claude, and David A. Sherman. "The Psychological Predicament of Women on Welfare." In *Cultural Divides: Understanding and Overcoming Group Conflict*, edited by David A. Prentice et al. New York: Russell Sage Foundation, 1999.

Tate, Katherine. *From Protest to Politics: The New Black Voters in American Elections*. Cambridge: Harvard University Press, 1994.

Taylor, Charles. "The Politics of Recognition." In *Multiculturalism: Examining the Politics of Recognition*, edited by Amy Gutmann. Princeton: Princeton University Press, 1994.

Taylor, Robert Joseph, and Karen D. Lincoln. "The Million Man March: Portraits and Attitudes." *Perspectives on African American Research*, 1998.

Tillmon, Johnnie. "Welfare Is a Woman's Issue." *Ms. Magazine* 1 (Spring 1972): 111–116.

Tin, Jan. "Who Gets Assistance?" In U.S. Bureau of the Census, *Current Population Reports*, July 1996.

Tyler, Tom. *Why People Obey the Law*. New Haven: Yale University Press, 1990.

U.S. Bureau of the Census. *Statistical Brief: Mothers Who Receive AFDC Payments: Fertility and Socioeconomic Characteristics*. March 1995.

———. "Money Income in the United States." *Current Population Reports for 1999*, prepared by Carmen DeNavas and Robert W. Cleveland. Washington, D.C., September 2000.

————. *Statistical Brief: Mothers Who Receive AFDC Payments—Fertility and Socioeconomic Characteristics*. Washington, D.C., 1995.

U.S. Department of Commerce. *Current Population Reports: Who Gets Assistance?* Prepared by Jan Tin. Washington, D.C., July 1996.

VanDijk, Teun. *Elite Discourse and Racism*. Newbury Park, Calif.: Sage Publications, 1993.

Verba, Sidney, Kay L. Schlozman, and Henry Brady. "Race, Ethnicity and Political Resources: Participation in the United States." *British Journal of Political Science* 23 (1993): 453–497.

————. *Voice and Equality: Civic Voluntarism in American Politics*. Cambridge: Harvard University Press, 1995.

Waller, Margy. "Don't Let Bush Bury Welfare Reform." *New York Newsday* (January 20, 2003): A21.

Walters, Kimberly Battle. "'They Think You Ain't Much of Nothing': The Social Construction of the Welfare Mother." *Journal of Marriage and the Family* 60, no. 4 (1998): 849–865.

West, Guida. *The National Welfare Rights Movement: The Social Protest of Poor Women*. New York: Praeger, 1981.

White, Deborah Gray. *Ar'n't I a Woman? Female Slaves in the Plantation South*. New York: W. W. Norton, 1985.

White, Geoffrey M. "Affecting Culture: Emotion and Morality in Everyday Life." In *Emotion and Culture: Empirical Studies of Mutual Influence*, edited by Shinobu Kitayama and Hazel Rose Markus. Washington, D.C.: American Psychological Association, 1994.

Wilcox, Clyde. "Racial and Gender Consciousness among African-American Women: Sources and Consequences." *Women and Politics* 17 (1997): 73–95.

Williams, Lucy. "Race, Rat Bites and Unfit Mothers: How Media Discourse Informs Welfare Legislation Debate." *Fordham Urban Law Journal* (1995): 1159–1196.

Williams, Melissa. *Voice, Trust and Memory: Marginalized Groups and the Failings of Liberal Representation*. Princeton: Princeton University Press, 1998.

Williams, Wendy W. "The Equality Crisis: Some Reflections on Culture, Courts, and Feminism." In *Feminist Legal Theory: Readings in Law and Gender*, edited by Katherine T. Bartlett and Rosanne Kennedy, 15–34. Boulder, Colo.: Westview Press, 1991.

Yin, Robert K. *Case Study Research: Design and Methods*. Thousand Oaks, Calif.: Sage Publications, 1994.

Young, Iris Marion. *Justice and the Politics of Difference*. Princeton: Princeton University Press, 1990.

————. *Intersecting Voices: Dilemmas of Gender, Political Philosophy and Policy*. Princeton: Princeton University Press, 1997.

Young, Iris Marion. "Inclusive Political Communication." Paper presented at American Political Science Association Meetings, Boston, September 1998.

Zaller, John. "Diffusion of Political Attitudes." *Journal of Personality and Social Psychology* 53 (1987): 821–833.

———. "Information, Values and Opinion." *American Political Science Review* 85 (1991): 1215–1237.

———. *The Nature and Origins of Mass Opinion*. New York: Cambridge University Press, 1992.

———. "The Myth of Massive Media Impact Revived: New Support for a Discredited Idea." In *Political Persuasion and Attitude Change*, edited by Diana Mutz, Paul Sniderman, and Richard Brody. Ann Arbor: University of Michigan Press, 1996.

Zucchino, David. *The Myth of the Welfare Queen*. New York: Scribner, 1997.

Index

African Americans: anti-welfare public opinion, 23, 26, 44, 53–54; commonalties with white public opinion and political values, 23, 26, 53, 55, 107, 110–111, 114; political culture, 2, 3, 5, 26, 40, 42, 44–45, 53, 55, 60; racial uplift, 32, 54. *See also* Black Women's Club Movement; Civil rights movement; Million Man March; National Welfare Rights Organization (NWRO)

Agency, 14, 20, 40, 45. *See also* Collective action framework; Democracy, democratic deliberation; National Welfare Rights Organization (NWRO); Welfare activism

Aid to Dependent Children (ADC), xiii, 28, 34–38, 42, 66, 112

Aid to Families with Dependent Children (AFDC), xiii, 9, 41, 50, 66, 88, 118, 123–124, 142

American Association of University Women, 107

American political culture, 24–25, 27, 31–33, 39–40, 42, 45, 47, 57–58, 60, 66, 123, 148; threats emanating from, 144, 148, 151

Bishop, Sanford (D-GA), 110–112

Black Mothers: in slavery, 26, 31, 63, 139; who receive AFDC/TANF, 125

Black Women's Club Movement, 16, 30–33, 39, 43, 61, 139

Block Grants, 69, 74, 82, 86, 93, 98, 102, 106. *See also* **Policy Options**

Boundary-drawing, 43, 50, 55, 60–61, 144

Bracey, Marie, 42. *See also* National Welfare Rights Organization (NWRO)

Breaux, John (D-LA), 95

Bridges, Bertha, 1, 2, 4, 9–10, 20, 22, 64, 117–118, 144, 154. *See also* Welfare recipients

Brisco, Sheryl, 127–130, 136. *See also* Welfare recipients

Brown, Amos, 134

Brown, Willie, 121, 133

Bush, George H. W., 51, 131

Bush, George W., 13, 22, 137, 137, 152, 154; administration, 13, 22, 152, 154. *See also* Welfare policy

Buzzwords, 8, 12, 51, 57, 94–95, 101; key, elite frames of, 90; "welfare as a way of life," 8, 94, 99, 111. *See also* *Culture of Poverty*

Calvert, Mildred, 46. *See also* National Welfare Rights Organization (NWRO)

Camp, Bill (R-TN), 101

Care for Children, 13, 33, 69, 78, 79–82, 84, 93, 97, 100, 102, 104, 111, 127. *See also* **Political Values**

Cavalier, Octavia, 122–124. *See also* Welfare recipients

Children's Defense Fund, 73, 81, 109

Christianity, 30, 69, 79–80, 82, 93, 100, 102. *See also* **Political Values**

Civil rights movement, 16, 39, 42–43, 45, 54, 148

Clayton, Eva (D-NC), 112, 114, 132

Clinton, Bill, 13, 54, 154

Coalitions, 156. *See also* Lack of solidarity with traditional allies

Collective action framework, 39–40, 42,
45–46, 62; agency, 4, 8, 29, 36, 40, 42,
45, 48, 63, 151; group consciousness,
39, 40, 45
Communicative context of gross inequality, 6–7, 13, 49–50, 62, 68, 87, 91,
100, 118, 136, 142, 145, 150
Congress, 1, 13, 41, 54, 59–60, 87, 91,
94, 99, 101, 104, 106, 108, 110–111,
115, 120–122, 124–127, 133, 146,
157; Franklin Roosevelt and southern
Democrats, 35, 36. See also House of
Representatives; Senate
Congressional Black Caucus (CBC), xiii,
59, 110–112, 140
Congressional Record: communicative
norms, 89; content analysis of, 1, 2, 7,
14, 19, 63, 89, 90–91, 93, 94, 99, 104,
107, 115, 124, 140
Consensus, 8, 13, 23, 25, 56, 63, 124,
135; as a requirement for democratic
deliberation, 147; as a variable, 13, 75,
79, 84–87, 91, 93, 104–106, 108;
Among American Public, 23, 56,
67–69, 84–86, 93, 105–106; Among
Branches of Government, 69; Among
Taxpayers, 69, 84–86, 93, 105–106;
Among Executive and Congress, 69,
84–86, 93, 105–106; Bipartisan Support, 12–13, 51, 59, 69, 84–86, 93,
105–106; regarding the public identity
of the "Welfare Queen," 59, 84
Content analysis: of Congress, 1, 2, 7, 14,
19, 63, 89, 90–91, 93, 94, 99, 104,
107, 115, 124, 140; of news media, 19,
22, 60, 65–66, 75, 81, 122
Contract with America, 67, 79
Controlling images of "welfare queen,"
24, 26–27, 56, 60, 64. See also Public
Identity of "Welfare Queen"
Correspondence bias. See Failure of representative thinking
Crime, 64, 69–70, 74, 77, 80, 85, 93, 96,
98, 100, 105. See also Public Identity
of "Welfare Queen"
Critical theory paradigm, 18
Cross-Generation Dependency, 51, 64,
69–70, 74, 77, 80, 85, 93, 96, 98, 105,
111. See also Public Identity of "Welfare Queen"

Cubin, Barbara (R-WI), 120, 154
Culture of Poverty, 8, 56–57, 69–70, 74,
77, 80, 85, 93–96, 98, 100–101, 103,
105, 111. See also Public Identity of
"Welfare Queen"

Dandridge v. Williams (1970), 60
Democracy, 3, 14, 17, 29, 115, 139–141,
142, 145–146, 148, 150, 152, 155; democratic attention, 3, 6; democratic deliberation, 3–6, 8–9, 15, 17, 19, 22,
138, 140–152; democratic theory, 8,
142–143, 147; liberal, 141; participatory, 3, 17, 22, 39, 48, 137, 141–143,
145, 148; perversion of, 3–4, 6, 9, 50,
106, 117–120, 136, 142; threat to, of
politics of disgust, 14, 25, 137–151,
154; threat to, of public identity of
"Welfare Queen," 24, 62, 137, 140,
144, 150, 155, 157. See also Politics of
disgust
Disgust, 7, 9–10, 87, 91, 106, 116, 119;
definition of, 9–11; impact of cognitive
cues of, 9–10, 144–147. See also Emotions; Politics of disgust
Domestic violence: policy recommendations from welfare recipients, 10,
136–137, 141; survivors, impact of
PRWA upon, 10, 11, 146, 153, 157
Don't Work, 64, 68–72, 74–78, 80, 85,
93–96, 98, 100–101, 105, 123. See
also Public Identity of "Welfare
Queen"
Drain on National Resources, 63, 64, 69,
71, 74, 77, 80, 85, 93, 98, 105. See
also Public Identity of "Welfare
Queen"
Drug Users, 68–70, 74, 77, 80, 85, 93,
96, 98, 100, 105. See also Public Identity of "Welfare Queen"
Duration of Welfare, 69–70, 74, 76–77,
80, 85, 93, 96, 98, 105, 130. See also
Public Identity of "Welfare Queen"

Economic Individualism, 23, 25, 30–32,
48, 50, 53–55, 67, 69, 79–80, 82, 84,
93, 100, 102, 104. See also Political
Values
Elite frames of key buzzwords, 90. See
also Buzzwords

Emotions, 4, 6–9; emotion cues, impact of, 147; feminist theory's embrace of, 6; political foundations and functions of, 6–9, 65, 119, 137; social psychological foundations and functions of, 7–8, 142. *See also* Disgust; Politics of disgust
Ewing, Thomas (R-IL), 97

Failure of representative thinking, 7, 10–11, 33, 61–62, 91, 107, 114–115, 118, 125, 130, 132, 136, 142, 146, 150, 156. *See also* Politics of disgust
Family Assistance Plan (FAP), xiii, 48, 58–59. *See also* Welfare policy
Family Caps, 51, 55–56, 69, 78, 82, 86, 93, 97–99, 102–103, 106. *See also* **Policy Options**
Feminism, 4, 39, 48, 52, 131, 137, 156; cultural, 28; feminist lawmakers, 13, 107, 109, 130–131, 133; feminist majority, 110; maternalism, 28–29, 33; National Organization for Women, 107, 110. *See also* Steinem, Gloria; Women legislators
Food Stamp Reform, 69, 74, 82, 86, 93, 98, 102, 106. *See also* **Policy Options**
Frank, Barney (D-MA), 120, 155
Franks, Gary (R-NJ), 110

Good Mothers, 69, 71, 86, 92–93. *See also* **Public Identity of "Welfare Queen"**
Grounded theory, 19

Helms, Jesse (R-NC), 103
Henderson, Anne, 40, 55. *See also* National Welfare Rights Organization (NWRO)
Heterosexual Marriage, 12, 13, 50, 54–55, 69, 79–80, 82, 93, 100, 102, 153–154; as a policy option, 12, 13, 73, 153–154. *See also* **Political Values**
House of Representatives, 1, 13, 22, 73, 78, 107–108, 110, 115, 120, 152; members, 3, 13–14, 16, 76, 88, 90–92, 94, 97, 99, 101, 107–108, 110–114, 117, 120, 126–127, 130–132, 154–155

Identity, 2, 3, 6, 12, 14, 144; intersecting or multiple identities, 15–17, 20, 24–26, 30, 33–34, 38–39, 47, 57, 68,

75, 87, 140–141, 148, 155–156; public identities, 15–17
Illegitimacy, 69–74, 77–78, 80, 85, 93–96, 98, 100, 105, 114. *See also* **Public Identity of the "Welfare Queen"**
Immigrant Benefits, 69, 74, 82, 83, 86, 93, 98, 102, 106; as a **Policy Options** variable, 30–31, 34, 38–39, 44, 47, 57
Individualism: as a political value, 25, 32 33, 50, 53–55, 61, 67; impact on explanation for sociopolitical problems, 25, 50, 53, 62, 139. *See also* **Political Values**
Industry, 23, 30, 36, 48, 50, 61, 65, 67, 69, 79–83, 93, 100, 102, 104. *See also* **Political Values**
Inner-City Resident, 69–70, 74, 77, 80, 85, 93, 96, 98, 100, 105. *See also* **Public Identity of the "Welfare Queen"**
Intersectionality, 16, 20–21, 26, 33, 44, 52, 57, 63, 65, 68, 87, 140–141, 148, 155. *See also* Identity

Jackson-Lee, Sheila (D-TX), 112, 114
Johnson, Nancy (R-CT), 107–108
Joint Center for Political and Economic Studies, 134
Judgment: choosing common conduct, 143; evaluating political legitimacy of claimant, 144–147; moral, 12, 15, 23, 36, 49, 51, 67–68, 72, 75, 78, 86–87, 91, 94–95, 114, 118, 144; public, 17, 141–147, 149–150; social, 11. *See also* Democracy, democratic deliberation; Public identity

King, Martin Luther, Jr., 44, 58. *See also* Civil rights movement; National Welfare Rights Organization (NWRO); Poor People's Campaign
King v. Smith (1968), 38

Lack of solidarity with traditional allies, 7, 13, 43–44, 49, 55, 61, 63, 91, 107–108, 110–111, 114–115, 133–136, 142, 146–147, 150, 156
Lazy, 60, 64, 69–72, 74–78, 80, 85, 93, 96, 98, 100, 105. *See also* **Public Identity of the "Welfare Queen"**
Long, Russell (D-LA), 41, 50, 57, 119

McInnis, Scott (R-CO), 3, 14, 117
Mead, Lawrence, 59–60
Medicaid Denial, 69, 74, 82, 86, 93, 97–98, 102, 106. *See also Policy Options*
Mica, John (R-FL), 119–120, 155
Middle class values. *See* Motherhood, relationship of, to transmission of political values; Motherhood, Victorian ideals
Mikulski, Barbara (D-MD), 13, 16, 108–111
Million Man March, 16, 53–54, 56
Milwaukee County Welfare Rights Organization, 40, 42, 46, 55. *See also* National Welfare Rights Organization (NWRO)
Motherhood: behavioral norms of good mothers, 29, 34, 61; compliance with/failure to comply with norms, 32, 34, 50, 65, 144; relationship of, to transmission of political values, 28, 30; single, 32, 44; Victorian ideals, 27–29, 31, 33–34. *See also* Welfare policy, regulation of maternal behavior
Moynihan, Daniel Patrick (D-NY), 51, 56–60
Murray, Charles, 59–60

National Association for the Advancement of Colored People (NAACP), xiii, 48, 58
Nationalism, 33, 53, 140; American, 28–29; gendered norms of, 29; maintenance of racial hierarchy, 28, 30, 33, 36; relationship to social welfare policy, 29, 53
National Welfare Rights Organization (NWRO), xiii, 27, 39–40, 45–50, 52, 56, 58–59, 61–63, 112, 115, 117, 149, 156; activism, local, 40, 42; activism, national, 27, 40, 42, 45, 48, 59–63; Marie Bracey, 42; Mildred Calvert, 46; challenges, financial, 43–44, 47–48, 52; challenges, political, 39, 43–44, 47, 50, 52, 56, 112; Anne Henderson, 41, 55; leadership, 46–47, 49; "Mother Power," 42, 48; Poor People's Campaign, 44; Garnette Reddic, 44; Johnnie Tillmon, 39, 41–42, 45, 48; George Wiley, 44; relationship with Martin

Luther King Jr. and the SCLC, 44. *See also* Milwaukee County Welfare Rights Organization
New Deal, 27, 34, 63. *See also* Welfare policy

Overly Fertile, 64, 68–70, 72–74, 77–78, 80, 85, 93–96, 98, 100, 105, 114. *See also Public Identity of the "Welfare Queen"*

Parental Responsibility, 69, 79–80, 82, 84, 93, 100, 102, 104. *See also Political Values*
Paternal Solutions, 69, 74, 82, 86, 93, 98, 102, 106. *See also Policy Options*
Personal Responsibility and Work Opportunity Act of 1996 (PRWA), xiii, 2, 7, 10, 12–13, 18, 61, 67–68, 79, 88–89, 91–92, 107, 111, 115, 124–126, 136, 152, 154; support of, 13, 111; votes against, 13, 112; votes for, 13
Perversion of democratic attention, 3–4, 6, 9, 50, 106, 117–120, 136, 142, 144, 150, 155, 157; animalistic images of welfare recipients, 50, 119–120, 144, 155. *See also* Politics of disgust
Policy Options: as a variable, 74–76, 79, 81–86, 88, 91, 93, 95, 97–99, 102–104, 106, 111, 114–115; *Block Grants*, 69, 74, 82, 86, 93, 98, 102, 106; *Food Stamp Reform*, 69, 74, 82, 86, 93, 98, 102, 106; *Family Caps*, 51, 55–56, 69, 78, 82, 86, 93, 97–99, 102–103, 106; *Immigrant Benefits*, 69, 74, 82, 83, 86, 93, 98, 102, 106; *Medicaid Denial*, 69, 74, 82, 86, 93, 97–98, 102, 106; *Paternal Solutions*, 69, 74, 82, 86, 93, 98, 102, 106; proposed welfare reform solutions, 8, 12, 51, 55, 65; *State Programs*, 55–56, 69, 74–77, 81–83, 86, 93, 97–99, 102–104, 106; *Teen Mother Policies*, 69, 74, 78, 82, 86, 93, 98, 102, 114, 106; *Time Limits*, 51, 69, 74, 82, 83, 86, 93, 98, 102, 106; *Workfare*, 74–76, 82–83, 85–86, 93, 97–98, 102–103, 105–106. *See also* Welfare policy
Political context, 2, 4, 6, 9, 14, 17, 61, 63, 79, 84, 90, 92, 99, 101, 104,

110–111, 139, 149–150, 152. *See also*
Politics of disgust
Political participation, 3, 17, 20, 24–25,
27, 39, 43, 45–46, 48, 62, 115, 137,
142, 144–145, 148–150, 152, 157
Political Values: as a variable, 75, 79–84,
86–87, 91, 93, 97, 99–104; *Care for
Children*, 13, 33, 69, 78, 79–82, 84,
93, 97, 100, 102, 104, 111, 127; *Christianity*, 30, 69, 79–80, 82, 93, 100,
102; conservative backlash against
NWRO, 51; *Economic Individualism*,
23, 25, 30–32, 48, 50, 53–55, 67, 69,
79–80, 82, 84, 93, 100, 102, 104; *Heterosexual Marriage*, 50, 54–55, 69,
79–80, 82, 93, 100, 102; *Industry*, 23,
30, 36, 48, 50, 61, 65, 67, 69, 79–83,
93, 100, 102, 104, *Parental Responsibility*, 69, 79–80, 82, 84, 93, 100, 102,
104; relationship to transmission of,
28, 30; *Small Government*, 69, 79–80,
82, 84, 93, 100, 102; *Welfare System
Accountability*, 69, 79–80, 82, 93,
100–103. *See also* Motherhood, relationship of, to transmission of political
values; Motherhood, Victorian ideals
Politics of disgust, 4–9, 12–14, 18, 21–22,
25, 49–50, 52, 57, 61–63, 68,
117–118, 121, 124, 136–137,
139–140, 142, 144–145, 147,
149–150, 152, 154–157; definition, 4,
6. *See also* Communicative context of
gross inequality; Democracy, democratic attention; Failure of representative
thinking; Lack of solidarity with traditional allies
Poor People's Campaign, 44. *See also* National Welfare Rights Organization
(NWRO)
Presidential election, 1996: political context, 13, 149; and consensus for welfare reform, 13. *See also* Clinton, Bill
Public identity, 4, 5, 7, 9, 14–15, 21–22,
39, 48, 56, 67, 77, 95, 97, 111,
114–116, 147, 151; conceptual definition, 8, 15; impact on democratic deliberation, 16, 22, 142, 147–149, 151;
impact on political participation, 14,
21, 22, 24–25, 52, 62, 142, 145,
148–150; impact on public policy, 6,

14, 16–18, 20, 22, 46, 49, 55–57, 62,
79, 86–91; moral judgment component, 16, 26, 36–37, 51, 61, 67–68,
71–72, 75, 78, 86–87, 91, 94–95, 114,
118, 144; stereotype component, 15,
17, 24, 31, 48, 52, 61, 72, 75, 86–87,
91, 94–95, 114, 118, 122, 133. *See
also* **Public Identity of the "Welfare
Queen"**
Public Identity of the "Welfare Queen,"
6–9, 16–17, 22, 24–25, 27, 33, 53,
56–57, 59–60, 63–64, 66–68, 73–76,
91, 93–95, 97, 103, 111, 113–115,
117, 120–122, 131, 137, 139–141,
143–146, 149, 151–152, 154–157; as a
variable, 64, 69–72, 74, 75, 79–81,
83–87, 91, 93–105, 110–111, 113;
Crime, 64, 69–70, 74, 77, 80, 85, 93,
96, 98, 100, 105; *Cross-Generation
Dependency*, 51, 64, 69–70, 74, 77,
80, 85, 93, 96, 98, 105, 111; *Culture
of Poverty*, 8, 56–57, 69–70, 74, 77,
80, 85, 93–96, 98, 100–101, 103, 105,
111; definition, 56; *Don't Work*, 64,
68–72, 74–78, 80, 85, 93–96, 98,
100–101, 105, 123; *Drain of National
Resources*, 63, 64, 69, 71, 74, 77, 80,
85, 93, 98, 105; *Drug Users*, 68–70,
74, 77, 80, 85, 93, 96, 98, 100, 105;
Duration of Welfare, 69–70, 74,
76–77, 80, 85, 93, 96, 98, 105, 130;
Good Mothers, 69, 71, 86, 92–93; *Illegitimacy*, 69–74, 77–78, 80, 85,
93–96, 98, 100, 105, 114; impact historical, on welfare recipients, 59; impact on other political groups, 23, 60,
63, 145; impact on public policy, 22,
56–57, 60, 66, 88, 131, 145, 154;
Inner City Resident, 69–70, 74, 77, 80,
85, 93, 96, 98, 100, 105; *Lazy*, 60, 64,
69–72, 74–78, 80, 85, 93, 96, 98, 100,
105; organizing theme of hyperfertility,
6, 21, 25, 31, 34, 37, 40, 48–50, 52,
55, 61, 64, 66, 71, 73, 75, 78, 139,
144; organizing theme of laziness, 6,
21, 25, 31, 34, 36–38, 40, 48–50,
60–61, 64, 66, 71, 75, 131, 133, 139,
144; *Overly Fertile*, 64, 68–70, 72–74,
77–78, 80, 85, 93–96, 98, 100, 105,
114; post-1996, 6, 18, 23, 46, 56, 92,

Public Identity of the "Welfare Queen"
    (continued)
    140, 145–146, 148–149, 151; *Single
    Parent Family,* 64, 69–70, 72, 74, 77,
    80, 85, 93–96, 98–101, 105, 131; *Sys-
    tem Abuse,* 60, 64, 69–70, 72, 74, 76,
    77, 80, 85, 93, 96, 98, 105, 106, 131;
    Teen Mothers, 64, 68–70, 72–74,
    77–78, 80–81, 85, 93–94, 96, 98–100,
    105, 114, 131. *See also* Social con-
    struction of target populations

Radanovich, George (R-CA), 99
Randall, Vernellia, 131. *See also* Welfare
    recipients
Rangel, Charles (D-NY), 92, 112, 114
Reagan, Ronald, 51
Reddic, Garnette, 44. *See also* National
    Welfare Rights Organization (NWRO)
Roman, Elena, 124. *See also* Welfare re-
    cipients
Roukema, Marge (R-NJ), 110–111, 113

Senate, 13, 50, 78, 108, 115, 119, 152;
    members, 41, 50, 51, 56–60, 95, 103,
    119
Shaw, E. Clay (R-FL), 90–91, 120
Single Parent Family, 64, 69–70, 72, 74,
    77, 80, 85, 93–96, 98–101, 105, 131.
    *See also **Public Identity of the "Welfare
    Queen"***
Small Government, 69, 79–80, 82, 84, 93,
    100, 102. *See also **Political Values***
Small, Rhonda, 122–124, 155. *See also*
    Welfare recipients
Social constructions of target populations,
    15–16, 61, 87, 89, 99; definition, 5. *See
    also* Welfare target populations
Solomon, Gerald (R-NY), 94
Southern Christian Leadership Conference
    (SCLC), xiii, 44, 58
State Programs, 55–56, 69, 74–77, 81–83,
    86, 93, 97–99, 102–104, 106. *See also
    Policy Options*
Steinem, Gloria, 107. *See also* Feminism
Stereotypes, 8, 14, 75, 86–87, 91, 94–95,
    114, 152; of Black women, 15, 24, 26,
    30, 31, 37, 51, 72; as a component of
    public identity, 14–17, 23–24, 31, 37,
    57, 67–68, 71–72, 118

Stewart, Desiree, 122–124. *See also* Wel-
    fare recipients
System Abuse, 60, 64, 69–70, 72, 74, 76,
    77, 80, 85, 93, 96, 98, 105, 106, 131.
    *See also **Public Identity of the "Welfare
    Queen"***

Target populations of public policy: mis-
    perceptions of target welfare popula-
    tion, 28, 35, 50, 66, 144. *See also* So-
    cial constructions of target popula-
    tions; Welfare policy
Teen Mother Policies, 69, 74, 78, 82, 86,
    93, 98, 102, 114, 106. *See also **Policy
    Options***
Teen Mothers, 64, 68–70, 72–74, 77–78,
    80–81, 85, 93–94, 96, 98–100, 105,
    114. *See also **Public Identity of the
    "Welfare Queen"***
Temporary Assistance to Needy Families
    (TANF), xiii, 9, 121, 156. *See also*
    Welfare policy
Tillmon, Johnnie, 39, 41–42, 45, 48. *See
    also* National Welfare Rights Organiza-
    tion (NWRO)
Time Limits, 51, 69, 74, 82, 83, 86,
    93, 98, 102, 106. *See also **Policy
    Options***

Urban Institute, 81

Washington, Booker T., philosophy of,
    32–33
Watts, J. C. (R-OK), 88, 90–91, 110–111,
    113
Welfare activism, 13; against discrimina-
    tory local implementation, 36; against
    national policy, 119; political outcomes
    of, 47. *See also* National Welfare
    Rights Organization (NRWO); Welfare
    policy
"Welfare as a way of life," 8, 94, 99, 111.
    See also Buzzwords
Welfare policy: alternative policy op-
    tions, 136, 141, 156; completion of
    high school education, 127, 130–131;
    discriminatory implementation,
    35–38, 62, 122; expansion of waiver
    process, 154; heterosexual marriage
    incentives, 13, 73, 153–154; regula-

tion of maternal behavior, 12, 27, 33, 38, 51, 99; regulation of work behavior, 38, 51, 65, 135, 153; renewal of PRWA, 13, 22, 117, 137, 152–154; welfare recipients' pursuit of higher education, 65, 118, 127, 129–131, 141, 153; widows' pensions, 12, 28, 29, 31, 33–34, 66. *See also* Family Assistance Plan (FAP); New Deal; Personal Responsibility and Work Opportunity Act of 1996 (PRWA); Welfare activism

Welfare politics, 16; explanations for poverty, 12; history, 12, 27–64. *See also Policy Options*; Welfare activism; Welfare policy

Welfare recipients, 1, 2, 4, 9–10, 20, 22, 64, 99, 101, 112, 117–137, 140, 142, 144–145, 152, 154, 155; alternative policy recommendations, 123, 132, 136–137, 141, 156; facts regarding, 35–36, 41, 65, 114, 124–125, 127, 130, 153; misperceptions of, 6, 23, 35, 50–52, 55, 61, 66, 131, 144; who work, 87, 92. *See also* Cavalier, Octavia; National Welfare RightsOrganization (NWRO); *Public Identity of the "Welfare Queen"*; Roman, Elena; Small, Rhonda; Stewart, Desiree; Wilson, Mary

Welfare System Accountability, 69, 79–80, 82, 93, 100–103. *See also Political Values*

Welfare target populations: in New Deal, 12, 25–26, 28, 34; in 1996, 18, 66, 75, 89–91, 94, 106; pre–New Deal, 12, 26. *See also* Social constructions of target populations

Wilson, Mary, 126. *See also* Welfare recipients

Wiley, George, 44. *See also* National Welfare Rights Organization (NWRO)

Woolsey, Lynn (D-CA), 76, 126–127, 130–131

Women legislators, 7, 10, 13, 16, 76, 107–114, 126–127, 130, 132, 146, 154. *See also* Feminism

Workfare, 74–76, 82–83, 85–86, 93, 97–98, 102–103, 105–106. *See also Policy Options*

About the Author

Ange-Marie Hancock is Assistant Professor of Political Science and African American Studies at Yale University. Her research interests cross American politics and political theory, with an emphasis on intersecting identities. She conducted the original research and wrote the original proposal for the Women's National Basketball Association. Currently, she is writing her second book, *The Double Consciousness of the Pariah: Identity, Citizenship, and Agency in the Work of Hannah Arendt and W. E. B. Du Bois.*